L14 - L15

RESPONSIBLE
GOVERNMENT:
AMERICAN
AND BRITISH

RESPONSIBLE GOVERNMENT: AMERICAN AND BRITISH

Stephen T. Early, Jr.
and
Barbara B. Knight

Nelson-Hall nh Chicago

LIBRARY OF CONGRESS CATALOGING IN PUBLICATION DATA

Early, Stephen Tyree, 1923–
    Responsible government, American and British.

    Bibliography: p.
    Includes index.
    1. United States—Politics and government.   2.   Great
Britain—Politics and government.   3.   Democracy.
4.   Comparative government.   I.   Knight, Barbara B.,
joint author.   II.   Title.
JK274.E16   321.8′04   80–29601
ISBN 0–88229–658–2 (cloth)
ISBN 0–88229–776–7 (paper)

Copyright © 1981 by Stephen Tyree Early and Barbara B. Knight

Manufactured in the United States of America

10   9   8   7   6   5   4   3   2   1

CONTENTS

Preface

This study grew out of a problem that confronts many instructors. While presenting a course on democratic government that focuses particularly on an analytical comparison of the processes and institutions of American presidential and British cabinet government, we discovered to our dismay that there is no title available to students suitable to that inquiry. There are many books on the American national government and an adequate number of titles describing the British government or political systems. None, however, combined the two and endeavored comparatively to introduce students to salient features of democratic organization and procedure by analyzing and contrasting them as they are found in these two prototypes. Using the analytical framework of responsible government, we approach the material on a subject by subject basis instead of describing first one system and then the other, leaving the integration and comparison to the students' unaided efforts.

This book is intended for students who have some knowledge of American governmental institutions and processes. For that reason we have not included extensive facts about American government, but we have sought to incorporate at appropriate points enough basic facts about the British system to make its content intelligible to students who have not completed any work in comparative government and politics. The study examines the two systems in light of democratic assumptions and processes. Our own students have responded to this approach in course by discovering that American ways are not the only ways and have entered upon more advanced study with keener perceptions and wider intellectual horizons.

Students who are accustomed to finding straightforward statements of factual assertions in textbooks used in their courses may be somewhat disconcerted by the content of this study. A fair amount of equivocation characterizes some of its sections. Comparisons contain numerous uses of qualifying words and phrases, such as "often," "usually," "mostly," and "virtually." Such expressions are employed to indicate discernible trends and dominant patterns, but they are also made necessary by data gaps and by the absence of analyses that if available would have facilitated greater certainty.

We must concede that our coverage is selective and our presentation is synoptic, although we have tried to incorporate as much depth as possible into the facts we set forth and our analyses of them in the context of democratic government. Nevertheless, the nature and scope of our task, its purposes and limitations of space, have compelled us to abbreviate our treatment. Some readers would doubtless have approached this task differently, chosen another pattern of organization, or given different interpretations to the aspects considered, but such is always the case with choices. We have necessarily made many subjective decisions about what to include and exclude and about how to treat our presentation. Some sources are suggested in the footnotes and bibliography for the interested reader to pursue subjects more fully. We have been oriented primarily toward the student and his needs as we have discerned them from our experiences with the subject matter in course. We have rigorously tried to exclude value judgments, explicit or implied, from our analysis of the two systems; we present them as different and indigenous and therefore not superior one to the other.

We have approached completion of the project as equals, neither of us pretending to the status of "senior" author. Although Professor Early was principally responsible for chapters 1, 3, 4, and 7 and Professor Knight for chapters 2, 5, and 6, we both read, criticized and revised all of them. We made a serious effort, however successful, to homogenize style, method of treatment and mode of presentation in order to eliminate distracting variations from the manuscript.

We alone are responsible for all sins of omission and commission.

CHAPTER ONE

POLITICAL CULTURES

INTRODUCTION

No governmental system can exist and operate entirely apart from the society which is subject to its authority, for some relationship exists between it and its social milieu. That relationship is a complicated and reciprocal one; the government affects the society, and the history, values, attitudes, myths, beliefs, etc., of the people condition the expectations and demands they make upon their government. The social framework also influences what the government can do and, often, how it can do what society will consent or acquiesce to its undertaking. A governmental system, then, both conditions and is conditioned by its environment.

The sum of the politically relevant attitudes, behavior patterns, myths, beliefs, and values of a people constitute its political culture. Unfortunately, it is not something that can be weighed or measured with precision. Because every politically organized people is different, there are many different political cultures. Within any given society there are many subcultures that produce distinctive politically relevant consequences but that collectively make up that society's political culture. To compound the problem further, a political culture is but a subset of a people's total culture.

Any effort to identify, describe, and compare the underlying beliefs, attitudes, values, practices, and institutions of societal

1

environments within which governments exist is faced with major problems. The reader should be aware of certain obstacles in the path of any effort to identify, analyze, and compare political cultures.

First, no society consists of a perfectly homogeneous people all of whom have the same politically relevant inheritance, perspectives, beliefs, attitudes, and values. A society has no corporeal existence. Like ideas of "property" and "corporation," it is a concept of the mind. It does not possess a single, self-directing center. Societies are aggregates of individuals having disparate personalities, prejudices, and interests and groups of individuals drawn together by shared interests and objectives. It is individuals who act and react, however predictably or unpredictably they do so. Hence, any effort to identify a feature of a political culture must be understood as referring to a dominant characteristic of that culture. When most people of a society most of the time act predictably to support a politically relevant value, that value can be considered to be a dominant part of the political culture. But to say that is to indulge a fiction, for to do so one must transfer the dispositions and behaviors of millions of individuals, separately and in organized groups, to the fictional collectivity and ascribe a personality to it as though it were a natural person.

Second, what is the controlling measure of dominance? Does it refer to a belief held by a majority of the people? By three-quarters of them? Of whom? Registered voters? All persons? All adults? To be dominant may it be a temporary whim, a passing idea, or must it endure over a long period of time and have demonstrable effect?

Third, what sort of evidence must be available to substantiate the existence of a politically relevant feature of a people's culture? Is the political culture limited to those features that operate within the structure and processes of government, or does it also embrace those features in the private arenas of a society that condition the structure, policies, processes, and behavior found within the authoritative public part?

Fourth, every society is a complex entity, particularly a modern, large scale, technologically based, industrial one. It contains an almost infinite number of interdependent, sometimes supporting but sometimes conflicting, diverse institutions that exert varied pressures upon individuals and cause them to view the same problems from different perspectives. At the same time, for any society to exist for very long, its people must accept a common core of agreement about fundamental values, aspirations, and expectations and give enough support to the governmental system to enable it to operate. Without general (not unanimous) acceptance of an underlying consensus, the society will be too unstable to provide an adequate foundation for the governmental system. This probably means little more, however, than that at any given time more people approve than disapprove of the government and what it is doing. No pattern of supporting consensus is free from internal tensions.

Fifth, any given political culture undergoes continual change and can be influenced by any factor that impacts on the governmental system. Analysis and comparison of political cultures is therefore an exceedingly venturesome undertaking. Richard Rose points out that, at any given moment, a political culture embraces a conserving of traditional features and an evolutionary process of change, and he suggests that in the English political culture the things that are stable are more numerous than those that are evolving.[1] Whether or not that is true of the American political culture is at least arguable. The most serious conflict within a system is likely to take place over those aspects of its political culture that are the focus of pressures for change, for people tend to distrust change and the uncertain consequences that it often produces.

Sixth, evidence of political cultures is found in different forms. Some elements of a political culture become incorporated in statute, but most remain as understandings, as norms taken for granted and reflected in dominant beliefs, in established practices, and in public demands and expectations. Many components of a political culture tend to remain sublimated until challenged by dissident opinion or action. They may affect any aspect of a political or governmental system, a fundamental constitutional principle as well as a lesser feature of local practice.

Seventh, the content and impact of a political culture change so that a measure of fluidity characterizes the substance and foci of its values, norms, and expectations. The more stable a political system is, the less will change occur in its political culture. Unanimity of acceptance is too much to expect; but in stable political systems there will be a high level of consensual agreement about the fundamental norms and values of the system, although in an open political system there will inevitably be some disagreement about any given feature. Policy differences are resolved through the operation of politics and the party system. They can strike acceptable balances on issues over which men disagree without precipitating violence only because most members of the body politic accept its basic norms, values, and institutions. Although the American Republican and Democratic parties and the British Labor and Conservative parties disagree basically about what government ought to do and the methods to be utilized to do it, neither believes that the other is evil or supports its elimination.

Differences of individual outlook on matters of policy are usually reflections of the social, educational, economic, religious, and other influences that have shaped the character, values, and personality of each of us. Because of these variables we hold different perceptions of and priorities about what is good, needed, and important. When individuals who share similar interests and perceptions coalesce into aggregations that play active parts in the political system, the resulting interest groups and political parties provide dynamic impetus to the system's parts, giving them life and direction and often forming subcultures within the broader political culture of the society.

Eighth, not only is a political culture composed of a great number of diverse elements, but those elements are also interrelated both as to origin and effects. Many can be traced to common beginnings, and often more than one will contribute to a single result. To identify their individual roots and consequences is difficult, as is separating the politically relevant from the irrelevant or insignificant. The elements are in constant flux. New ones emerge, and old ones weaken and disappear. It is often difficult to understand their meaning, for many rest on emotion, myth, superstition, error, half-truth or some other irrational base. Many elements of American and English political cultures, for instance, are surviving forms, holdovers from earlier times and different conditions that originally generated them and gave them meaning and purpose. Inconsistencies abound among them—for example, in Britain, the presence of monarchy in a democracy, a hereditary legislative chamber in a representative law-making assembly, or working-class voters who support "silk stocking" candidates of an upper class political party. Also, for example, in the U.S., people who support democracy in principle will advocate or condone undemocratic acts; people prefer simple rural life-styles, but 72 percent live in urban complexes; people prefer local self-government, but accept remote large-scale, impersonal government; or people may be strongly individualistic but demand collective governmental action, or be charitable and champion the underdog but often be violent, antagonistic, and aloof.

Ninth, almost by definition, political cultures in open democratic systems of government lack philosophical consistency. They are not made up of a closed systems of ideas, but rather embrace the myriad different responses that result when people evaluate political beliefs, actions, conditions, and institutions in light of their personal perceptions, experiences, and interests. Subjection of individuals to the cross-pressures of interests makes any response to a momentary decision highly transitory. The pragmatic bent of Americans elevates the needs of the moment above consistent adherence to a philosophical position, producing such anomalies as a laissez faire business community demanding protective tariffs, governmental subventions, cost-plus contracts, and loss-proof ventures backed by governmental guarantees.

These examples illustrate the uncertainties that confront any effort to identify and evaluate the significance of the principal elements of a political culture. But governments are in large part the products of psychological, religious, sociological, and other forces that operate in any society; governments, particularly democratic governments, do not function in a vacuum isolated from society's vital forces. Political cultures probably do not determine political action and behavior but influence only the frequency and intensity of individual political involvement.[2] Although to rely on analysis of political cultures as a basis for understanding political forms, programs, or behavior is to lean on a weak reed, it nevertheless has some utility for understanding and making comparisons between features of different systems.

It is not possible here to present a complete analysis of the American and British political cultures, but attention can be directed to some of the principal values and beliefs operating in those societies. To borrow a phrase, major value orientations[3] exert an easily discernible influence over what those governments can do. American preference for practicality, individualism, equality, democracy, pragmatism, and efficiency has de-emphasized planning and commitment to ideological conformity in favor of an ad hoc experimental approach to public economic problems. Public planning, on the other hand, has been a major activity of Labor governments in Britain and has become so widely accepted there as to lose most of its former controversial character. In similar fashion, British accommodation of governmental activity has permitted socialized medicine and extensive public ownership that the American political culture will not yet condone.

In this chapter we will endeavor to identify and gain some understanding of selected major aspects of the American and English political cultures, for it is these political cultures that have determined and continue to influence the nature and growth of their respective political systems. Such an undertaking is to a large extent a highly subjective effort, for what one identifies as a major element of a political culture depends somewhat on how it is viewed in relation to other components. The importance to be attached to its influence is even more a matter of individual judgment and interpretation. This treatment will necessarily be an abbreviated and simplified one, but one that nevertheless will provide a sounder foundation for understanding succeeding chapters than would exist without it.

AMERICAN POLITICAL CULTURE

INFLUENCE OF NATURAL SETTING

To some extent a political culture reflects the physical characteristics and location of its national home. The large size of the United States makes essential some form of decentralized government if all the details of a greatly diversified society are not to be administered from one point by a single jurisdiction. American federalism is a direct result of an effort to organize a general government for dealing with common matters of national concern while leaving particular matters of diverse natures to the attention of localized authorities more directly in contact with them. In this instance the psychological preference for localized government brought to America by English colonists reinforced the practical need for geographical decentralization. While the United States was establishing itself as an infant nation and later, while it was preoccupied with its own internal development, its geographical position separated it from the powerful nations of Europe. Moreover, it was bounded by colonies or weak governments, and, although we worried for a while about European imperialism in South America and French conquest of Mexico, its geographic position largely eliminated the need to devote natural resources and manpower to providing and maintaining large armies and navies. In consequence, public policy makers were able to respond to the wants and demands of the American people differently than the consequences of a more danger-laden geographical position would have permitted.

Not only was the United States endowed with a large land mass with a predominantly temperate climate, but it was also richly provided with natural resources. Throughout its existence, until recent years, its domestic and foreign policy and programs could draw upon an economy of abundance. That same abundance has provided a growing economy, usually accompanied by high employment and a steadily rising standard of living. While some use has been made of tax laws to redistribute income in the United States, the increased standard of living has been realized mainly by drawing on the abundant resources of the nation rather than by redistributing the wealth of some for the benefit of others. Hence, ability, enterprise, endeavor, and leadership—the usual generators of material reward in our system—have been stimulated by knowledge that their successful application would not go unrecognized.[4] In turn, the expectation of success has fed an impetus to succeed and fostered a rags-to-riches mythology in America.

Assuming that all natural characteristics of the United States relevant to its political culture could be identified and their results traced to their causes, the task would exceed the scope of our need. However, the above examples sufficiently illustrate that a relationship does exist between nature and politics, and, as it has in the past, it will continue to affect American political culture.

Other elements of that culture reflect human as well as natural inputs. A number of them will be examined now.

INFLUENCE OF JOHN LOCKE

Americans do not subscribe to a closed system of political philosophy that presents "right" answers to major questions about the nature of man and the relationship of man to government. Nevertheless, the influence of John Locke, political philosopher of the peaceful Revolution of 1688 in England, on the American political culture cannot be overemphasized. Although most Americans have probably never heard of John Locke, they have read or heard and perhaps even memorized portions of the Declaration of Independence that might have been written by him, so well do they capture many of his key ideas. Although most Americans probably cannot articulate their understanding of those ideas or identify their source, the ideas nevertheless underlie the political culture and influence the political thinking and behavior of most of us. Most of the basic liberal principles of the American governmental system are derived from Locke's formulation and from the central core of underlying consensus on which the entire system is built. Locke and the Declaration of Independence embrace those facets of American political culture often referred to as equality, individualism, natural laws, natural rights, popular sovereignty, government of delegated powers, doctrine of consent, ascendency of legislative over executive power, separated powers (primarily derived from the Frenchman Louis de Secondat Montesquieu, however), right of revolution, majority rule, government by law, republicanism, economic free enterprise and preference for rights of property. The emanations of these ideas penetrate most of the fundamental concepts of the American political culture in different degrees and in different ways. It is impossible here to trace their penetrations and interrelationships, but their influence is inescapable and determines much contemporary American political thought and practice.

AMERICAN COLONIAL EXPERIENCE

The experiences of American colonists under British rule made indelible impressions on local governmental institutions and values.

Examples come easily to mind. The arbitrariness of colonial governors produced a reaction against strong executive authority, so that under the Articles of Confederation no separate executive was provided for, and under the Constitution the powers of the president were limited and checked, and a short term was attached to his office. Experiences with British courts and justice contributed significantly to insistence upon the addition of a Bill of Rights to the new Constitution and went far to determine the specified guarantees of the first eight amendments. Elected representative colonial legislatures emerged as the popular organs of colonial governments because they were directly elected and because, in contrast to governors who spoke for royal authority and interests, they championed the people's interests. Later, the colonial assemblies spearheaded the expression of popular dissidence that culminated in the exercise of Locke's right of revolution. Much of that course of events came to pass because conditions in America had long been conducive to self-government and to the development of indigenous leaders, native institutions, self-confidence, and political maturity.

Culture at the time of the Revolution launched Americans on the path toward egalitarianism. Egalitarianism received a strong boost by the absence in America of any form of social stratification on the model of European feudalism. No hard class lines existed, and once titled Englishmen left for America such differences as distinguished man from man were of an acquired, not hereditary, character. Opportunities for economic fulfillment held out the promise that they could be eliminated by an independent, enterprising, imaginative and self-reliant person. The world's most liberal suffrage of that day gave added thrust to colonial egalitarianism by giving an equal vote to each free, white, adult male citizen. The underlying ideology of the American future was set out by John Locke and captured in the Declaration of Independence. Colonial charters served as the antecedents of assembled, documentary constitutions which were widely accepted as social contracts establishing governments of delegated powers by consent of the governed. The disallowance of colonial statutes by royal veto and the reversal of decisions of colonial courts by the privy council in London doubtless conditioned American thinking to accept judicial review, first under state constitutions and later under the United States Constitution.

CONSTITUTIONAL DEVELOPMENT

No sharp demarcation separates the political influences of the preconstitutional and constitutional eras. The drafting of the Constitution was only another step in American political development and built on much that went before it. Had there been no Articles of Confederation there could have been no Constitution of the United States as it came out of the Philadelphia convention. Hence, fear of too-strong government accounted, at least in part, for divided authority—divided between the three branches of government, between a general government and the states, and between two chambers of the national legislature. Representative democracy was provided for in a Congress, only one house of which was popularly elected, however. The spirit of republicanism produced an elected executive with a fixed term of office in place of hereditary succession, life tenure, or some other arrangement providing for less accountability. Popular sovereignty was recognized by providing for periodic direct elections of representatives, but fear of majority tyranny resulted in an indirect system for selecting presidents. Popular sovereignty was also expressed in the spirit of the Constitution's preamble, which declares that "We the people . . . do ordain and establish this Constitution for the United States of America."

To prevent abuse of power, the framers provided not only specific limitations but also a partial overlapping of separated powers so authority could be used to check authority within the tripartite division among the legislative, executive, and judicial branches. The legacy of intercolonial separateness and of state sovereignty, explicitly recognized by the Articles of Confederation, was accommodated by the establishment of federalism. But the nature of the new union was not resolved at Philadelphia and endured until the American Civil War settled the argument about whether a state could secede from the union.

These arrangements and their philosophical underpinnings have become deeply ingrained parts of American political heritage and culture. They are fervently endorsed by persons who do not understand them but who know they came from the founding fathers and must therefore embody the essence of political wisdom. The Constitution was widely regarded as a social contract, as an expression of the consent of the people to be subjected to governmental authority delegated and limited by themselves. Its vitality was proof that just government could be created among men according to natural law and natural rights. Although this philosophical underpinning current during Revolutionary and formative America has lost much of its rational appeal, it remains part of the American political ethic and culture. Today, Rosenbaum, citing Daniel Boorstin, points out that Americans accept the basic constitutional values as a given, a fact that Rosenbaum calls a particularly notable feature of our political culture.[5]

ABSENCE OF SOCIAL CONSCIOUSNESS IN AMERICANS

Most Americans feel only a vague sense of social consciousness or obligation. Most of us are, however, intensely preoccupied with our private, personal, and individual selves; the goods we pursue are overwhelmingly private goods of a material kind. Although we individually respond charitably and with empathy for the downtrodden, disadvantaged underdog, we still stand by and let even murder be done rather than get involved. Typically we have little sense of social obligation, of values of a nonegocentric nature to be served by private voluntary actions of individuals. So time, energy, and interest are consumed largely by family and job, with little if any of either left over for devotion to civic service. Private, not public, values govern most of our actions. Our concept of the individual's relationship to society is all too often perceived as atomistic, like separate pebbles in a pile, each of which retains its individual identity, rather than as having a corporate or cooperative identity in society.

DYNAMIC ELEMENT IN AMERICAN POLITICAL CULTURE

Americans like dynamic change. The strong strain in the English political culture of resistance to rapid social transformations exists in the United States only in a minority faction that espouses a return to classical individualism of the nineteenth century. There is little room in a society like the American for retrospective traditionalism. Here, the principal measure of merit of a person, institution, idea, or process is success. Will it work? Does it get results?

Here, also, history is too short and the pace of life too rapid to produce a reverential attitude for what has been. Americans tend to be of prospective rather than retrospective outlook. The future lies ahead: Look forward, not behind! American stress on accomplishment assumes change, and change leaves little room for sentimental attachment to the past. Institutions of the present are generally assumed to be temporary and deserve to survive only until displaced, as they inevitably will be, by something better. The doctrine of progress is as much a part of the American political culture as the doctrine of tradition is of the English. Whereas the past permeates almost every phase of English political culture, it has little value or permanent impact in the American. Indeed, we have brought into being several examples of "instant history" to strengthen our weak sense of heritage and continuity with the past.

MATERIALISM

American culture places a heavy value on material wealth. The roots of this emphasis are several. It drew sustenance from the vast area of the United States and its abundant wealth; from the immigrants' dream of making a better material life than could have been achieved at home; from the Lockian stress on the creation of property by mixing human labor with the bounty of nature; from Locke's teaching that government was created by men to make more secure their natural right to possession of property accumulated through individual effort; from the spirit of American capitalism with its advocacy of individual initiative, free enterprise, and profits, as reinforced by the laissez faire doctrines of nineteenth century Social Darwinism; and from the nineteenth century era of corporatism. From all of these sources has come a pronounced tendency to regard material possessions as objects of competition, as objects whose possession is good in itself (an end in itself), and also a tendency to use accumulation of material things as the measure of an individual's success and of his worth as an individual.

INDIVIDUALISTIC CONCEPTION OF POLITICS

Individualism permeates the American's conception of political, as well as of economic, man. There lingers among many Americans an ingenuous acceptance of the classical ideal of the motivated, informed, statesmanlike citizen who is an independent, meaningful entity in the political process. According to that ideal, each political participant seeks all possible alternatives, identifies probable consequences of each, rationally evaluates general good, and opts for the alternative policy that most closely approximates realization of the desired end. Furthermore, it is politically active individuals, not pressure groups, political parties, power brokers, or decisional elites, who are the motive force of the mechanism. Political involvement, according to this conception of the political relationship, is a privilege and obligation of citizenship in a democratic system. Some of its flavor is captured in the one man, one vote principle; some of it is reflected by democracy's reservation to each rational adult of the right to determine for himself what obligation to obey the law exists when its mandate clashes with the individual's conscience. But when voters realize that the system responds to group power and that decision making is vested in multiple centers rather than in aggregates of discrete, informed, publically motivated, citizen voters, apathy, disillusionment, or alienation typically sets in. Because bossism, corruption, and elitism do exist, disillusioned American citizen-voters tend to associate organized politics with those and other evils. Politics and assumption of public office become dirty business that good honest people avoid, even though the right to hold public office and to conduct the public business is democratically open to everyone instead of being the prescriptive right of a small group.

SOCIAL EQUALITY

The openness of access to public office reflects another aspect of American culture having far-reaching political importance. A sense of the social equality of each person is deeply ingrained in the cultural ethic. That it is reserved in practice for whites is, of course, a contradiction and blot upon the purity of the ideal, but its message is rooted in John Locke's legacy to our political culture, trumpeted by the Declaration of Independence, reinforced by the Protestant emphasis on the equal worth of every individual in the eyes of God and the possibility, equally open to everyone, to attain salvation. The ideal is further strengthened by the abundance of opportunity for individual material betterment. The Constitution's repudiation of titles of nobility, the absence of class-stratified society on the European model, the influence of America as the land of opportunity, and the influx of millions of immigrants seeking to attain material well-being could only have operated throughout their history to enhance a sense of social equality and promote social mobility among Americans. All of those forces reinforce an ingrained insistence that although we differ in many discernible ways, no person is worth more than another as a person.

The ideal of equality has practical meaning as well as moral force. Economically it has come to mean equality of opportunity —the concept that each person ought to have an opportunity to make of himself whatever he has the luck, incentive, good judgment, and ability to succeed in doing, free from artificial constraints arbitrarily imposed by society. Further, the ideal of equality translates legally into the Constitution's guarantee that no person shall be denied life, liberty, or property without due process of law or be denied the equal protection of equal laws. Equality before the law (equal justice under law) means at least that the law ought not advantage or disadvantage anyone by virtue of capricious, arbitrary, or whimsical substance or application.

But the ideal of equality has not prevented a strong strain of racism from developing in American culture. Although the institution of slavery was destroyed by the Civil War, that war did not eradicate from our beliefs the moral, religious, economic and pseudoscientific arguments put forth to justify the "peculiar institution." Moreover, abolition by bayonet left behind a bitter legacy of reciprocal distrust. It did not eliminate a consciousness of white superiority, and it left behind an unassimilated depressed minority whose presence in American society gave the lie both to philosophical assumptions of equality of men and opportunity and to the "melting pot" thesis.

Furthermore, the ideal of equality in American society conflicts with the ideal of freedom, for freedom to assert one's capabilities as one's goals and initiative to lead produce unequal results because all men do not start even. The more favored will probably emerge ahead of the less favored competitors in a free struggle, so that inequalities of possession, power, status, and influence will be produced among the members of society. Conversely, equality can be maintained only by constraining individual freedom. Philosophically, the conflict can be resolved by saying that neither freedom nor equality is an end in itself, but both are means to the development of individual personality, which is the ultimate end of social life. Americans, however, hold a decided preference for freedom and show a pronounced willingness to tolerate the resulting inequality.

OPPORTUNISTIC DISREGARD FOR THE LAW

In spite of their professed belief in equality and the fact that Americans are probably the most litigious people in the world, they individually and collectively show a disposition to opportunistically disregard the legal processes and to take direct and even violent action. Locke taught and the Declaration of Independence proclaimed a natural right of men to act in a revolutionary way—outside the law—in order to throw off injustice. The revolutionary tradition of eliminating oppression or other social evil by acting outside the law has had a long presence in the American political culture. In recent and contemporary times it has appeared in many forms, among them lynchings, intimidation, vigilantism, passive resistance, sit-ins, riots, marches, bombings, and assassinations. The tendency to act on the assumption that a just end legitimates almost any means that might be chosen to attain it, and to assume that a virtuous motive excuses perpetrators from normal punitive processes and sanctions, runs strong in American political character. To cheat on one's income tax or to run a stop sign on a deserted road are parts of the game of citizenship.

STRONG CONSENSUAL SUPPORT FOR THE SYSTEM

Notwithstanding the ready willingness of many to take illegal action to attain their ends, most Americans register strong support for the basic principles of the constitutional, political, and legal systems. They place heavy stress on ideals of the founding fathers and profess to endeavor to fulfill them in practice. Typically, our political culture shows little tolerance for nonconformity to approved political beliefs and practices, and advocates of alternative systems have traditionally met with a cold reception. We declare the benefits of liberality, but all too often we exhibit strains of developed political intolerance. Most amendments to the Constitution have concerned only mechanical aspects of its operation and have left its basic principles untouched, for much of the systemic support stems from the tendency to attribute to the Constitution's framers the wisdom and status of demigods and to transfer the presumed virtues of the document's drafters to the institutions and principles of government embodied in it.

Systemic support is also derived from the promise of American constitutionalism—the promise it held out to millions of foreign-born persons for a better life of toleration, economic freedom and opportunity, and social equality and mobility, all made more realizable by the existence of an open system of tax-supported general public education. Outside the ranks of such groups as the Weathermen and the Symbionese Liberation Army, little condemnation of basic constitutional principles and institutions is heard. Support remains high in spite of increased political alienation among Americans brought on by the Viet Nam War, Watergate, and existing economic and social problems. Withholding of support is clearly a principal reaction directed against specific partisan politicians, organizations, policies, and programs. Of course, the strength of systemic support varies among groups. It is stronger, for example, among whites than among blacks, among middle-aged Americans than among young adults.

SELF-CONFIDENCE AND OPTIMISM

Self-confidence and optimism are two facets of American character, individual and national, that appear and reappear in many forms. We take for granted that the future will always be bright; problems can always be overcome by application of American know-how, initiative and ingenuity. "Where there is a will, there is a way" might appropriately be made our national motto. A mobilization of science, resources, and common sense can triumph over any national adversity. In their efforts to solve their problems, Americans place their confidence in the lessons of practical experience and tend to distrust proposals generated by exercises in abstract intellectualism. Behind these characteristics are frontier self-reliance and individualism and the collective spirit of a barn raising magnified and applied on a national scale.

AMBIVALENT ATTITUDES TOWARD POLITICS

Although most Americans will give strong systemic support to their constitutional order and readily affirm their belief in democratic principles, most also reveal a negative attitude toward partisan politics and government and exhibit low levels of civic activity, for politics are widely regarded as "dirty." Politics are widely assumed to require politicians to engage in dishonest, demeaning, selfish, self-serving, degrading, and shameful activities that "nice" people will not undertake. Partisan politics have the widespread reputation among Americans of being a haven for unscrupulous individuals; persons who are pillars of the community, at least in their own eyes, often dislike becoming involved in an activity so widely held in disrepute. Preoccupation with private affairs and the bad public reputation of elective politics combine to cause many Americans to refuse to seek public office. Thus, at the same time that most Americans strongly support the institutions, principles, and symbols of democracy and hold them in high regard, the personnel who man public offices are often perceived as scoundrels.

American disdain for political involvement extends to the mechanism for choosing officers of government, enforcing accountability, and conferring consent—the electoral process. Although voting in national elections is the most prominent form of political activity engaged in by most Americans, the nonvoting rate in national elections is high compared to the participation rates of electorates in other democracies. Few Americans campaign on behalf of candidates, make donations, or work for a political party, and fewer still seek elective public office under a party label. Party identification is at best a tenuous thing in the United States, and a growing proportion of the American electorate does not identify with any political party. Frustration, alienation and apathy run strongly through the political outlook of large segments of the public, especially among young adults, members of minority groups, and the poor. Nonetheless, most American voters in all societal components feel that their political participation is meaningful and can exert a discernible effect upon decision makers and processes of government.[6] Although the political cultures of both American and British citizenry reflect high levels of confidence in their constitutional systems, Rosenbaum concludes that Americans are more suspicious of and more disposed to distrust politicians and public officials and more apt to challenge authority and insist on accountability than the British are.[7]

THE OPEN SOCIETY

The American political culture places heavy emphasis upon the virtue of individual freedoms, particularly those associated with the open expression and communication of politically relevant ideas. The First Amendment's guarantees of free speech, press, association, and petition, and the privilege of voting in frequent elections brought on by short terms of office reflect the combined influences of colonial experience and Jacksonian democracy. American society has remained relatively free from governmentally imposed censorship, even in wartime. But despite efforts to use the channels of political communication to pass on the values of an open society to successive generations of Americans, those values inevitably encounter situations in which their meaning and applicability are cloudy; because their idealism makes them inherently somewhat unrealistic, respect for and adherence to them is far from perfect. It is a paradox of American political culture that whereas we give individual freedoms generous lip service in principle, we are often willing to condone outrageous departures from their conscientious implementation. Even the Supreme Court of the United States has on occasion appeared to collapse in the face of public opinion hostile to claims of these basic rights.

ECONOMIC ORIENTATION OF THE AMERICAN POLITICAL CULTURE

Capitalism has been and largely remains the economic foundation of American political democracy. Once again, the origins of this belief lie deep in the philosophical and historical foundations of the system. Locke taught that property originated when men mixed labor with natural goods and thereby acquired title to as much as could be used or stored without waste. The right to property was one of Locke's enumerated natural rights and found its vay into the Fifth Amendment along with "life" and "liberty." The principal reason men created government was to protect property, Locke wrote. The message of free economic enterprise also came through from the philosophers of the American Revolution. The Constitution devotes so much attention to property rights that Charles A. Beard, one of America's most eminent historians, in his *Economic Interpretation of the Constitution* concluded that its framers regarded the new plan as essentially one to safeguard the interests of property owners. Adam Smith's *Wealth of Nations* was published in 1776 and preached the gospel of individual pursuit of economic self-interest, maintenance of a free-market economy, and preservation of a competitive economic mechanism free from governmental interference left to operate according to unimpeded functioning of natural economic laws. The search for a better life in America by economically deprived immigrants was partly a response to the promise of material betterment through application of individual effort to land and resources in a setting of abundance free from barriers to economic endeavor. If human incentive and philosophical justification were insufficient to bestow respectability on capitalism, the Protestant message that material gain was evidence of God's favor ran strong through the land and could be invoked as divine approval of temporal materialism and its mode of acquisition.[8] And although William Graham Sumner's *What Social Classes Owe to Each Other* was published in America more than one hundred years after independence and *The Wealth of Nations,* it carried the message that in the competitive struggle, the most fit would survive. Conversely, success was evidence of fitness. Hence, by means of competition's eliminating the unfit, society would be benefited and strengthened, and all would be accomplished through natural processes of selection. Moreover, just as laissez faire economics taught that natural laws ought be left by government to operate freely, so the Social Darwinism of Sumner taught that the ineluctable processes of natural selection should be free from governmental efforts at social reform. Otherwise, puny misguided efforts of administrators would produce nothing but social deterioration brought on by government's interference with the wisdom and processes of nature.[9] Classical economics and Social Darwinism made a powerful impression on American thought in the late nineteenth and early twentieth centuries. The rapid industrialization of America and its emergence by the end of the nineteenth century as an exporting and manufacturing nation seem irrefutably to prove the validity of the free enterprise gospel of laissez faire capitalism. Its message of do-nothing government became a part of the political culture and today remains a strong current of thought affecting the attitudes of many Americans about the role government should play in society, particularly regarding its relationship to the economy and to business. Its proponents are among the most vigorous opponents of social welfare and other reform legislation, of the welfare state, and of governmental involvement in the lives of Americans and their organized interests. The traditions of free competition, of an unregulated market economy, of the profit motive, and of curtailed government reinforce existing American suspicion of governmental power and involvement in spite of the contemporary dominant expectation that government will play a positive role to enhance the material and psychological well-being of the citizenry.

DIVISIVE FORCES IN AMERICAN SOCIETY

The American political culture also reflects the fact that the American people present a bewildering variety of diverse components. Women demand equal treatment in a male-dominated society; many blacks feel they are second class citizens in a white-dominated society; the rural-urban cleavage endures in the minds of millions of small town residents who even in 1981 regard cities as sinks of evil and city dwellers as condemned; labor and management continue to struggle, often in an atmosphere of mutual distrust and suspicion; Catholics and Protestants contend not only for men's souls, but often acrimoniously and with deeply ingrained suspicion over the issue of public aid for parochial schools; and millions of Americans suspect and distrust their governmental leaders. Ethnic divisions endure and refute the concept of American society as the great melting pot, receiving waves of immigrants, changing them in its crucible, and recasting them into that new being—the American. Ethnic subcultures and old allegiances resist transformation and absorption. They have long been a source of tension, disquiet, and disharmony in American society and are reflected in our public policy, partisan politics, and political behavior. Perhaps because of the great size of the United States, ethnic, religious, and racial differences survive and resist the processes of societal homogenization.

But the worst failure of America to live up to its ideals is probably found in its treatment of blacks, native Americans, hispanics, and orientals. The record of governmentally endorsed discrimination against these domestic populations needs no elaboration and stands as testimony to the extent that unreconciled hostilities have permeated the American political culture. The presence of religious, ethnic, racial, and cultural diversity has impacted heavily on it and left many scars that are politically relevant today.

That same diversity, however, has influenced our political culture for the good by stimulating the development of attitudes and values in our national character that help overcome the disintegrative consequences of diversity. By unifying and homogenizing our outlook and practices toward one another, attitudes of equality, tolerance, mutual acceptance, moderation, cooperation, good will, compromise, self-restraint, and at least a modicum of national good humor, have enabled Americans to attain a high level of political development and self-government. At the same time, ours is the most pluralistic society in the world, and deep divisions that strain the democratizing influences of the above attitudes constantly threaten the social fabric and occasionally result in temporary losses of effective social control.

ENGLISH POLITICAL CULTURE

In spite of all that the British and American people share by way of similar experiences, stable democracy, common cultural heritage, legal tradition, and devotion to constitutional government and political liberalism, there is a common political culture only to the level of principles and values. At the level of specific institutions, attitudes, and practices, there are many divergent aspects in the two political traditions attributable to differences of geographical position, size, social structure and characteristics, values, and economic and political history.

Although America is young and Britain is much older, both political cultures are highly integrated, which, according to W. A. Rosenbaum,[10] means that they exhibit the following features:

1. possession of a strong national government supported by general agreement that it is entitled to receive its citizens' primary loyalty, albeit active local governments and associated loyalties are present;
2. general agreement about the legitimacy of governmental institutions, their structures and modes of operations, limits of authority, methods for choosing governors, and methods of enforcing accountability; and other fundamental norms of the system;
3. existence of a high level of mutual trust between competing interests, agreement on legitimate methods of conflict resolution, and sustained ability to govern society unmarked by major outbreaks of lawlessness;
4. diffusion of political power among a wide diversity of centers that attain temporary dominance by constructing alliances of support based on compromise, persuasion, and bargaining in an atmosphere mostly free of sharp antagonisms and deeply rooted fears;
5. strong allegiance to and trust in the system undiluted by a significant measure of apathy toward or alienation from the constitutional regime.

Rosenbaum suggests that no other nation matches the United States and Britain in the degree to which integration of the political culture has been attained and political stability maintained.[11]

ENGLISH UNITY

The English system is often held out as one of the most stable systems of government, and the reason often advanced to account for that quality is the cultural homogeneity of its people. England, in contrast to the large expanse of the United States, is a small entity whose people are characterized by a high degree of political integration.

A strong sense of national identity has developed among them hat separates them from the peoples of continental Europe. The population is overwhelmingly white, Protestant, English speaking, and ethnically distinct from Europe's.[12] They support a dominant national Church of England, read a half-dozen nationally distributed newspapers available in all parts of England on the day of publication, have a strongly developed sense of trust and confidence in their governmental institutions, and are divided into numerous subgroups that generally do not regard one another with hostility or distrust. Their politically important internal cultural differences have not required recognition in the form of specially created subnational political units. In other words, their significant differences within the political culture have not exceeded the capacity of the national government to handle them. Societal cleavages generated by differences of race, language, ethnicity, religion, or other potential sources of hostilities have been successfully subliminated or eliminated in the political culture so that their disruptive force has been largely subordinated to the requirements of national unity. They no longer seriously fragment society or undermine the basic consensus essential to stable general government in a unitary system. Socialization of successive generations of Englishmen has instilled in most of them acceptance of the dominant institutions, values, and beliefs of the political culture. Whereas localism is a prominent feature of American government, the unitary English government, utilizing parliamentary delegations of authority to parliamentarily created local authorities, has not weakened the centralization of law, policy making, or administration established centuries ago at the expense of independent local authority.

Every social system, however, is divided by some criteria into subsystems. It should occasion no surprise to find that English cultural homogeneity on closer inspection is found to embrace some sharp internal divisions, many of which have significant political consequences. Within the broader political culture of Great Britain, those of Northern Ireland, Wales, and Scotland differ from that of England, and within that broader context Welsh, Irish, and Scottish nationalism have exerted an increasingly strong divisive force since the election of 1974. The political culture of England is also torn by an element of racial tension injected into the body politic by the presence of large numbers of immigrants from non-Anglo Commonwealth countries who comprise a distinct subculture within the dominant one.

In addition, the English political culture presents a pluralistic aggregate of diverse interests striving to gain recognition, influence, or material or psychic gain for their members. Although religion was once an influence more divisive than nationalism is in today's political culture, England, like the United States, is a highly secularized nation. Religious tolerance is now set deep in the political culture so that religion in English politics produces no sharp tears in the social fabric. But it does have considerable impact. The established church and much of its membership tends to align with the Conservative party and to support the values and institutions of the traditional system. The nonconforming sects and their adherents have been pronounced supporters of governmental innovation and reform, critics of conservative action, proponents of mass political participation, supporters of trade unionism, advocates of socialist policies and programs, and generally attractive to the lower classes. The nonconforming sects have played a modernizing role in English politics, challenging traditional elitism and its foundations, stimulating greater democratic political participation, and weakening the force of ingrained deference as a proper attitude of the governed toward their governors. Particularistic interests abound within the English political culture, and those differences are politically significant.

SOCIAL MOBILITY

Upward social mobility is not difficult in England, but compared to America, not many Englishmen are driven by a desire to better their socio-economic status. The capitalist work ethic has not had anything like the impact on the British that it has had on Americans. Large numbers of working-class families are content with their social status, and, while the parents of English working-class youths feel that their children enjoy greater opportunity for upward mobility than existed when the parents were young, most of the parents and offspring are satisfied to stay in the working class. English parents do not seem to be anxious for their children to take advantage of educational reforms that might make it possible to escape their status for a better one. Their outlook contrasts with the American ideal that each generation should enjoy greater advantages in life than its predecessor did. British class stability produces easier political socialization by exposing individuals to fewer conflicting pressures and discontinuities and increases regularized political behavior.[13] Most members of English society hold a realistic perception of their social status and pursue education for work appropriate to their station, so that upper-class children attend grammar schools for entry into a university and ultimately a profession; middle-class and upper middle-class children tend to attend the same secondary schools, but may or may not go to university before entering employment in business, finance, commerce, or public service. Working-class children mainly attend comprehensive or vocational schools, often dropping out as soon as they are of age to enter a trade, agriculture, or other work. There are, of course, some individuals in every class who are either upwardly or downwardly mobile. But there is no question that, regardless of class, the educational pattern followed by a young person will significantly influence his chances in later life and may even permanently brand him as inferior.

INEQUALITY AND DEFERENCE

A sense and acceptance of social inequality is deeply rooted in British political character.[14] Government historically has been in the hands of a few persons drawn from a small segment of society —"the rich, the wise, and the well-born." Popular sovereignty has never been a fundamental principle of the British constitution, as it is often cited to be of the American. The franchise in England was tightly restricted and extension to the masses of voters came slowly. Four hundred and two years passed between the suffrage act of 1430 enfranchising "forty shilling freeholders" (owners of real property having the then substantial rental value of forty shillings per year) and that of 1832 extending the vote to a growing middle class. The Reform Bill of 1832, however, was not enacted to promote democracy in England but was a pragmatic response to shifted political power. The Whig party astutely enacted it to take advantage of an opportunity to strengthen its political base among the people. The English did not recognize the principle of one man, one vote until 1948, when plural voting privileges for graduates of Oxford and Cambridge Universities were abolished. The egalitarianism of Andrew Jackson's frontier democracy in America stands in sharp contrast to Edmund Burke's formulation of a doctrine of natural inequality and inequality of rights and status. Inequality remains a value of Conservative party philosophy, and efforts of Labor governments after World War II to level income disparities, democratize education, increase mass political activity, and raise the social position of working people brought forth renewed expressions of the value of social inequality from conservative quarters in England.[15]

The basis of inequality in British political culture is the attitude of deference to one's betters that is widely held among its middle-class and lower-class members. Whereas an American would probably automatically bridle at the suggestion that his opinions were not worth as much as the next person's, many Englishmen accept without resentment the premise that some members of society are superior to many others.[16] Democratization of the franchise and broadened access to education have not appreciably weakened that attitude. British decision makers are not expected to be back-slapping men of the people, but individuals recognized as possessing outstanding qualities of maturity, judgment, and responsibility that place them above the common man.

The American's sense of egalitarianism is to be contrasted to the Englishman's acceptance of deference and inequality. Many Americans who tend to identify themselves with some stratum of society, one usually denominated in economic terms, hold a degree of class consciousness in their social outlook. American class identity, however, is not held with much intensity; does not provide a class base for a political party; is not reflected in differences of dress, manners, speech, education, and recreation; and does not divide Americans into "us" and "them." Americans of one class do not typically acknowledge that members of a higher status possess some right to rule that is superior to that of persons in a lower status group. American egalitarianism overrides the American sense of class and eliminates from American political culture many deferential attitudes that promote the existence of a hierarchical society. The American attitude is that no person can claim a right to rule another that the second cannot assert with equal justification against the first. Americans do not accept the idea of a hierarchically structured society. The American political culture assumes that each person lays claim to possession of as much innate right to self-determination as he grants to each other person; that no one possesses superior political wisdom amounting to a right to rule; and that even the most ignorant person can make a contribution to the good order and operation of the political system in the form of common sense and intuitive rightmindedness.

DISTRUST OF INTELLECTUALISM IN BRITISH POLITICS

Richard Rose reports that English political culture is suspicious of clever men whose political policies are determined by intellectualism unguided by practical experience.[17] Rationalism is regarded as having definite limits, and intellectuals, whether of the right or left, are not readily trusted as practitioners of the political arts. English resistance to intellectualism in political life shows up in one form as the Burkean conservative's dislike of sudden change; such conservatives see nonevolutionary change as a process that tears up old institutions root and branch so that they can be replaced by intellectualized substitutes, untested by practical experience and the acceptance of generations of men. The English can never escape the past, nor do most of them want to. Gradualism is the keynote of English political change. The Conservative party yields to changing conditions that produce pressure for accommodation so that it will not be engulfed by political forces it refused to acknowledge. Although the Labor party champions socialism and nationalization, it is a state socialism that will be established by using existing parliamentary processes and machinery, not by the forcible destruction of the status quo and the substitution for it of a proletarian dictatorship. Communism is too extreme for most members of the British working class. To date, the nationalization brought about by the Labor party has been selective; no general takeover of the instruments of production, distribution, and exchange has been attempted. Just as the Conservative party has learned to live with national health insurance and nationalization of the steel, transport, and other industries, the Labor party has learned to tolerate a large, private enterprise, capitalist sector in the British economy. Whereas Americans seem to prefer dynamic change, the English seem to believe that virtue is on the side of age and the test of time. This ability of each English political party to endure features of the other's programs has promoted systemic stability, gradual evolutionary change, and moderation. It is also testimony to the mutual trust that English political parties exhibit toward one another, but that is not to say that either party endorses what it pragmatically assimilates of the other's programs.

PRAGMATISM

The stable, responsive, and effective governments found in the United States and England are pragmatically oriented, although both contain numerous ideological threads running through them that tie together groups of individuals who find their various pre-scriptions compatible. By pragmatic is meant an outlook toward government and its activities that is essentially based on trial and error, instead of on a preconceived comprehensive belief system that purports to set out prescribed ends and means for government and society. A pragmatic approach judges policies and actions by their consequences, rather than by their conformity to abstract principle.[18] It responds to practical problems of men in society rather than to the problems of implementing and remaining true to the ideals of a more or less closed system of beliefs. It is open-minded because it is not committed to one true way to virtue. It is able to respond more readily to problems of urban decay, rising crime rates, mass transportation, unequal rights, and the like without having to force policy choices into conformity with a pattern of ideological prescription. But neither Americans nor Britons are devoid of systemic beliefs that influence the ways individuals per-ceive public problems and policies. Some measure of consistency and predictability in the political culture is essential, for example, to the existence of political parties. All that American and British pragmatism can mean, therefore, is that the dominant outlook of both political cultures is free of ties to an all-pervasive frame-work of principles to which the system of government, its values and programs are subordinated, as in Hitler's Third Reich or the contemporary Soviet Union. Like Americans, the British people agree to disagree in an atmosphere of good-natured accommodation, to tolerate different concepts of the general good and policies to realize it, and to support the legitimacy of political opposition.

British pragmatism can be observed in numerous features of their constitutional system. The common law represents an accommodation to the practical needs of governmental centralization and legal uniformity in a country previously characterized by Anglo-Saxon localism; the Conservative party, despite its elitist preferences, extended the suffrage to working-class Englishmen after the Liberals had done the same for the middle class. The Conservatives merely bowed to the fact that their party could not survive on a foundation of only aristocratic support. The monarchy has been retained in spite of its paradoxical position in a democratic system of government because of its recognized value, symbolic and practical, for that system. But authority to govern has been shifted from monarch to Parliament consistent with the principles of political liberalism; from Parliament to cabinet in response to needs for centralized planning, enactment and implementation of public policy and for responsible party control; and as yet partially from the cabinet to the prime minister in acknowledgement of the fact that party government in a modern industrialized society needs party identification and centralized leadership focused in the office of a single leader.

EVOLUTIONARY DEVELOPMENT

British political culture and its political and governmental institutions are the products of a long series of ad hoc responses to the recognized needs of forces in society that had to be accommodated. Of all extant liberal governments, that of England is probably most often cited as being the epitome of the evolutionary type gradually refined through a long course of history. In contrast, that of the United States was produced by a small group of men at a specific time and place following the revolutionary overthrow of a previous allegiance. The essence of the evolutionary tradition does not lie in the absence of revolutionary events from national history, for the English have experienced two such events. Neither, however, broke the main thread of evolutionary development toward constitutional monarchy and political liberalism. Conversely, the American government has felt the soft influence of gradual change during its relatively short life in, for example, the slow transfer of power to the presidency from the Congress, in the rise of political parties, and in the establishment and rise to primacy of judicial review.

RELIGION

The English people are 90 percent Protestant and are not divided by a politically significant religious schism. It is a commentary on the prevailing high level of religious tolerance and mutual trust that there is no Roman Catholic political party in England. In the United States, the constitutional wall of separation between church and state assures that no official religion such as the Church of England can be set up. Although English religious freedom and tolerance are much valued today, their official national church, the Church of England, exists. The Queen is its formal head; its archbishops are appointed by the Queen and sit in the House of Lords. Since the days of Henry VIII, the first monarch to head the Anglican church, there has been a close political association between the Anglican hierarchy and the temporal rulers of England. In contemporary terms, the Church of England, being hierarchical and traditionalist, has been the choice of many supporters of deference, status, and authority who mainly support the Conservative party.

Nonconformist Protestant religions enjoy no similar relationship to the state. They are congregational rather than hierarchically organized and permit their individual congregations to govern the separate churches within the denomination. Their members have latitude for the interpretation of scripture and can withdraw from one church and form a new congregation in the event of irreconcilable internal differences. These features of non-Anglican Protestantism inculcate values of independent thought and action in their members, teach and accept a type of revolutionary right in the form of congregational division, encourage the development of independence of action and self-governance on a congregational scale, and imply that governance of the congregational church is by consent of the members subject to it. Hence, nonconformist chapels have served as breeding places for the virtues of democracy and equality in the English political culture and as a means for instilling them in the people. Those circumstances made a special affinity develop between first the Liberal party and later the Labor party and the supporters of nonconformist denominations. They are also less tradition bound, more liberal in their attitude toward change, and less supportive of state authority than Anglicanism has been. Whereas the Anglican church has traditionally been the spiritual home of the ruling elite of England, the nonconformist sects attracted the support of the lower classes and, by aligning with the Liberal and Labor parties, played an important role in English politics and the formation of English political culture.[19]

EDUCATION AND CLASS

To understand many aspects of English political culture one must understand something about the class structure of the society and the relationship of the educational system to it, for the first is largely dependent on the second.

English society is hierarchically stratified into a still clearly differentiated lower class, lower middle class, middle class, upper middle class, aristocracy, and nobility. It is a deferentially oriented society in which the mass of people generally concede that a small elite group has a legitimate superior claim to hold important public office and to make decisions affecting the public business. English upper classes enjoy a largely ascribed status.[20] Deference translates into the idea that the small segment of society advantaged by money, influence, education, status, culture, and family heritage ought to govern. That idea is particularly attractive to persons of a conservative persuasion but is not widely held today in the ranks of Liberals and Laborites.

The educational systems in relation to class structure play contrasting roles in the United States and England. The American system of public education is a bulwark protecting democratic egalitarianism. One of its major purposes is to remove from the public consciousness any inclination toward social stratification. However, the English social structure is tied to and in large measure maintained by the British educational system. Rose asserts that the educational system has always stressed inequality of intellect, opportunity, and social status.[21] Despite many educational reforms undertaken in recent years by Labor governments, English society remains a basically stratified society; the dominant attitude of acceptance seems unweakened by the efforts at educational democratization[22] and the class structure of British society continues to be firmly anchored at both ends.

Different ideas toward the value of access to education operate in the United States and England. Americans feel they have the right to a public tax-supported education from primary school through college. Requirements for admission are generally moderate and can usually be met by most secondary students. Entry into post-secondary education is taken for granted by the sons and daughters of millions of working-class families in America as well as by those of parents in white-collar and professional occupations. But in England, access to higher education has traditionally been restricted to a relatively small percentage of the college-age population. Carter reports that before World War II only one person out of every thousand had received advanced education.[23] Efforts of recent Labor governments to broaden access to higher education have brought it closer to the general population, however.

The British have ended use of the "eleven plus" examination to discriminate between pupils who possessed academic ability and were eligible for preuniversity education and those who did not and could go only into vocational training. The "eleven plus" examination was long a crucial determinant of the British youngster's educational future. It was taken on completion of primary school at about age eleven and stressed general knowledge and the development of logical, verbal, and other skills. It was successfully passed by only about 25 percent of those who took it.[24] Because success on the examination was a prerequisite to college preparatory education, failure prematurely but effectively cut off three-fourths of the potential university population from entry into higher education. Those who failed could, of course, go into a comprehensive secondary school and prepare for entry into a middle-class occupation, but they could not go beyond it to college or university.

Theoretically, the "eleven plus" examination had the same effect upon all pupils regardless of family position. Most of those who stood the examination, however, were children from working-class families who were less likely to have absorbed in their home environment the types of skills and knowledge that enhanced prospects of success on the examination. Pupils from more advantaged backgrounds often had attended private primary school where the curricula were more consonant with the "eleven plus" examination. Hence, most of the pupils who failed it were those from state primary schools and particularly pupils from less advantaged backgrounds.

Understanding of this background is made important because of the longstanding and deeply ingrained British tendency to draw social, political, and civil leaders from an elitist group partially identified by its educational attainments. The practice meant that those persons who finished university education were the most likely candidates for future positions of influence and power. Those who did not gain entry were foreordained to secondary positions of influence and power. Hence, while education in the United States is open to all who would take advantage of it without state imposed barriers and direct linkages to class identification, in England the "eleven plus" examination functioned to limit social mobility, curb equality of opportunity, and perpetuate a class-based pattern of leadership selection. Those effects, moreover, endure in spite of efforts of Labor governments to end the channeling effects of the "eleven plus" examination by abolishing it, to democratize entry into the top levels of the British civil service, to weaken the influence of the prestige "public" schools such as Eton, Harrow, and Winchester, and to broaden the composition of university student bodies.

None of those efforts has produced a marked increase in the democratization of British society. Hierarchy and deference remain deeply ingrained in British social consciousness. The assumptions of inequality and the idea that the "best" ought to rule in society and government continue to be widely accepted although strongly denounced by the Labor and Liberal parties. Moreover, it seems unlikely that the reforms of the avowedly egalitarian Labor party leadership will bring about significant changes in the political cultures, at least in the immediate future. There seems to be no national surge of support for egalitarianism. The Conservative party, which generally supports the prevailing pattern of British education and gains most from existing attitudes, draws approximately one-half of its electoral support from working-class voters. By their adherence to the Tory party they seem to register their acceptance of the prevailing values, for without their votes the Conservatives could not gain office on the strength of their elite constituency, a steadily declining portion of the electorate.

This discussion would not be complete without notice of the "public" schools and of their role in preserving class distinctions, deference, and elite rule in the English political culture. Despite their name, English "public" schools are expensive, socially selective, private boarding schools of the secondary level. The prestige "public" schools have been the major gateway for entry into Oxford and Cambridge universities. They have been the early training ground for large numbers of cabinet members, prime ministers, members of Parliament, and members of the top-level administrative class of the British civil service. The requirements of academic and scientific education necessary for success in the "public" schools, plus the expense of attending them, place their advantages beyond the reach of most children from the working classes. Only a small percentage of British secondary school pupils attend these schools, but they come overwhelmingly from the "best" families and produce a disproportionately large share of future leaders. They are patronized by the most advantaged segments of English society and in turn serve them by teaching the virtues of a stratified, hierarchical society to their pupils. Mayer and Burnett assert that education at a "public" school continues to be accepted as important if not indispensable to attainment of power and prestige in contemporary public life.[25] They have been instrumental in melding the hereditary upper class of older English society with the newer politically and financially important business and professional groups into a new upper class of birth and wealth, all portions of which are linked by education, marriage, clubs, money, and other advantages.

Closely allied to their attitude of deference, and in contrast to American egalitarianism, is the Britishers' love for distinctions of class, title, and honors.[26] The Crown, House of Lords, privy council, royal family, honor's list, and the penchant of Englishmen to use letters after their names to designate various honors and recognitions they have received attest to their regard for distinctions setting men and women of merit apart from their fellows. On the one hand those symbols of inequality are the basis for a claim to deference, and on the other hand, they are a justification for extending it. A contrary dislike in American society for such distinctions readily permits only medical doctors to place the initials of their profession after their names. Public display of honors, awards, recognitions, and achievements is generally regarded by Americans as evidence of immodest self-esteem and self-proclaimed importance, especially if done by a person seeking elective public office. This is not to suggest, however, that American egalitarianism is of the excessive variety that produces political instability. It is only to suggest that Americans have a more pronounced disposition than do the British to distrust persons in positions of power, to make them operate in a brighter light of exposure to public knowledge and scrutiny, to measure closely official actions and statements by the public opinion of the moment, and to permit exercise of official discretion only when it is adequately confined by accountability.

DEFERENCE AND ADMINISTRATION

The deference of the British is also manifested in their attitude of tolerance toward bureaucracy engaged in the day-to-day administration of government. Whereas it is in the spirit of American political culture to regard government as a hostile force, a threat to individual freedom, a source of remote impersonalism bearing excessively on our lives, a source of regulation, and a force to be constrained, vigilantly watched, and diminished when possible, the British prevalently regard government as a positive agency, an instrument for enhancing the public good by collectively mobilizing societal resources for cooperative action. British decision makers are, of course, subject to the rule of law applied through administrative tribunals and the regular common law courts, and they are held regularly accountable through an effective system of electoral control. The British people expect the government to rule, and they recognize that governance necessarily means constraint, rules, regulations, and taxation. As long as government discharges its responsibilities in an orderly and legitimate manner according to public expectations and established norms, the British citizenry is generally willing to let it cope with the daily chores of administration free from parliamentary intrusion and nit-picking public inquiry. Regardless of which party is in power, it is expected to serve the general good, to act responsibly, and, when necessary, to yield to accountability. But as might be expected from their respective value structures, deference plays a more prominent role in the citizenry's attitude toward the Conservative than toward the Labor party, and is more effective within the ranks of the Conservative party toward its leadership than within the Labor party ranks toward its leaders. Deference encourages the British to concede extensive discretion to their governors in a centralized and integrated system and to subject them to far less close scrutiny in their performance of official duties than do American media and other organs of public opinion in the context of our political culture.

CHAPTER TWO

CONSTITUTIONAL GOVERNMENT

Both the British and the American governments are constitutional governments. A constitution is that body of fundamental law, the plan of government, which defines the basic institutions of government, sets forth their functions and interrelationships, and establishes the basic relationships between the government and its citizens.[1] The democratic tradition in which the British and the American governments are grounded calls for limited, responsible government, centering upon the primacy of the individual. In this tradition, government serves as a means toward an end, not as an end in itself.

Although not all democratic governments require specific, uniform institutional arrangements, they do depend upon both constitutional government and constitutionalism. Constitutionally limited government is a means of approximating the democratic ideal of "rule by law, not by men." This is possible, however, only when the value of constitutionalism widely pervades a public. Constitutionalism is a particular set of ideas and beliefs about the kinds of constitutional rules a nation ought to have and a reverence for those ideals and rules. It serves as a conserving force within a political community, a deep and long-held attitude of respect for and deference to the substance of the constitution.[2] Whatever the formal differences between them, the American and British political systems are both characterized by constitutionalism. Important

37

differences exist in British and American constitutional forms, bu
they should not be permitted to obscure the basic constitutiona
similarities that underlie both governmental systems. Although the
forms do differ, there is much similarity in their substance.

An understanding of the British and American governments as
constitutional governments, albeit different in form, may be enhanced by taking note of two related but separable meanings of the
term "constitution." In both a political and a nonpolitical sense
the constitution of anything refers to the proper arrangements of
its several parts to form a unit or a system in which the separable
parts are integrally interrelated. For example, the constitution of
a human being is that arrangement of such parts as the cells,
organs, muscles, and nerves which make up what is conventionally
called a human body. The constitution of any object consists in the
proper ordering of its parts to impart to it its essential characteristics, those attributes that make it what it is, enable it to perform
its proper functions, and distinguish it from other things. In this
sense, then, everything has a constitution, whether it be a body, a
chair, or a government.

A second, but strictly political, meaning of the term constitution
is that which Americans are accustomed to employ in a more specialized sense to refer to a written, documentary plan that by common agreement is known as the Constitution of the United States.
To distinguish clearly between these two uses of constitution, the
formal document will be referred to as the Constitution, and constitution will refer to the proper ordering of the parts of anything.

In the first, generic sense of the term both the United States and
Great Britain have constitutions. When the term is considered in
its second meaning, differences become apparent. While there is
one specific document that can be identified as the United States
Constitution, this is not true for Britain. The largely unwritten and
unassembled constitution of Great Britain does not resemble in
form the American document. Hence, the distinction between form
and substance illuminates the basic difference between the two
constitutions and causes Americans rather superficially to suggest
that the British have no constitution. The Americans' preoccupation with formal documentary content underlies the intense concern in the United States with what is or is not specifically included

in the constitutional document and with what is or is not compatible with the documentary provisions. By contrast, there is no formal documentary Constitution in Great Britain, with the result that substance must be the measure of what is constitutional. There is, therefore, among the British no concern with the sorts of constitutional formalities that so raptly engage the attention of many Americans as the U.S. Supreme Court considers the constitutionality of statutes or of official actions.

It should be noted carefully, however, that although attention to constitutional form in the United States contrasts with concentration on constitutional substance in Britain, the American constitutional government as well as the British must be understood in the generic constitutional sense. To accept the legal document as the only element comprising the constitution of the United States will produce only a partial and highly legalistic insight into the actual nature of the American governmental system. The student who confines his attention to that document alone will be misled about the actual nature of the system itself. But seen in the broader context of its generic relationship, the Constitution of the United States becomes an historic document which together with certain customs, organic statutes, and interpretations collectively determine the structure and functioning of the American system of government. With this in mind, the student can understand better the basic similarities between the American and the British constitutions. Substantively, the two systems are fundamentally alike in that both are limited, responsible governments, albeit the institutional forms that are employed in each country to govern, to limit the government, and to hold decision makers responsible for their actions differ.

SOURCES OF THE CONSTITUTIONS

With this background, it is now possible to see a high degree of similarity in the sources of the British and the American constitutions. In spite of the fact that the United States Constitution differs in form from the predominantly unwritten and unassembled British constitution, it is crucial for a full knowledge of both political systems that their constitutions in the broader, generic sense be examined. This is easier to do in the British case than in the

American because, since no one formal document exists, the tendency to focus only on one such source does not inhibit the broader view as it does in the American case.

Both constitutions consist of similar elements that play similar roles, for in any governmental system, even one like the American with a written constitutional document, informal procedures and relationships necessarily evolve which variously add to, circumvent, or alter the formal arrangements. Just as the British constitution is characterized by its evolutionary, flexible nature, so the United States constitutional document has been supplemented by evolving customs, laws, and judicial interpretations.

Many elements of the unassembled British constitution are ancient in origin. Some can be traced back to the aftermath of the Norman Conquest of 1066, but the much younger American constitutional document had its beginnings only in the eighteenth century. The constitution of Great Britain is unwritten only in the sense that historic documents and other written elements of which it partly consists have not been assembled into one document. Moreover, it consists largely of certain uncodified, often ancient, conventions and usages. Conventions and customs also constitute parts of the American constitution, but they comprise a far greater portion of the British constitutional fabric. Their greater prevalence in the British than in the American constitution manifests the lengthy persistence in Britain of age-old traditions which give a marked historical continuity to its constitution, tying the present to the ancient past. For constitutional conventions there is no formal documentary basis. They emerged with the following of practices that even today are continually evolving and adapting to changing circumstances. But in spite of this difference, the two constitutions are flexible and adaptable to the changing needs of society.

CONVENTIONS AND CUSTOMS

Conventions of the British constitution refer to those special customs that developed originally to curb the royal prerogative. Such a convention of the constitution is that which permits the monarch to act only on the advice of a responsible minister. Customs more generally understood refer to those practices which originally developed as a matter of political convenience and work-ability, for example, the custom of resignation or parliamentary dissolution by a government in power when it can no longer command the confidence of the House of Commons. These customs rest upon utility and persist as long as they fulfill their original purposes. Although they are not legally enforceable in themselves, they are engraved in the force of tradition, continuing to be binding because they serve important needs and because they are perceived widely to be legitimate. They are so fundamental to the British system that to violate a constitutional convention or custom would jeopardize the workability of the government. For example, a convention has evolved that the British monarch does not take political actions independent of the cabinet. If this convention were violated, the cabinet would be likely to resign. Cabinet resignation under these circumstances would probably result in one of two consequences: no one would agree to join a new cabinet or, if any one did, the House of Commons would refuse to support it.[3] Thus, although a particular practice that is followed for a long period of time receives no formal designation as a constitutional convention, one who departs abruptly from the accepted practice will be denounced for taking unconstitutional action.

Among some of the more important of the British constitutional customs are: cabinet collective responsibility, individual ministerial responsibility, the fusion of powers in Parliament and its cabinet, and the resignation of the cabinet or the dissolution of the Parliament and call for new elections if the cabinet loses the confidence of the House of Commons.

Customs and usages also form part of the American constitution, often fleshing out the bare bones of the basic framework that is set forth in the constitutional document. Neither political parties nor judicial review is mentioned in the constitutional document itself, but their evolution and functioning clearly form parts of the American constitution, broadly understood.[4] The development of American constitutional customs is inevitable, for wherever a written constitution or statutory or common law is silent or ambiguous, the force of custom may enter.[5] Hence, all codified constitutions are supplemented to some degree by custom and usage. What is unusual in this respect about the British constitution is that its conventions and customs are so numerous and so important relative to its written elements.

COMMON LAW AND JUDICIAL INTERPRETATION

Common law and judicial interpretation of written constitutional components also form parts of the constitutions of Britain and the United States. An important source of British and American constitutional principles is to be found in court decisions. As they apply common law to particular cases and interpret the provisions of various statutes and charters, judges inevitably define them and develop their meanings more fully. Judges give life and shape to statutory law as they interpret its meaning and apply it to particular circumstances.[6]

Especially in the area of civil rights and liberties, common law provides some of the most important of the British constitutional principles. These principles originated in common customs or precedents as applied by courts to the decisions of individual cases, and over time the number of such principles of general application increased, growing stronger and more comprehensive. Today these are an essential component of the protections constitutionally afforded British subjects, including such fundamental rights as trial by jury and writ of habeas corpus. Because Britain has no Bill of Rights comparable to that found in the American Constitution, common law and judicial interpretation contribute substantially to the British constitution. However, common law and judicial interpretation are also important sources of rights in the United States, because the substantive rights formally listed in the first eight amendments are neither comprehensive nor self-defining. The Ninth Amendment leaves room for development of rights to be constitutionally protected although not specifically included in the other amendments. In addition, rights specifically listed have been held to imply the similar protection of other related ones. In this way both the right to privacy and the right of free association have been interpreted to belong in the list of those constitutionally protected even though they do not appear in the constitutional document in so many words. The meanings of specifically listed rights, such as protection against cruel and unusual punishments and unreasonable searches and seizures derive from judicial interpreta-

n. Such interpretations and applications put life into the constitu-
nal listing.

STORICAL DOCUMENTS

In the course of British history, a number of major govern-
ntal crises have produced great documents such as Magna
rta, the Bill of Rights, and the Act of Settlement, which contain
e terms of resolution of the crises. Most of these documents are
ts of Parliament, but what sets them apart from other important
rliamentary acts is both the context of the major constitutional
uggles in which they originated, and the fact that the settlement
ms contained in them affect the character of some part of the
sic governmental machinery or relationships.[7] In this respect
ey are not unlike the Thirteenth, Fourteenth, and Fifteenth
nendments to the United States Constitution adopted after the
vil War, which place limitations on certain actions of the states.
th the British documents and these American constitutional
nendments are alike in that their primary purposes and effects
e to place constraints on the exercise of governmental power.

STATUTORY LAW

Although most British parliamentary and American congres-
onal statutes never acquire the status of great historical docu-
ents, some of them (often called organic acts) do stand in a
osition above ordinary statutory law because the subjects with
hich they deal are of intrinsic importance to the constitutional
brics. An example of such statutes, going to the core of basic
overnmental institutions and processes, is the set of Reform Acts
ginning in 1832, initiating the revision of the franchise in
ritain. Statutes of similar constitutional importance in the United
ates are the Judiciary Acts, establishing and later modifying the
tional court system, and statutes creating and restructuring
binet-level departments. It should be noted that no special legis-
tive machinery or process for enactment of statutes of constitu-
onal status is required in the United States or in Britain, except
at in a few specific cases Parliament has provided for more
mplicated enactment procedures.

With this understanding of the varied sources of constitutional

principles and provisions in both the United States and in Gr[...]
Britain, it is now possible to examine the various ways in wh[...]
constitutional change takes place in the two countries. In this c[...]
text it is again important not to let formal differences obscure [...]
important substantive similarities. Neither political system co[...]
survive long in a complex and rapidly changing environment wi[...]
out having developed means of achieving necessary constitutio[...]
change. The ability to undergo constitutional change while ma[...]
taining fundamental principles has enabled both Britain and [...]
United States to endure as stable political systems in the mod[...]
era.

CONSTITUTIONAL CHANGE

It should not be surprising to the thoughtful student that ame[...]
ing the American constitutional document involves a precise [...]
of complex and time-consuming procedures which are themsel[...]
constitutionally prescribed. This is in keeping with the Americ[...]
bent for formal and legalistic concerns with respect to the Cons[...]
tution and with the existence of American federalism. The bel[...]
in the importance of the states as subunits within the federal s[...]
tem is manifested in the role given to them in the ratification p[...]
cess. By contrast, because Parliament is legally supreme in a unit[...]
system and because the British constitution does not consist of o[...]
basic codified document, there are no fixed, special procedures [...]
altering it. The British concept of constitution, it will be recall[...]
emphasizes matters of substance over those of form, so set forma[...]
ties for amendment are not viewed as necessary. The fact th[...]
American constitutional change occurs by means other than th[...]
prescribed for making formal changes in the language of the c[...]
stitutional document points up the extent to which form and su[...]
stance of their constitution is of importance to Americans.

A secret of the long endurance of the American Constituti[...]
throughout much social, economic, and political change will n[...]
be found in the formal amendment process, but rather in the mo[...]
flexible processes of constitutional elaboration and adaptation su[...]
as action by the legislature and the executive, judicial interpre[...]
tion, and custom.[8] In both countries, flexible methods of achievi[...]

onstitutional change include revision by statute, by judicial interpretation of law, and by changes in conventions and usages. Thus
he processes of constitutional modification in the United States
nd in Great Britain are more similar than they appear at first
lance, in spite of the presence of formal amendment procedures
n the United States and their absence in Great Britain.

MODIFICATION BY STATUTE

An act of Parliament, passed by the same simple majority pro-
edures as any other piece of ordinary legislation, becomes part
of the British constitution solely by virtue of adding to, modifying,
or altering the body of British constitutional law. What sets such
cts apart from other legislation is their substance, not the pro-
edures for their enactment; they become part of the constitution
ecause they deal with fundamental institutions, processes, and
machinery of government. In the British constitutional framework,
he complete supremacy of Parliament—formally Crown, Lords,
nd Commons in Parliament assembled—is the basis of this
power. This contrasts with the American legislative subordination
o the fundamental law contained in the constitutional document.
Thus, in America no ordinary process of enacting statutory law
can result in formal additions to the Constitution. It also follows
hat no law which is in conflict with a provision of the United
States Constitution may be enforced.

According to the mandate theory the power of Parliament to
amend the British constitution by majority vote is qualified by the
need for a mandate from the electorate before Parliament can
make any fundamental constitutional change. Acting on this theory,
ome prime ministers have refrained from proposing legislation
hat contains the substance of a constitutional change until the
voters have expressed their position on the matter in general elec-
ions. However, the mandate theory has never fully replaced the
concept of independent authority, and crucial policy decisions have
been made with no mandate without upsetting the voters' constitu-
ional feelings.[9] Some persistence of the feeling that alteration in a
British constitutional principle ought to be enacted by a government only if it has fought and won an election on it resembles a

principle underlying the complex American formal amendmen ratification procedures—that the population in general should con cur in any major change.

It appears that what is not formally constitutional in the Unite States may be substantively constitutional, that is, part of the con stitution, in Great Britain, whereas in the United States no ord nary statute is part of the formal document and in Britain n every statute is constitutional in substance. For example, elector reform in Great Britain has been carried out through the proces of passing legislation; in the United States, suffrage was grante to women and to eighteen-year-olds by formally amending th Constitution, while similar extension of the suffrage in Britain too place by majority vote in Parliament.

Although legislation enacted by the United States Congress doe not formally become part of the constitutional document, the sub stance of the constitution is modified or added to by congression statutes. Congress has created new executive departments and con solidated or demoted others from cabinet rank. Also, it has mad changes in the size of the Supreme Court, altered the scope of i appellate jurisdiction, and established the regulatory commission Such legislative actions have produced changes in the America constitutional system of significance at least equal to the change brought about by formal amendment. In fact, in many ways th formally rigid United States Constitution has proved to be highl flexible by methods of informal change, in contrast to the seem ingly flexible British constitution, changeable by ordinary statute which can in practice be very difficult to alter. For example, i Britain where suffrage can be changed by ordinary legislation, n such extension of suffrage took place from the time of the earl 1430 Forty Shilling Freeholder Franchise Act to the 1832 Grea Reform Act.

MODIFICATION BY JUDICIAL INTERPRETATION

In addition to change by statute, constitutional revision in bot countries occurs by means of judicial interpretation of the law Judges must interpret the meaning of the constitution when it i at issue in disputes litigated in the courts. It is clear that whoeve interprets the law with authority sets the measure of the law

hether it be constitutional law or otherwise. Also, in both coun-
ies, common law is derived from judicial decisions and each such
cision, though following precedents established in previous cases,
btly modifies the common law.[10] Whenever judges interpret the
eaning, scope, and application of law, the law undergoes a degree
change. Because the formal amendment procedures in the United
ates are so cumbersome and time-consuming and do not respond
adily to felt need for change, constitutional change is often accom-
ished by means of judicial interpretation to meet altered circum-
ances in the modernizing society. The generality of the American
onstitutional provisions presents an opportunity for such modifi-
ation through reinterpretation.[11] By this process, for example, an
xpansion of the meaning and scope of the interstate commerce
lause has fundamentally changed the social and economic life of
merica, and interpretation of the meaning and application of
due process" since the addition of the Fourteenth Amendment to
e Constitution has basically revised the protection of the individ-
al and his relationship to the state.

The power of judicial review is of major importance to judicial
terpretation of the Constitution of the United States. But, in
ritain, the legal supremacy of Parliament operates to place its
atutes beyond the invalidating power of all courts. American
dges possess the authority to declare unconstitutional the statutes
nd acts of the national legislature or executive. This very power
f judicial review, now an integral part of the basic constitutional
amework, was self-generated and resulted from the Supreme
ourt's interpretation of its own authority according to the pro-
ision in the Constitution for the establishment of the judicial
ranch of government.

EVISION BY CUSTOM

Since conventions and customs form such a large portion of the
ritish constitution, it is apparent that modification by new and
evised conventions and customs is a major means of change in the
ritish constitution. However, it is also an important form of con-
titutional change in the United States. Such change occurs as a
natter of growing and adapting to new developments in the social,
conomic, and political life of a country. Because of the evolu-

tionary nature of such changes, it is impossible to know precisel
when they begin or to date the moment at which an old conventio
or tradition has largely given way to a new one. When it become
more workable to alter ways of acting politically, change take
place, and a new convention or usage remains in effect so long a
it is practical and acceptable, according to the realities of politica
life. For example, at the beginning of the twentieth century, con
vention changed to selecting a prime minister from the House o
Commons, no longer from the House of Lords, because of th
greater political convenience and practicality of having the prim
minister present in Commons, to which body of Parliament politi
cal power was shifting. Monarchs originally chose whomever the
wished to serve as advisers or ministers, but once it was politically
necessary for the monarch to have the support of Parliament fo
his decisions and actions, the convention arose that ministers mus
be advisers who are supported by Parliament. To insure that thi
be the case, they are chosen from among the leaders of the politica
party which fills the majority of the seats in the House of Commons

Although such traditions and conventions, contributing to th
workability of the government in Britain, evolve slowly and are no
in themselves legally enforceable, they can be enacted into law i
violated. Over time, the custom that Lords exercise no veto powe
over a piece of financial legislation approved by the House o
Commons had developed. In 1909, after Lords departed from tha
practice and rejected the budget voted by the House of Commons
the Parliament Act of 1911 converted the custom into a statute.

Because customs may be part of the American constitution
their alteration over time or by statute will have constitutiona
significance. For example, the development of the political party
system slowly modified the workings of the government, altering
such institutions as the electoral college and the internal organiza
tion of the legislature. As in Britain, in the event that an estab
lished custom or usage is violated, it may be codified. The tradition
begun by the first American president, that the chief executive
serve no more than two terms in spite of the fact that the constitu
tional document itself was silent on this matter, was informally
binding until the administrations of Franklin Roosevelt. After his

iolation" of the tradition, a constitutional amendment was ssed, legally limiting future presidents to two terms.

The foregoing modes of informal constitutional modification are sponses to societal forces. As power relationships change in re- onse to altered societal circumstances or to attitudinal shifts, new ationships and practices evolve. Such changes in and adapta- ns of constitutional custom can take place more flexibly and sily than change through more formally prescribed methods, and y permit smooth adaptation of the political systems to their vironments. But such flexible constitutional change presupposes nation that is sufficiently steeped in tradition and naturally cau- us in its approach to change, lest the whole political structure come unstable and collapse.[12] Both Britain and the United ates seem to fulfill these conditions. It should be noted, however, at although the possibility of constitutional change through such ormal means does afford necessary flexibility to the political stems, change in traditional ways of doing things does not take ace quickly or easily. The force of tradition and custom is very ong, and long periods of time may elapse before there is suffi- ntly widespread acceptance and support for a change to legiti- ize the altered patterns of action. In fact, formal change is some- nes easily obtained, but years may pass before the change in nstitutional forms can effect any real alteration in customs and ages, as in the case of the addition of the Fifteenth Amendment the United States Constitution. That formal amendment granted nstitutional voting rights to male citizens regardless of race, but is did not become a political reality in many areas of the country til a century later.

CONSTITUTIONAL PRINCIPLES

When viewed as meaning the proper arrangements of units thin a system rather than as a particular document, the term nstitution refers to the fundamental principles that are part of e nature and essence of a particular system. The constitution of ch country is different from that of any other because of the rticular mix of fundamental principles of which it is composed. cause both Britain and the United States are liberal democracies, and because the British political background and experience we[...] major factors shaping the founding and early development of [...] American system, many of the fundamental principles underlyi[...] the two political systems are similar. Others differ, however, b[...] cause of the differences in political culture and experience. A[...] though both systems are grounded in the principle of limit[...] government, different forms and institutions have evolved [...] achieve this common goal. On the principles of territorial a[...] functional division of powers, the two systems exhibit contrasti[...] patterns. This stems partly from the fact that the principle of sta[...] sovereignty differs from that of popular sovereignty, the form[...] found in Great Britain and the latter in the United States. Ho[...] ever, on the principle of the protection of civil rights and liberti[...] great similarities exist in substance, in spite of some importa[...] differences in the forms of their protection. Another key differen[...] stems from the fact that the constitutional principle of judicial [...] view which underpins the American political system is absent [...] Great Britain. Although each of these major constitutional pri[...] ciples is complex, and treatment in this context is necessarily bri[...] some consideration of each and of its shaping of the political sy[...] tem in which it is found will follow in order to understand bett[...] the similarities and differences in the constitutions of Great Brita[...] and the United States.

TERRITORIAL DISTRIBUTION OF POWER

One way of dividing power and authority in an effort to a[...] proach the ideal of limited government—putting limitations on t[...] exercise of power and its potential abuse—is by territorial divisi[...] of power. When power and authority are divided territorially [...] the constitution, territorial or spatial regions are given powers [...] their own, and authority and functions are divided among differe[...] levels of government. However, all political frameworks, whatev[...] the basic formal pattern and whether or not explicit constitution[...] division of power is made, are characterized by some distributio[...] of power among political authorities at the various levels [...] government—national, regional, and local. The unitary politic[...] system of Great Britain and the federal system of the United Stat[...] exemplify the two major constitutional patterns of territorial d[...]

tribution of power. Despite the differences in the constitutional distribution of power among levels, however, in both systems there is some degree of division of authority and function among national and local levels.

UNITARY AND FEDERAL SYSTEMS

The two systems embody unitary and federal structures. In the British unitary system, the central, national government has the constitutional authority to determine the degree of decision-making power and the type of functions which it will delegate to the local governmental officials, because the national government is legally supreme in all areas of political decision making. In contrast to this, the American political system is federal in nature. The Constitution divides power between the national government and the several state governments, granting delegated powers to the national government and leaving reserved powers to the states.

Each pattern of allocated authority in turn reflects its historical setting. The American setting differed from the British and led naturally to the adoption of the federal system. Originally, the American colonies were separate from each other. At the time of independence from England, one of the major decisions to be made was that of determining a workable and acceptable form of relating the thirteen states to each other and to a central political authority. The original autonomy of the separate states and the intense level of identification which the citizens had with their own states made it necessary to preserve some measure of separate identity for the states within any union. Because the arrangement under the Articles of Confederation proved to be unworkable due to the lack of unity and central direction, the need arose for a plan of union that combined needed unity with some degree of autonomy for the diverse states. The federal structure in America was designed to combine and balance unity and diversity.

Great Britain did not originate in the coming together of initially separate, autonomous units, comparable to the American states. A smaller and less diversified geographical and cultural entity, it does not require the more politically complex federal arrangement in order to accommodate regional diversity. Both historically and geographically, it presents a more homogeneous setting than that in America, in which a unitary system naturally evolved. Although the British nation includes (along with England) three regions that were originally separate—Northern Ireland, Scotland, and Wales —the relationship of these with the rest of the country is both in form and in substance unlike that between the individual American states and the United States national government. The fit of the four units within Great Britain will be discussed briefly below.

As is generally the case in a unitary system, the national government in Great Britain maintains its authority over politics at the lower levels principally by the control it exercises over finances— taxes assessed, collected, and reallocated to local governments.[13] By contrast, in the American federal system the national government and the state governments have independent tax collection and resource allocation functions and authority.

It has been suggested that one of the major reasons why Britain has been able to manage well without a written codified constitutional document is that it has a unitary form of government. In a federal system such as that of America, where powers are divided between national and state governments, complex relationships obtain, and it must be clearly laid down what powers the different authorities possess. A convenient way of defining this division of powers territorially is by means of a written constitution.[14] One benefit of the federal arrangement is that there is a clearly defined basis for the decentralization of political decision making which it involves.[15] But the clarity of the decentralization arrangement might well be lost if there were no document to establish in clear and explicit terms the authority division between the national government and the governments of the states. Without the Constitution as a reference in national-state authority disputes, even though the constitutional provisions are open to varying interpretations, the resulting ambiguity could lead to great conflict between the two levels of political authority.

LOCAL GOVERNMENTAL UNITS

Although there is territorial variety within Great Britain, the much more homogeneous country and population and the greater national orientation in political outlook permit a degree of centralized planning and direction which could not be tolerated in the

United States. The higher level of localism and regionalism in the American political culture resists centralized political planning and decision making in most areas of life. Local authorities, however, are neither nonexistent nor impotent in Britain. In that country, local governmental institutions do indeed exist and have an ancient history. But, in contrast with the American federal arrangement in which constitutional sanction is given to the territorial division of powers, control over the scope of authority and the role of local government in Britain lies with the national government. Parliament has been very willing to delegate as much competence to local units and authorities as they have shown the capacity and willingness to assume. Nevertheless, and regardless of the actual degree of decentralized administration, local authorities are constitutionally free to act only in areas in which specific power to do so has been granted to them by the central government, and they must perform those tasks that Parliament makes obligatory on them.

Because the units of local government in Great Britain have limited independence and financial resources, in contrast to the relatively greater resources of the American states, they have less freedom for autonomous action. They are dependent on the national government for grants and loans to provide essential public services. They also lack the authority to enter into new areas of governmental activity, unlike the states in America which often experiment and pioneer in new functions and arrangements which, if proven workable and successful, may be adopted by other states or the national government. Because of their scarce resources and limited authority, British local officials are unable to take the initiative to respond to new problems and to changing public needs independent of the central government. Yet the local leaders often enjoy considerable influence as a practical matter over the policies germane to their own localities. The central government must rely on the cooperation of local officials for the successful implementation of many programs and policies. It may prove difficult to compel local leaders to do what they do not want to do and to prevent them from doing what they are determined to do.[16]

Within the British unitary structure, Northern Ireland, Scotland, and Wales have enjoyed a special degree of regional independence from the center, but this does not extend to the creation of a federal relationship. For example, until the recent crisis of unrest, Northern Ireland sent representatives to Westminster, but also had its own Parliament, cabinet, and governor-general. It was in practice virtually self-governing in local matters, but even so, Northern Ireland was ultimately subject to the legislative supremacy of the Parliament at Westminster. Scotland and Wales have a degree of local autonomy and have special committees in Parliament for their affairs.[17] But a recent proposal by a Labor government for legislative devolution for Scotland has met with strong government opposition, and the ultimate outcome of the proposal remains unclear.

In sum, the unitary system in which power is concentrated constitutionally at one level of government is appropriate for the particular British political and cultural setting. The concentration of power at the governmental center is balanced by the disposition on the part of Parliament to grant authority and functions to localities for administrative convenience. In the United States the different cultural and political setting calls for the more complex federal arrangement. What centralization, coordination and control at the center is lost in the United States because of the territorial distribution of power is gained in the amount of local autonomy and diversity permitted in a large and heterogeneous political environment.

In addition to the differences between Britain and the United States with respect to territorial distribution of power, differences also obtain between the two countries on the matter of the functional distribution of power on the national level of government. The differences between the constitutional principles of fusion of powers and of separation of powers will now be examined.

FUNCTIONAL DISTRIBUTION OF POWER

There are two major patterns for organizing political institutions democratically and allocating political power to them—parliamentary systems and presidential systems. The British political system is parliamentary in organization, whereas the American system is presidential. The key point of difference between the two

ypes is found in the concentration of power in the British system
nd the separation of power in the American. At the heart of the
distinction is the functional distribution of power which estab-
ishes the relationship between the executive and the legislature.
While in the United States the institutional arrangements divide
power between the executive and the legislative branches of the
government, giving them coequal and independent constitutional
tatus, in Britain the legislature and the executive, though distinct
rom each other, are "fused" institutionally and have reciprocal
power to dismiss each other.

The reciprocal dismissal power in Great Britain between the
egislature and the executive is absent in the United States. The
American legislature and executive are elected separately by the
voters for fixed terms of office. Neither depends upon the other
or continuing in office, although they do have some reciprocal
powers of lesser magnitude to bring into effect mutual checks and
balances.

The British parliamentary system constitutionally locates all
political authority within the Parliament. Members of the majority
party in the lower house select a cabinet and a prime minister from
the members of Parliament. Since Parliament is legally supreme,
t can force the executive to resign from office by showing a lack
of confidence in its refusal to enact into law a vital legislative
proposal from the cabinet. Recently, a reciprocal power on the
part of the cabinet has developed; the cabinet response to the lack
of confidence from the legislature may be to request the monarch
o dissolve the House of Commons and call for new elections,
theoretically taking the issue "to the country" to be resolved by the
voters. In the United States, in contrast, the system of separated
powers enables the legislature and the executive to disagree on
policy, with the president exercising his veto to kill congressional
measures or the legislature defeating presidential proposals, but
both remaining in office, at loggerheads.

The British chief executive is thus chosen from and remains in
and responsible to the legislature, unlike the case in the United
States where, for example, it is constitutionally necessary for a
member of Congress to resign from that post in order to accept a

cabinet position. In Britain a cabinet member remains in tha[?] executive position only so long as he is also a member of Parlia[?] ment; in the United States no one may belong to both branches o[?] the government at the same time. The American separation o[?] functions is bolstered by a strict separation of personnel, but th[?] British fusion of power is brought about in part by the overlap o[?] personnel in the executive and legislative branches of government[?] A look at the different ways in which the two types of system came into being and the reasons for the differences in their origin and courses of development will make clearer the nature an[?] functioning of each.

ORIGINS AND DEVELOPMENT OF THE
PARLIAMENTARY AND THE PRESIDENTIAL SYSTEMS

The British political system may be the world's best example o[?] an evolved system, growing out of changes that have occurred ove[?] a period of nine hundred years.[18] The major historical change in the evolutionary development of Britain were the subordinatio[?] of the church to the state, the centralization of political authority and the differentiation of the legal and political institutions. I[?] contrast to this long period of evolutionary growth, the America[?] political system was created at a specific moment in history, a[?] Philadelphia in 1789 by the founding fathers who drew up the con[?] stitutional document.

In Britain by the seventeenth century, in the course of lon[?] struggles between the Stuart monarchs and Parliament, a simple and more unified government resulted, taking the place of th[?] greater governmental complexity and diffusion of political powe[?] which had existed since the period of the feudal system. The over all centralizing tendency steadily brought local business under th[?] control of the central government. However, the monarchical ab[?] solutism which the Stuarts sought to effect, along the lines of tha[?] on the continent, did not come into being; the end result of th[?] monarchical-parliamentary struggle for the newly centralized politi[?] cal power was the emergence of Parliament as the victor. Fro[?] that time to the present, although the location of decision-makin[?] power within Parliament has shifted, it has remained centralize[?]

wherever it was located. Changes in the terminology used to refer to the British government reflect the historical power shifts: "monarchy" was replaced by "parliamentary government," and then "cabinet government" became the term accepted as more descriptively accurate. Some now suggest the substitution of "prime ministerial government" to denote the increasing importance of the role of the prime minister within the cabinet.

The Americans managed to miss the seventeenth century revolution which occurred in England, in part by a quirk in the timing and sequence of various events. Basically, the principal leaders of political thought and activity in the colonies had departed England before this revolution took place, and so it can be said in part that they simply missed it because they left when they did. This timing was not altogether a chance one, since some of the same forces that brought the changes in England contributed to the departure of the colonists for America. In any event, it was basically the old sixteenth-century Tudor elements of the British constitution underpinning medieval institutions which were brought to America. At roughly the same time that these institutions were being abandoned in England, they were established on American soil where they took firm root. Among the more important and lasting of these generally medieval principles and institutions were the subordination of government to fundamental law and the close intermingling of the legal and political realms. To this day, Americans are a litigious people, taking to courts to settle problems normally handled in England by political institutions without judicial involvement. Also among the important transplants were a firm belief in the fitness of a balance between the legislature and the executive and a great vitality of local governmental institutions with considerable powers of their own. Authority or sovereignty, collected and concentrated in Britain, was never brought into a single institution or individual in America, but remained dispersed throughout society and among the many organs of the body politic. The continued supremacy of law was joined to a decisive rejection of the concept of state sovereignty as it had developed in Great Britain. The concept of sovereignty was either rejected altogether in America or sovereignty was viewed as popular, located in the people. This American concept of popular sovereignty leads to a wide dispersal of authority, in contrast to the concentration of authority which the British concept of state sovereignty calls for.

LOCATION OF POLITICAL AUTHORITY

Important changes in basic beliefs and attitudes took place in Britain during the seventeenth century which ultimately resulted in a shift away from the traditional view, based in natural law theory, that men declare law but do not make it. This view was replaced by a rationalization of authority, a belief that the state itself is the source of all political authority, taking the place of fundamental law as its source. In the United States, however, the old viewpoint, based on natural law, that law is not made but discovered by men, and that fundamental law is thus beyond human control, was brought to America where it persisted. When this notion became partly identified with a written Constitution, codifying fundamental law, it followed that man-made, statutory law was viewed as subordinate to it. In 1789 the Constitution was seen as essentially a codification of limits already imposed on the government by custom and reason, not as something invented or created by men. It stems from this basis that sovereignty remains diffused among the people, not concentrated in a Parliament as in Britain. The concept of judicial review grows out of and bolsters this primacy of fundamental law. If this law is felt to be codified within the written Constitution, as in the United States, then the Constitution becomes the touchstone with which to measure the legality of actions and statutes. If a conflict arises between the law of the Constitution on the one hand, and statutes or actions of governmental officials on the other, then the American Supreme Court exercises the power of judicial review to insure the supremacy of the Constitution. Since the Constitution is viewed as an expression of fundamental law, it must limit the actions and policies of political officials.

In Britain, a modernizing trend grew; men developed a sense of their own competence. From this derives the more modern view that in fact men make law, rather than discover it pre-existing and external from themselves. Parliament came to be a law-*making* body, and hence Parliament can "amend" the British constitution simply by enacting a law. Behind this is the concept of state sovereignty, mentioned earlier, which developed in Britain. Sovereignty was originally held to be lodged in the monarch, but the transfer of final decision-making authority to Parliament made that body the single, absolute source of law for Britain. Today, cabinet and Parliament in Britain are interrelated elements; each exercises independent authority, not, as in the United States, authority delegated by the voters.[19] The notion of state sovereignty was rejected in America, and to the extent that sovereignty is accepted there, it is felt to be lodged in the people, not in the state. It has been suggested that the argument of the colonists with Britain in the eighteenth century was basically an argument against state sovereignty, and in particular against the legislative supremacy of Parliament. Pollard suggests that the colonists' fundamental objection was to sovereignty vested in any state whatever, even in their own. Americans revolt even today against the concept of state sovereignty, in favor of the vague and elusive ideal of popular sovereignty.[20] The nebulous concept of popular sovereignty is essentially latent and passive, in contrast to the positive and active concept of state sovereignty.

INSTITUTIONS AND FUNCTIONS

The rationalization of authority and concentration of power in Great Britain were accompanied by the emergence of functional differentiation and more specialization in the governmental institutions and bodies. This differentiation and specialization of function was largely a result of the response to the growing complexity of society and the corresponding increase in the demands placed upon governmental functions. As the power was concentrated, the functions performed were dispersed among increasingly specialized institutions. Executive power was the first to emerge in England in the process of specialization, followed by the judicial, with the exchequer, king's bench, and common pleas courts, and the like. The last to emerge was the legislative power. In this process of specialization of function and division of labor, greater power and authority came to rest in the law-making function than in the law-enforcing function. Administrative, legal, judicial, and military bodies became specialized, achieved semi-autonomy, and were subordinated and made responsible to political bodies which exercised sovereignty.

Whereas in Britain, governmental functions were dispersed among many specialized institutions and power was concentrated within Parliament, in the United States, functions were combined in many institutions and power was dispersed. The Constitution established a government of separated institutions, sharing functions, with power divided among them in order that a complex system of checking and balancing would result. The primary motive was to prevent tyranny by checking power with power, ambition with ambition. Hence, the presidency was created as a set of roles with many functions to perform—policy initiative, rule making, rule enforcing, and administration of the entire executive branch. Legislative functions were dispersed among several institutions as well, to both houses of the legislature, to the president with legislative initiative, as well as to state governments. At the same time that Parliament was becoming functionally unicameral as the House of Lords lost most of its political power, the United States Congress remained fully bicameral, with each house of the legislature equal in power, and further diffused the legislative functions and authority to congressional committees and subcommittees.

The irresistible forces to bring about unity of authority in Britain grew out of conditions in English society that did not obtain in America. In seventeenth century England, as in most of Europe at that time, civil and religious strife accelerated and led eventually to demands for strong, centralized power to re-establish and maintain political order and security. The breakdown of order in English society that was behind the drive to achieve unity through governmental means occurred before any wide expansion of democratic political participation had taken place. When the expansion of political participation did begin later, it was marked by discontinuities on two levels. First, there were discontinuities on the institutional level. In England democratization meant, institutionally, a shift of power from the monarch to one house of the legislature—the popular assembly. Second, on the electoral level, democratization meant extension of the vote for this popular assembly only. From aristocracy to upper bourgeoisie, then to lower bourgeoisie and peasants, and finally to urban workers, the right to vote was broadened through the classes. This extension of the franchise meant an expansion of suffrage for one institution in which political authority had become centralized to all of the classes within the English society.

The framers of the American Constitution believed that divisions and conflicts within the society were so potentially dangerous that a complex system of institutional checks and balances was necessary to mitigate the evils of faction. Yet the American Constitution has proved to be successfully workable largely because this view which the founding fathers had of American society was in error. In actual fact, the society in America was free of the kind of strife and conflict which had developed in England. The absence of significant societal divisions, such as the class stratifications which in Europe were the remnants of the old feudal social order, permitted the transformation of political issues into legal ones and made the centralization of political power, so crucial in England, unnecessary in America. Largely because there was no aristocracy to dislodge from a position of power, there was no impetus to call into being centralized governmental authority to dislodge it. Therefore, while in England the franchise was democratized by extending the vote for the one body in which political power was concentrated to more and more groups within the population, in the United States the popular franchise was liberalized for many different institutions, for example state governorships and legislatures, the Senate and House of Representatives, the presidency, and local elected offices.

Given these very diverse origins and lines of development, it is not surprising that the present parliamentary fusion of power in Britain differs on many counts from the separated legislative and executive powers in the presidential system. It is to these constitutional points of difference between the two political systems today that the discussion now turns.

FUSION OF POWERS VS. SEPARATION OF POWERS

Fusion of powers refers to the joining of the powers of policy making and policy executing, combining the legislative and executive functions of government. By contrast, separation of powers describes the division of these two powers. The American system, which was founded on the organizing principle of separated powers, has autonomous, competing power centers, whereas the British political system emerged with a concentrated authority. The political history of Great Britain since the seventeenth century has consistently reinforced the underlying social and cultural tendencies to unity.

Walter Bagehot contrasted what he termed the "simple" British form of government, in which final authority on all political questions is in the hands of the same person, with the American "composite" government, wherein the supreme decision-making authority is divided among many branches and functionaries.[21] In Britain, the executive, legislative, and judicial powers are not divided; on the contrary, fusion of executive and legislative powers obtains in Britain. The cabinet is the institution which joins the legislative and the executive parts of the state.[22]

In legal theory, all authority of the British government is fully vested in a composite body styled the "crown-in-Parliament." But the supreme power which Parliament possesses has come in political reality to rest with the House of Commons, the lower house of the British Parliament. Inside this body it is concentrated in an inner council of ministers, the cabinet.[23] Indeed, British political institutions in the late twentieth century are still simple in Bagehot's meaning of the term, as contrasted with the more complex composite American government.[24]

Government in Britain has thus become, in constitutional reality, party government, for the concentration of political authority was followed by the rise of the modern British party system. The development of the strong British two-party system must be understood in combination with the marked growth of the executive power. Only then will it be clear that the British power to govern is concentrated in the elected leaders of the majority party assembled in the cabinet, and that parties and elections are the means for controlling their use of power. Thus the parliamentary leaders of the party which controls the majority of seats in the House of Commons exercise the concentrated political authority so long as they maintain their legislative support. The party government is implemented through the cabinet which serves as the pivot around which all of the country's political machinery revolves. Led by the prime minister, the cabinet directs the affairs of the country until its party support in the representative elected House of Commons disintegrates.[25]

American government, on the contrary, cannot be properly termed party government. Although political parties emerged early in the country's political history and remain a crucial democratic political force today, they developed within the framework of separated powers. Federalism and the separation of governmental decision-making authority in the United States have brought about a corresponding fragmentation within the political parties, whereas the concentration of decision-making authority in Great Britain exerted an integrating force on the political parties. National parties in the United States, unlike the case in Britain, do not always control the separately elected executive and legislative branches of government at the same time. Even when they do, their fragmented condition precludes the degree of cohesiveness and control needed to achieve responsible party government. Moreover, attempts to bring unity and cohesion into each of the American parties have failed to overcome the centrifugal forces of federalism and separated powers.

In contemporary Great Britain, while it is indeed possible to distinguish between the executive, legislative, and judicial *functions* of government, there is no rule that insists that these specific functions shall be performed by distinct and separate persons and bodies.[26] In fact, the office of one political official combines all three powers of government at the same time. The lord chancellor is a member of the executive cabinet, the legislative House of Lords, and as Britain's highest judge is a member of the judiciary.

The fusion of the executive and the legislature in Britain means that the executive is chosen by Parliament. There is in Britain no separate popular election for the executive as is the case in America; after the British general election is held, the parliamentary members of the party with a majority of seats in the House of Commons choose a prime minister to head the executive branch. By contrast, the American method of selecting legislators and highest executive officers brings into the functional separation a type of sociological checking and balancing. Elected officials in the two branches of government are chosen from different constituencies, for varying staggered and overlapping terms of office, and by different sets of voters. They are thus responsive and responsible to different combinations of groups within the electorate, so that interests can be checked by other interests in the policy-making process. These conditions and the structure of American government preclude the concentration of political responsibility in the political parties as it exists in Britain.

If the British cabinet loses the support of its party's members in Commons, it must resign or request the monarch to dissolve Commons and call for new elections. This custom, which is now an integral part of the British constitution, developed so that there can never be the kind of prolonged disagreement between the executive and legislative branches that occurs almost routinely in the United States.[27] The British executive and legislative officials never follow conflicting policies; the two must always be in agreement in order to govern. In spite of the fact that there is no formal separation of the executive and legislative powers in Britain, as there is in the United States, there is a very real and clear distinction between the cabinet and Parliament. A key to the British governmental system is the continually maintained balance between the legislative and executive initiative of the cabinet on the one hand, and the consideration of the cabinet's policies and programs by Parliament on the other.

The pluralism which Americans tend to view as the key to achieving and maintaining limited and responsive government is carried directly into the national institutions by means of the diffusion of political decision-making authority. Americans are very wary of concentrated power and believe that the only way in which government can be limited is through institutional checking and balancing. However, this arrangement inevitably results in a blurring of the lines of political accountability. The British take a different view of limited government. In the British system, the key to achieving limited government is believed to lie in the clear-cut lines of political responsibility that run from the electorate to the political decision makers through the intervening institutions, the political parties. Hence the British are willing to let their elected decision makers exercise a great degree of concentrated power because they feel confident that the political parties provide the means of calling the decision makers to account in the next election.

Because the constitutional principles considered thus far and the political cultures differ between the two countries under study, there are also major differences in the ways in which the constitutional protection of the rights and liberties of the individuals is carried out in each. These differences, including the presence of judicial review in the United States and its absence in Great Britain, will now be examined. But the contrasts which come to light in the course of the discussion ought not obscure the basic importance accorded to the protections for individual rights and liberties in both countries. After all, both Britain and the United States share a common heritage of political liberalism and democratic ideals out of which protection for these rights and liberties developed.

PROTECTION OF INDIVIDUAL RIGHTS
AND LIBERTIES

Although Britain is thought of as the spring of modern political liberalism, and much American mythology concerning the nature and sources of individual rights was derived from British sources, the political and legal cultures of the two countries have evolved to produce very different syntheses of these rights and their protection.

DIFFERING ATTITUDES TOWARD PROTECTION
OF RIGHTS AND LIBERTIES

American emphasis upon legalism precipitates a significant difference between British and American conditions. British citizens rely very little on lawsuits and legal rights to control their law enforcement and administrative personnel. Deep seated traditions about the proprieties of authority and its legitimate exercise are more powerful constraints on power wielders in Britain than are constitutional provisions, statutes, and decisions of judges, which provide the key American constraints. British citizens are more willing to leave the protection of their liberties from abuse of authority to the force of public opinion than are Americans, who tend to view the courts, especially the Supreme Court, as their first line of defense for individual rights. This may help explain why, in times of emergency, the British exhibit a more flexible and spontaneously tolerant attitude toward necessary abridgments of selected rights, whereas Americans tend to insist that such abridgments be identified, enunciated, and legitimated by politically non-accountable judges rather than by politically accountable decision makers. The British police, courts, and citizenry do not exhibit the tendency toward finely drawn distinctions in law that are so much a part of the Americans' bent toward government by judiciary, especially when civil rights are at issue. In this area, Americans seem to trust their appointed judges and to distrust their elected decision makers and tend to favor the resolution of controversies arising over the protection of their rights by litigation and adjudication rather than by majority vote.

This American preference for litigation may be in part due to the existence of the codified Bill of Rights in the Constitution of the United States. The British do not have a comparable listing. Most definition and protection of the rights of Englishmen are the products of sporadic, almost casual and haphazard responses to ad hoc situations that have developed throughout the course of British history. Ancient confrontations, national emergencies, casual litigation, and principles of common law have all contributed, and continue to contribute, to the development of civil liberties in Britain. The British are not bothered by the absence of a written Constitution or a listing of their rights in something known as a Bill of Rights. Certain historical documents clarify or reaffirm various rights, but, for the most part, these rights were not created but invigorated by the phrases recorded on parchment. More than the Americans, the British seem comfortable in their belief that what is crucial to the maintenance of freedom for individuals is the spirit in which authority is exercised. Written protections guarantee nothing in practice unless decision makers, tax collectors, anonymous bureaucrats, and other power wielders operate in the spirit of the guarantees. If they do, the argument runs, the written guarantees are not necessary; if they do not, documentary enumerations will accomplish nothing.

The British outlook toward individual rights is not characterized by the emotionalism that has aroused so much passion over civil ights in the United States in recent years. Their political and legal cultures do not impel them to go to law for the purpose of protecting rights, and the British courts do not approach the rate of American tribunals in deciding cases imposing limits on abusive authority. Nevertheless, the British are neither indifferent nor casual in their esteem for the value of individual rights. They assume, as do Americans, that people should be free to do what the law does not forbid and that punishments should be imposed only upon conviction of a breach of its prohibitions. But they are less preoccupied with the precise definition of these rights and their application to particular situations of alleged deprivation than are Americans. The general policies and attitudes of respect for liberty, not specific consequences in individual cases, are held to be most important for the preservation of meaningful rights and liberties for individuals.

Because of the different approaches to the subject, in Britain there is almost no literature that deals with civil liberties, while in America there are thousands of books and articles that directly treat the subject. This provides evidence of the Americans' intense preoccupation with giving individual rights exact definition and specific protection.[28] In addition, the British are only just beginning to form organizations such as the American Civil Liberties Union, the NAACP, and the Anti-Defamation and Defense League which have become important in America as watchdogs of individual rights. Such organizations play key roles in providing counsel and defense for individuals involved in litigation concerning civil rights controversies. Their absence in Britain stems partly from the subordinate role of the judiciary in defining civil liberties, in contrast to the heavy American reliance on the judicial system to provide the definitions. Although groups that publicize oppression and champion rights do exist in Britain, they cannot use the courts as such groups do in America, and they are legally prohibited from financing litigation on behalf of aggrieved plaintiffs. Also in contrast to the United States, the British have no body comparable to the American Civil Rights Commission, charged with the enforcement of specific statutes safeguarding individual rights. No offices such as the civil rights division of the Department of Justice or the civil rights section of the Department of

Health and Human Services exist in Great Britain to receive, investigate and act on complaints of discrimination.[29]

In addition, there are no lawyers in Britain specializing in civil rights cases; this subject area is not significant enough to attract profitable interest in either the practice of civil rights law or in its special study in universities or legal societies. In Britain, cases are rarely litigated for the purpose of establishing a civil right; that results almost by chance, as a secondary product of a verdict reached in a particular case. This contrasts directly with the focus of the U.S. Supreme Court's decisions on the definition of civil liberties in cases in which they are at issue, with secondary importance attached to the disposition of the particular case in question at that court level.

Thus, the protection of civil liberties in Britain depends principally upon the British respect for limited government, deeply ingrained in the political culture. This allows the British to leave the issues surrounding civil rights and liberties to the parliamentary processes. Although in both the United States and Britain the line separating public policy making (a function of executives and legislatures) and adjudication (that of the judiciary) is clear in principle, it is much more controlling in practice in Britain. There, judges go to great lengths to avoid entering the public policy arena, whereas American judges often appear to reach out for policy issues. This is in line with the tradition of litigation and disposition to sue so characteristic of Americans, but lacking in Britain. There, policy implications for the protection of rights and liberties of individuals are debated in Parliament, especially by the opposition, and generally in the public press before legislation is enacted. After enactment, any effects adverse to individual rights that may stem from administrative application may be raised in the parliamentary question hour and inadequate replies from ministers may be made the focal point for the debate on adjournment. However, the arena is still the parliamentary, not the judicial, one.

It is significant to note in this connection the differences that obtain in the two countries in the processes for protecting individual rights stemming from the presence of judicial review in the United States and its absence in Britain. In the course of reaching decisions concerning individual rights, the U.S. Supreme

Court may reach the conclusion that a particular statute or action violates a protected right specifically listed in the Bill of Rights. Such a violation is thus ruled unconstitutional. Courts in Britain play no such role, a lack which tends to disturb Americans, who are much more suspicious of any governmental actions than are the British. Because the British are inclined to look upon their government with a high degree of trust, to expect it to govern, and to rely upon the political accountability underlying the system for their basic protections, they accept the fact that government inevitably imposes restraints on the individual's freedom of action. Americans, on the other hand, tend to demand the best of both worlds, positive government action and freedom from its consequences for individuals. Americans mark off the private realm from the public more definitively than do the British. The preoccupation of Americans with freedom *from* government is largely absent in Britain, where freedom *under* responsible government is the more characteristic attitude. A strong, positive role for government is regarded by the British as entirely proper, and a disposition to view government as a partner in achieving the common good contrasts to the American attitude which holds government as alien, often enemy, to be constrained and curbed lest it infringe on individual rights.

CURRENT PROBLEMS IN THE PROTECTION OF INDIVIDUAL RIGHTS

Like the United States today, contemporary Britain is confronted by a number of problems in the realm of individual rights. Such changes as the encroachment of the government into the arena that was previously private, the emergence of politically controversial groups within the society, and the arrival of divergent ethnic groups into Britain from the Commonwealth countries have precipitated challenges to the traditional understanding of individual rights and their protection. Nonconformist groups of whatever type by definition do not share the established values, and their members often feel that they are outside the scope of traditional institutions. For them, the accepted ways are not usually sufficient to provide the protection they feel they need. In some cases the slow processes of piecemeal legal change are adequate for their protection—as when abortion and homosexuality between consenting adults were decriminalized by statute in Britain—but more often nonconformists are forced to endure inadequate recognition of and protection for their special positions and interests which lie outside the mainstream of British culture and values.

Increased administrative activity in both Britain and the United States poses special problems and has raised renewed concern for individual rights. This is an old problem, recognized early in both countries. The habeas corpus writ, an important protection for individuals in both the United States and Britain, originated in the British courts well before the Habeas Corpus Act was passed by Parliament in 1679. Control of arbitrary power exercised by agents of the executive has long been the subject of concern to common law courts of England. Today, British courts, like their American counterparts, have a great responsibility for keeping the bureaucracy within the scope of its delegated authority and limited to legitimate proceedings. New problems sometimes strain traditional interpretations of long-accepted rights and their protection; for example, the development of technically sophisticated electronic eavesdropping equipment put a strain on the accepted American interpretation of the Fourth Amendment protection against unreasonable search and seizure which had always been applied to material objects only.

Particular difficulties which promise to persist have arisen in both countries surrounding traditional areas of privacy. The growth of administrative structure and authority has brought the bureaucracy increasingly into conflict with areas traditionally considered private. Social service programs require information that many persons regard as personal in nature, but that administrators view as essential to measure the needs and effectiveness of the programs. As government intrudes further into the lives of individuals and amasses more and more data about many phases of their lives, it stores that information in data banks, from which it is readily retrievable. The growth of executive power, usually over the citizenry, is a phenomenon of British as well as of American government, and in both countries raises a spectre that threatens civil liberties. Its most threatening form is not rank abuse of authority but the exercise of legitimate discretion delegated by vaguely worded statutes incorporating nebulous policy goals. Hence, there is growing cause to question whether reliance upon statutes, common law, and judicial decisions can continue to give adequate protection to civil liberties in Britain. There and in the United States the first line for defense of individual liberties is not in the courts, legislature or executive, but in public opinion, in the desire of the common man that government remain subservient to him and answerable to him through the mechanisms of open political processes. There is in the United States more than in Britain, however, a pronounced tendency to rely heavily upon the judiciary and on litigation. Americans probably rely excessively on their courts; the British may be compelled by the course of events to turn to their judiciary more than they have done in the past for protection of their rights and liberties.

CHAPTER THREE

PARTIES AND PRESSURE GROUPS

No democracy in recorded history has thus far existed without political parties nor, in more recently developed pluralistic societies, their close allies, interest groups that are politically active. Someone has suggested that if political parties had not come into being spontaneously with the emergence of democracy, they would have had to be invented, so essential are they to its existence. Modern societies are highly complex, and individuals in them have many distinct politically relevant interests associated with their numerous social roles.

REPRESENTATIVE FUNCTION

Individuals who share interests and who desire to promote them by establishing relations with government need a mechanism for doing so. The mass of citizens whose consent is supposed to be the source of a democratic government's legitimacy needs a means for granting and renewing it. A way must be provided so that the politically active public can choose its governors, indicate its preferences on matters of public policy, and hold its governors accountable for their conduct of public business, for democracy is based on the assumption that government must be responsive and responsible to the governed. But, government cannot respond to the needs and wants of a politically organized people unless those requirements and desires can be identified and expressed so that policy makers can understand and act on them. Given their multiplicity, diversity, and often conflicting character, the mechanism for mobilizing and articulating perceived demands of societal interests must be reasonable, accessible, open, and moderate. If it is not, the mechanism cannot function as a representative agency for comprehensively reflecting and transmitting public opinion on matters of social policy to government.

The normal machinery for accomplishing these and other objectives is the political party system, but because political parties cannot represent all of the myriad demands that groups bring to bear on the governmental process, their capacity to identify, mobilize, articulate, and transmit the public's needs and wants is supplemented by the ability of political interest groups to do so. However, the interest groups cannot actively transform expressed demands into public policies and programs, because they do not control public power through the exercise of authority in office. Hence, as will be brought out in detail later, interest groups work through political parties, legislatures, bureaucracies, and courts to attain their goals. They may sponsor candidates for public office or be otherwise closely identified with political activity, but only political parties have getting control of public office and exercising public authority as their principal goal.

ROLES OF POLITICAL PARTIES

Party systems in the United States and Britain fulfill the foregoing roles and in addition perform other functions typical of party systems in democracies. In America, principal responsibility falls on the candidates, with degrees of party help. In Britain, it is the parties that are primary; the campaign planners and candidates select issues for voter attention, simplify them to aid voter comprehension, and educate the electorate about them. Parties mobilize electorates and endeavor to aggregate political support by building coalitions of interest out of diverse groups. In doing so, they moderate extreme demands and bring about compromises in competing and conflicting expectations. Parties serve as channels for communicating demands and supports to governors and thereby reflect public opinion. Parties identify candidates, conduct elections, link the electorate to the government, stimulate citizen political

tivity, assume real or nominal responsibility for government,
itimate the system, legitimate issues and candidates, and demon-
ate the vitality of democracy and its political processes. By con-
cting elections and antecedent activities prior to them, parties
lp bring the political branches of the government into being and,
cording to the system at hand, facilitate their operations. Party
stems must either actually take responsibility for government,
in Britain, or give the appearance of doing so sufficiently to
isfy public expectation, as in the United States. Finally, but
ost importantly, democratic party systems must provide major
litical parties opportunity to gain access to political power, per-
it the "out" party of the moment knowledgeably and meaning-
lly to criticize the "in" party as its opposition, and stand ready
take over responsibility for government whenever the electorate
cides to make a change in party control. In different ways and
different degrees the American and British political party sys-
ms pursue the goals or perform the functions associated with
mocratic government.

GENERAL SIMILARITIES OF
ANGLO-AMERICAN PARTY SYSTEMS

In both the United States and England, political party systems
e national, competitive, two-party systems. But American parties
e more significant as agencies for identifying and transmitting
blic needs and expectations to government for enactment and
plementation than they are for enforcing accountability of
vernors to the electorate. The British political culture and system
signs the government and cabinet in power the principal role in
at arena. The British electorate does not expect to be a primary
urce of policy proposals but to serve as a sounding board for
licy initiatives taken elsewhere. The American electorate, on the
her hand, expects its parties to operate as major lines for com-
unicating public expectations and demands to decision makers
government. British political parties are superior to American
rties as agencies for developing policy and enforcing responsi-
lity, but not for transmitting policy preferences from the elec-
rate to governors. American political parties are expected to mir-
r public opinion regularly and accurately.

In the nature of things, American political parties cannot atta
the degree of consistent policy development achieved by Briti
parties. Given the lack of discipline; the influence of localism; t
decentralization of authority, decision making, and structure with
them, there can be little wonder that disunity over policy a
failure of elected representatives to follow the executive's poli
leads exists. Another defect lies in the fact that American nation
party platforms are prepared by committees of the quadrenni
national coventions, but the party machinery thereafter loses
direct control and almost all influence over their enactment in
law. The platform committee writes the statement of party pri
ciples and programs—which no one regards as important a
binding—but translation of its generally ambiguous planks in
law rests with the party's legislative members, who may not const
tute a majority of their house of Congress. At best, a preside
with a working majority of his party in both chambers can on
propose legislation with knowledge that Congress will dispose
his legislative program. Depending on his personality, perceptic
of his office and power, party strength, and working relations wi
congressional leaders, the president can play a significant or negl
gible role over how Congress disposes of his proposals. But l
must negotiate, compromise, and bargain; he cannot comman
and any success he achieves will be the result of his efforts ar
those of his lieutenants, not the consequence of a system of di
ciplined, responsible party government spanning the separatic
between legislative and executive branches.

Each is a two-party system consisting of two major parti
competing for national offices, each having a realistic chance
coming to power so that a reasonable pattern of alternating contr
of government emerges. Nominally, majorities determine electic
results, but both systems endure pluralities. In fact, since Worl
War II, most British and American executives have been chose
by less than fifty percent of the popular vote, and in both system
a shift of from 5 to 10 percent of the vote could have change
party control of the national executive office. Appearance
majority rule in the American system is preserved by the fact tha
the candidate chosen president always receives a majority of th
electoral college ballots. In Britain, control of the government go

o the party that wins or can control a majority of the seats in the House of Commons. Hence, each system in choosing its executive preserves some element of majority rule. Both party systems serve as the foundation on which stable, moderate, responsible, and responsive governments are built, although British parties are internally more cohesive, disciplined, and accountable than are American.

The parties of both systems are moderate, complex, and popular. They each try to attract support from the widest possible range of electoral interests. Of the four major parties—Democratic, Republican, Conservative, and Labor—Labor most clearly emerges as ideologically centered, but it avoids rigid doctrinaire positions on national policy issues and readily compromises with practical necessity as political fortunes demand. However, its commitment to state ownership of the instruments of production, distribution, and exchange sets it apart from the other major parties; they have policy preferences but no consistent ideological framework that defines and confines their policy orientations and operations.

SOCIOLOGY OF PARTY SUPPORT

British political parties have an easily distinguished class bias that American major parties largely lack. The sociological composition of the Labor and Conservative parties contrast sharply. Conservatives draw heavily from professional and well-to-do elements of the population and somewhat less strongly from the white-collar category. Labor receives support from only approximately 20 percent of the nonmanual groups of the British population. Jean Blondel points out something of a paradox resulting from the social composition of British parties—only about 60 percent of the working class supports the Labor party, and the middle class, which purports to be free of class bias and consciousness, supports the Conservative party, the party of elitism and hierarchy. Labor, therefore, substantially represents only the working class, but the Conservatives draw heavy support from manual workers, small business owners, higher type white-collar employees, middle and high professional people and business and upper-class voters.[1]

Some similarity of support can be discerned by pairing British and American parties. Both the Labor and Democratic parties appeal to working-class voters. Albeit the Democratic party has successfully broadened its appeal to the middle class, both attract votes from the economically and socially depressed, from urban voters, from young professionals, and from white-collar groups. The ethnic and racial bloc votes that in America go heavily to the Democrats have not figured in British voting patterns, but nonconformist Protestant voters in Britain tend to support Labor just as American Catholic and Jewish votes go largely to the Democratic party. The British Conservative and American Republican parties have some common bases of electoral support. Both are associated with the more economically, educationally, socially, and occupationally advantaged portions of the respective electorates. Both draw rural votes and votes from business, commercial, financial, professional, and manufacturing segments of the suffrage. But a large proportion, varying from 33 to 40 percent, of Britain's largest social class—manual workers—votes Conservative and represents a source of electoral support unmatched in the Republican party's electoral base.[2] The Episcopalian vote in America has long been associated with the Republican party, as Church of England membership has traditionally been aligned with the Conservatives.

The principal class bias among the four parties is that of the British Labor party. As will be noted in some detail later, many formal links exist between the Labor party organization and British trade unionism, for the party is dedicated to the interests of the laboring class, draws most of its membership and financial support from British unions, and provides labor with heavy representation in the central structure of the party. The privileged status of unionism in the Labor party reflects the fact that the party originated outside of Parliament as a pro-labor political activist movement launched to obtain for labor a larger share in national policy making. Although no formal links exist between either major American party and organized labor, the leadership of American labor is cultivated by the Democratic party, the labor vote is a substantial part of its electoral base, and influential labor leaders are heard in and influence the councils of the Democratic party. The party is also indebted to financial support from labor sources. Nevertheless, the British Labor party is avowedly more ocialistically motivated than the Democratic, whereas the Democratic is more middle class, less doctrinaire, and less egalitarian. This is not to suggest, however, that British parties are monolithic or that American parties are necessarily internally divided into contending factions. Instead, British and American parties are alike in that all contain deep and wide internal divisions. But, because the British governmental system demands that the party in power be united and cohesive, British party divisions normally produce far less negative effect on the governmental mechanism than do splits in the major American parties.

MINOR PARTIES

Both systems accommodate minor parties, but they suffer the usual fate of lesser parties in two-party systems. In each they are alternative parties, often dissident, narrowly focused, gadfly organizations. In an average American presidential election year, a dozen or more will enter primaries, and perhaps as many will place candidates on the ballots of different states, but rarely does one succeed in capturing a single electoral college vote. An exception in recent years has been regionally based movements that sought to win sufficient electoral college votes to throw the presidential election into the House of Representatives, where the faction hoped to be decisive in the process of choosing a president by the House.

The British Liberal party emerges most prominently in British national elections after the two major parties. The party usually gains approximately a half-dozen seats in the House of Commons, but the effect of its popular vote is dissipated by the operation of the single member district. Since the election of 1974, the Scottish, Welsh, and Northern Ireland Nationalist parties have also exerted a strong but localized effect in general elections, but they also have won only a few seats in the House of Commons. Because of the strength of the major British parties and the obstacles in the path to minor party success, third parties rarely elect more than a token number of members in either party system. Third parties, therefore, do not often impair the stability of governments. It is a tribute to the political maturity of party leadership in Britain that the Callaghan Labor government was able to maintain stable effective control in spite of its dependence upon the coalition support of Liberals to give it the thinnest of working margins. The situation is also evidence of the discipline, cohesiveness, and unity of the party membership and the effectiveness of leadership within the system.

DIFFERENCES IN PARTY SYSTEMS

Just as there are general similarities between the respective systems and their component parties, so there are significant major differences attributable to differences of political culture within which they operate and to certain variation of principles and structure in the two constitutional frameworks. For example, British unitary versus American federal government; parliamentary sovereignty opposed to American popular sovereignty; and British fusion versus American separation of powers. Because both party systems fulfill the same roles as agencies of democracy, most differences that will be brought out in these pages will be of secondary importance. At this point, however, we will attend to several major ones.

PARTY CENTRALIZATION

One striking difference between British and American political parties lies in the centralization of party organization and control in England and the diffused decentralization in America. The difference, of course, is attributable to party characteristics attuned to a unitary government and those appropriate to a federal system. The evolution of governmental authority in England involved a movement to the center followed by political liberalization and democratization for governmental institutions that required fully integrated and systematized responsibility. Cabinet government, majority control, individual and collective ministerial responsibility, accountable political leadership, and existence of a formal opposition all necessitate centralized political parties. In contrast, American federalism alone is sufficient to guarantee decentralized parties in the United States, but it is reinforced by such other centrifugal political forces as separation of powers and its corollary, checks and balances; state control of the suffrage and election

national legislators; the electoral college system; and the spirit
localism that pervades American politics. E. E. Schattschneider
[cal]led the decentralization of power in American parties their most
[sal]ient characteristic, one that clarifies almost all of their other
[fea]tures.[3] Candidates for Congress who fight primaries without
[pa]rty help, who fight campaigns and get elected largely without
[na]tional party aid, and who develop their own local power bases
[ba]ck home may have little reason to feel party loyalty, indebted-
[ne]ss, or gratitude above the constituency level. Their independent
[po]litical power bases free them from being in servitude to their
[pa]rty.

[ST]ABILITY AND CONTINUITY

[The] British political parties are characterized by a high degree of
[co]ntinuity and permanence of operation. Organizations of British
[pa]rty structure do not virtually disappear between elections and
[re]quire reconstitution before being able to conduct the next cam-
[pa]ign as American parties do. In part their continuity and perma-
[ne]nce are due to the fact that a national election can be set by the
[pr]ime minister at any time he feels one is necessary or desirable,
[w]hereas American elections occur according to a fixed timetable
[re]gulated by constitutionally prescribed terms of office. The need
[of] the British to conduct elections to fill vacant seats in the House
[of] Commons in the interval between national elections also pre-
[se]nts a continuing reason for party preparedness. American par-
[ti]es, however, are called upon to operate fully only at election
[ti]mes, depend heavily on volunteer help that falls away rapidly,
[h]ave little to do between scheduled elections, are highly localized,
[an]d virtually dissolve in the politically quiescent interludes between
[ca]mpaigns. Moreover, if a party leader is to lead; to optimize his
[p]arty's chance of victory in the next election; to maintain his own
[p]osition at the head of his forces; to control his party's units and
[it]s office holders; to direct policy formulation, enactment and
[im]plementation; and be accountable to the electorate, he must
[h]ave a party to lead. Increasingly the British party leader is gain-
[in]g recognition as the party's sole authoritative spokesman and as
[th]e living embodiment of the organization's philosophy and pro-

gram. To fulfill the expectations held of him by the public, part
and government, he must have a stable, united, integrated, an
disciplined party organization behind him.

By contrast, an American president may be only titular lead
of his party, but strong or weak, he will have many public riva
for power. He will be secure for four years, but as Jimmy Carte
learned in 1980, he cannot ignore the impact of his image ar
record on his own and his party's electoral fate. The party whic
lost the presidency is assured no less than a minority role in th
houses of Congress, but there its members are joined only by
common party label and do not act in concert as a disciplined o
position. In the 1980 campaign, however, the Republican Nation
Committee (RNC) transferred impressive amounts of its fun
to selected House and Senate races, successfully wresting contr
of the Senate from its rival party and substantially increasing R
publican strength in the House. A sustained infusion of nation
party resources and influence into the selection of its congression
members may operate upon those so aided to increase their d
pendence, enhance their sense of loyalty or obligation, and mal
them more aware that their political fate is closely linked to th
of their party's presidential candidate. Whether increased cohesic
can be achieved remains to be seen. Neither party central org
plays much role in party affairs until presidential election effo
resume, for state party units and congressional constituency c
ganizations created by candidates act to fill vacancies in the Hou
by special election. Those in the Senate are usually filled
gubernatorial appointments.

Withal, the American national party is built on a foundation
party identification and commitment felt by millions of individu
voters. That sense of identification and support keeps the parti
alive and helps span the gap separating the formal structures of t
national and state parties. But it is rendered uncertain by t
strong sense of disdain for political parties and partisan politi
that runs through the American political culture. Fully a third
the American electorate identifies with no political party. Ame
cans have little understanding of responsible party governme
and the American party system rests on an insecure foundation
public trust and acceptance.

Even in England, in spite of the high level on which party competition is conducted, public mistrust of parties makes a policy attributable to the prime minister and cabinet more respectable than one identified with their party. Merkl contends that in the American and British systems of party rule, the electorates prefer to believe that decisions are made, not by party organization and influence, but by means of spontaneous nonpartisan choices.[4]

Moreover, while the British always choose a national executive and legislature at the same time, Americans do not. The terms of our representatives are renewed each two years, along with one-third of our senators, and only every four years is a president chosen, the elections coinciding only in presidential election years. The events within party ranks are linked only by a common concern to gain control of the House, Senate, and presidency, whether by the coattail effect or by intraparty organizational and financial relationships. Because of the separation of powers and fixed terms of national office, the political fortunes of a presidential candidate are not controlled by the success of congressional hopefuls, as the fate of a British party leader who hopes to become prime minister is tied to the fate of his party's constituency candidates. A president is president with or without party control of one or both Houses of Congress. On the other hand, the candidates for seats in the House of Commons are dependent upon the party's finances, label, organization, and electoral effort, and the price they pay for that dependency is their individual legislative initiative and autonomy after election. American legislators of the president's party can and often do kick off the party's traces and with virtual impunity go their own ways on policy and other matters of concern to the executive, largely free from presidential control.

The separation of presidential from congressional elections is increased by the impact of localism, candidate perception, and issue orientation on voters in the congressional districts. They evaluate candidates for Congress by one scale of values and presidential candidates by another, and they are probably more influenced by their perceptions of a candidate's personal qualities than they are by his party label or his party's national program and philosophy.

At the same time the stability and continuity of America's major

parties are only slightly enhanced by the increasing but still minor
extent to which national issues and proposed solutions are being
injected into national electoral politics at the state and congressional district levels. The British tradition that representatives in
Commons represent the interests of all persons for whom they
enact national laws, not just those of constituents who return them
(the principle of virtual representation), has never gained ascendency over the forces of parochialism in American congressional
politics. American parties still operate on the principle that representation must be directly and closely related to constituency needs
and interests, because most American voters feel that their interests must be served by their individually elected representatives.
The way that American electoral districts are created and used
reinforces that feeling, which in part vitalized the American
Revolution, as does the custom that requires a Representative to
live in the congressional district from which he is elected. This is
not to suggest that British MPs (members of Parliament) ignore
their constituents—the realities of practical politics prevent them
from doing so—but it is to say that they and their electorates
understand that local interests can properly be accommodated only
when that action is compatible with party program and government policy. They can vote their convictions and their constituencies contrary to party position without suffering dire consequences
but only after making careful preparation to determine that their
defection from a party vote will not affect its fortunes in the
House.

PARTY COHESION

The members of British political parties elected to office exhibit
a high degree of cohesiveness; those elected by American parties
do not do so to a high degree. But British parties must exhibit
cohesiveness, for, if party members in Commons went their independent legislative ways, ignored their party's leadership, or voted
unpredictably on measures transforming electoral pledges into law,
the stability of the government would be jeopardized by its uncertain ability to command the support of a majority of its members
in Commons and to remain in office. Hence, in the British system,
a high degree of party cohesiveness—bloc voting according to

party identity and leadership—is required and obtained. In contrast, in Congress, party leaders usually make little effort to induce party cohesion on any but the most important measures, and even then persuasion unbacked by meaningful sanctions is the principal measure. Neither party in either the House or the Senate has the ability to bind its members to stand together behind legislation. The force of parochialism in congressional politics and elections is very strong; little sense of party loyalty or obligation ties the district party to the national party leadership; legislators are socialized to vote independently on legislation consistent with campaign promises, constituency interests, and vote trading among themselves. Furthermore, separated powers forces the president to rely heavily on persuasion and horse trading—giving political favors and collecting on political debts—and relying on publicity to overcome the gulf between himself as party leader and the legislative leadership of his own party on Capitol Hill. Inability to marshal his own party may force him to depend on the minority legislative party for help in enacting his administration's policy measures, and it is not unusual for the legislative leaders of the president's party to oppose his policies.

PARTY DISCIPLINE

Discipline is the antidote to party factionalism. Reasons why British parties are highly disciplined are not hard to identify.

1. They can control from the central party offices the choice of party nominees at the constituency level if they desire to do so to protect party regularity.
2. They can withhold their party labels from unacceptable local party choices.
3. They are based upon electorates that are politically socialized to regard party affiliation, not the personalities or policy positions of individual candidates, as all important. Voters vote party labels according to the national program of the party as enunciated in election manifestos and in statements by its leader and top-level spokesmen. Increasingly, the leader is accepted as *the* spokesman of his party, and electioneering done by other prominent party figures

usually reflects agreed-upon positions on national issues. All candidates are accepted as speaking to the party positions, not as individual vote getters seeking personal success at the polls.

4. British party structure is nationally organized and centralized. Little formal autonomy is vested in constituency organizations. Constituency organizations are also socialized to understand their place in the scheme of party success, to respond to the political complexion of the constituency, and to select politically reliable and compatible candidates to wear the party's label. A candidate knows what is expected of him as a candidate and as a member of his party.

5. In British party politics a successful career is built on a record of party service, regularity, and discipline. For an individual member of Commons to have real impact on the policies of his party, he must escape the ranks of the backbenchers by being selected by current party leaders for future positions of influence and power.

6. The British party system makes clear to the individual MP that the system of party control, of which he is a small unit, ties his political fate to that of his party. For his party to remain in the majority and in control of the government, he knows that he and his fellow members cannot act with such disregard of party cohesion and discipline that the stability of the government is jeopardized or a fall from office is precipitated. The system does not require him to act like a mindless automaton, but it does demand that he generally support the party on major issues and subordinate his personal orientations on issues to those fixed by the cabinet and embodied in the government's legislation.

7. British party discipline and cohesion may be strengthened by the MP's knowledge that failure to support the government of their party may bring on a national election, with its attendant inconvenience and expense. This explanation is not thought to be very weighty on the minds of most MPs today, but fighting an election is bound to have some nuisance value that will be a stimulant to party support.

8. A British party may deny its label (withdraw the whip) to a recalcitrant member who becomes a maverick and thereby

force him to abandon his seat or run as an independent candidate. Either course would probably bring an end to his political career, for party label is so important in British electoral politics that a candidate running without party endorsement would have virtually no chance at the polls. However, expulsion is a rarely imposed sanction. Neither expulsion nor the threat of it is a major cause of party regularity among backbenchers.

9. In the last analysis, what probably keeps most private members true to their party's leaders and principles is the knowledge that if they do not support them, the opposition party will succeed to power and office. That prospect for any reasonably committed party member should be sufficiently reprehensible to guarantee a high degree of party support on his part.

It is British party discipline and cohesion which assure that the party dominant in Commons and the prime minister will wear the same party tag. They assure that national issues, not local interests, will be the focus of electoral concern. They enhance party responsibility by enabling the prime minister to rely on his party's members without having to elicit aid for his legislation from the opposition, as American party leaders must sometimes do, and thereby cloud the issue of who should be held accountable at the polls for what.

Thus, the integrated symmetry of British cabinet government does, but the fractionated and separated powers of rival legislative and executive officers in the American presidential system do not, inherently require party discipline and unity. What happens at the polls to presidential candidates is constitutionally, and may be politically, unrelated to the outcomes of legislative elections. The nomination of American congressional candidates is controlled at the congressional district and state party levels, as is the selection of presidential electors. The latter, especially, are often selected by rank-and-file party members voting in primaries or by committee or convention, but, regardless of the means employed, without national party control. The political fate of an American senator or representative is determined in most instances by the votes of state or congressional district. The influence of a president may affect the outcome of a legislative race in a closely divided two-party constituency, but the political fortunes of members of Congress are not directly tied to that of executives, as they are in the British system of party accountability. This situation results from the fractionated condition of the American party's structure. A nominal national party machinery exists, but it has only weak links to the operationally effective state party organizations. Success of the party in a national election is due to the ability of the state party organizations to carry the election at the grass-roots level.

The American system does not depend upon partisan support aggregated in the houses of Congress to produce legislation, for the president's party may not control one or both chambers. No formalized opposition exists in the American pattern of legislative-executive relations, and a successor executive is not identifiable until a national election has been held. Political stability is provided by fixed terms of office that dictate the timing of legislative and executive elections, not by the need for political parties to maintain stable majorities in order to remain in control of governmental office and power. The principle of separated powers rules out the president's having the ability to dissolve sessions of Congress and bring about consultations of the national electoral will. Because American legislation is enacted by ad hoc coalitions of support, often built across party lines, it is virtually impossible to demonstrate that policies are enacted with clear claims to majority electoral support. It is impossible to speak meaningfully about majority party control of Congress; no source of organized opposition to the incumbent administration is provided within the system. Responsible party government does not operate in the American constitutional system. Consequently, disciplined political parties are not necessary to its operation.

PARTY WHIPS AND PARTY DISCIPLINE

Party discipline in Britain is also reinforced by the roles of party whips and by information flow. Localism in British politics is very weak force compared to its disintegrative influence in American national politics. MPs are elected from local constituencies to be sure, but everyone concerned with British elections assumes that the purpose of an election is to take an appeal to the country o obtain a popular verdict on the majority party's program and record, not to choose persons to be delegates of electors. British candidates cannot stand for election to executive office or be presented as agents of their constituencies. Nevertheless, MPs cannot ignore their constituencies. By visits to their political home bases, maintaining offices there, and keeping in close contact with their local party agents, they keep in touch with their constituents' attitudes toward party leaders and programs.

The link between MPs sensitive to voter opinion at home and the party's leaders are the whip and assistant whips of each party. It is their duty to notify their members about the seriousness of pending legislation and about what the leaders expect from them by way of unity and support on the votes. The whips keep in touch with the backbenchers to determine their feelings about the same measures and transmit the attitudes of members and constituencies to the party leadership. It is the function of the whips to enforce party discipline, to mobilize party support in Commons, to promote party solidarity, and to apprise party leaders about backbench objections so that policy adjustments can be made off the floor instead of in response to a venture into insurgency by fractious MPs on the floor of the House. Majority party dominance and its leader's position of control largely depend upon the successful functioning of the whips.

American legislative parties in the houses of Congress also employ whips. They function as liaisons between the members and floor leaders of the parties, try to promote party unity and win votes for party policy, sound out opinions on pending legislation, endeavor to mobilize members on important votes, and generally aid the floor leaders of the houses. But, because the operating environment and party roles in the chambers of Congress are so different from those features of the House of Commons, the significance of American party whips in maintaining party cohesiveness and close legislative-executive relations is but a pale shadow of the British pattern.

MAINTENANCE OF CONSTITUENCY RELATIONS

Members of Commons and Congress maintain close relations with their local party organizations. The American representative and, to a lesser degree, senators as well, are spokesmen for the interests of their electorates. That kind of direct, almost personal, representation requires detailed knowledge of constituents' needs. If the American legislator fails to serve his constituency to its satisfaction, it will turn on him at the polls in favor of someone it believes will represent it more faithfully. Hence, members of the House and Senate cultivate their political bases, not to promote party strength but to protect their own political flanks from attack. Their principal objective is to retain their individual seats and further their own careers. But the independence and virtual autonomy of the members from party control, the lack of party regularity and discipline, and the absence of party program and control all render procedures like those employed by British parties unnecessary.

Maintenance of discipline among MPs is enhanced by these procedures. Constituency organizations and voters understand that the obligation of a member is to support his party; in fact, constituency committees impose constraints on errant backbenchers under prodding by local electorates. But an unknown shift of local opinion or a miscalculation by central policy makers could bring on disharmony and even defection from the party ranks. To prevent those consequences from occurring, MPs occupy a middle position between the central party organization and the consitituency organizations. They inform the whips and central executive organs of the party about any widespread dissatisfaction with party programs and leadership at the local level of the party structure. They alert party leaders to the need for policy revision before the private members feel driven to desert the party on a vote. The network of political communication between the local organs and central party authorities is a two-way system of persuasion, explanation, and compromise that operates with a high level of effectiveness in both British political parties.

INTRAPARTY DEMOCRACY

American party partisans enjoy more opportunities for directly controlling the choice of party officials, for indirectly affecting the parties' policies, and for choosing candidates than do supporters of English parties. American party members select party officials, committee members, and convention delegates by participating in party primaries held at various levels of the party structures, including candidates for seats in the houses of Congress. But British parties do not nominate candidates for Parliament or select party leaders by vote of the members. To democratize relations between a party and its members by permitting them to make such choices would be incompatible with the character of the British party and its role in the governmental system. Candidates are selected by party units, not by rank-and-file members. Except for the annual conferences, nothing like an American party convention is assembled to fix party rules, slate or nominate candidates, or set policy in Britain. No means are used to assure that a candidate designated by a central executive committee is acceptable to the rank-and-file members who will be asked to vote for him, for they never determine the candidates for Commons. It has been estimated that local party leadership for all British parties involves no more than a few hundred thousand partisans from a national electorate of approximately forty million voters. But in a typical constituency, actual capacity to determine party business resides in the hands of a half-dozen people who, at best, have been only indirectly selected by a handful of the full constituency membership.[5]

The greater degree of intraparty democracy in American parties is required by the American political culture. American parties are not expected to take responsibility for the policy statements or personalities of candidates who bear their labels or for incumbent executive officers and legislators. Parties in the United States do little more along that line than provide mechanisms for identifying and electing individuals to office and for holding them individually accountable at periodic intervals. American political parties do not assume collective responsibility for them or for their records in office. English political parties, of course, do accept that responsibility.

The absence of primaries from British party practice eliminates certain difficulties that afflict American parties. Bitterly fought primaries can produce intraparty wounds that heal slowly and impair unity and harmony. The primary system also produces for American parties candidates whose views are diverse and reflect the interests and orientations of the local electorates which chose them instead of reflecting the party positions on national issues.

Such diversity in British parties would be incompatible with the unity of party appeal to the electorate, with party control of candidate selection in local constituencies, and with party responsibility.

PARTY IDEOLOGIES

British political parties, in contrast to the parochialism of their American counterparts, are committed to the national interest before party advantage,[6] but, of course, each party has its version of what the national interest is and how to serve it.

Like major American parties, those of Britain struggle for the support of a single national electorate and pursue the uncommitted voter. They are prone, as are American parties, to moderate extreme positions and to offer programs that will appeal to that group. Each major party in England, Rose suggests, has been influenced by the experiences and, especially, by the successes of its rival.[7] In spite of genuine policy differences setting them apart in each party system, the major parties of each society exhibit tendencies toward integration of leadership positions, rank-and-file members, and the public at large. Differences exist at the levels of short-term particulars and long-term principles, but grounds of agreement within each system can also be found.

THE CONSERVATIVE PARTY

The major British parties are distinguishable by salient differences of ideology and implementing programs, but neither is a hard-core ideological party. The Conservative orientation is markedly different from that of the Labor party. The Tories are not committed to a precisely stated comprehensive doctrine. Instead, like American major parties, the Conservatives are dedicated to a number of broadly stated principles of indefinite meaning and scope which lend themselves to easy adaptation to specific societal needs and demands. Each major party does accept certain principles that it prefers to serve when political realities permit. Hence, Conservatives accept the ideas of a religiously founded society and the virtues of free enterprise and of private business, industry, finance, and commerce. The party is less appreciative of the interests of organized labor, but it cannot ignore the heavy support it receives from working-class Tories. Therefore, it accepts, however reluctantly, a substantial degree of Socialist-inspired national policy—national health protection; nationalization of steel, banking, transport and other areas of economic activity; national housing, and other programs. It accepts measures of social welfare but not of socialism. The party has traditionally supported and drawn support from old established institutions such as deference, a hierarchical society, elitism, the Church of England, the monarchy, the nobility, and the House of Lords. Its preferences are for the virtues of moderation, for slow, conserving change, and for a Burkian conception of society existing independently of the individuals that compose it—a society of unequal individuals in which government establishes only the conditions necessary for individuals to attain the good life for themselves by their own efforts, a society in which each person finds his own place according to his ability to make the most of his talents, opportunities and luck. Conservatives tend to oppose big government as associated with the welfare state and as being disruptive of the natural order that, if left alone, will most beneficially develop society.

Nevertheless, the Conservative party is a national party that draws support from all quarters of the electorate. Its strength with the voters lies in its pragmatism. It is committed to neither unyielding principle nor program. It takes an expedient approach to party principle and programmatic activity, bending principle as necessary to fit the changing nature of policy needs. Its ideology is not deeply rooted and is able to attract approximately two million voters to direct membership in its party. Like major American parties, the Conservative is a cadre party that permanently retains a small number of professional party workers who are aided by periodic infusions of volunteer help at election times.

THE LABOR PARTY

Perhaps because it originated outside of Parliament in a social movement that was heavily influenced by intellectuals—particularly those of the Fabian Society—the Labor party has a more ideological and programmatic character than do the Conservative or major American parties. Labor is the party of egalitarianism and is more committed to a program to implement its ideology than are the other major parties. But the party is not dedicated to orthodox Socialist doctrine accepted as a hard core of party principle. The party lacks the doctrinal rigidity that typifies a true ideological party.

Labor party attention focuses on individual well-being, especially that of the working class and the economically and socially depressed portions of society. As its title suggests, it is the workingman's party, although it welcomes electoral support from any quarter. The party rejects the deference of the Tory working-class supporter and the hierarchical view of society favored by the Conservatives in favor of advocating social and economic equality. Labor believes that it is the proper role of government to provide relief from poverty, illiteracy, and other social ills by direct action, not by merely providing conditions in which individuals can find their own ways by their own efforts out of their disadvantaged status. The resources and authority available to government should be utilized to provide fulfillment, security and happiness for people. The Labor party, therefore, uses the power of taxation to redistribute wealth and to eliminate wide disparities of personal wealth from society. Labor believes that class distinctions should be eradicated and that the social institutions that sustain them must be reformed or abolished; social services should be extended, prices and rents controlled, and the means of production, distribution, and exchange should be gradually nationalized to achieve better distributive justice by ending economic inequities created by capitalism. Big government is not anathema to the Labor party.

MAJOR PARTY ORGANIZATIONS

In Britain one pattern of centralized organization is adhered to with fair consistency by both major parties. They are mass-based popular parties and have unified structures from top to bottom under a single elected party leader. However, the Conservative party structure faithfully reflects the unitary nature of the constitutional system, but the Labor party provides internal representation to trade unions, cooperatives, and Socialist organizations in a sort of federalist arrangement. American major parties are federally structured to correlate with the existence of the states in the Union. It is that difference of party structure which makes comparison of British and American party organizations so difficult, for whereas the British parties extend from the constituency to the party leader, the American party is a truncated pyramid. The base consists of fifty state party organizations, each of which is legally and administratively separate from the others and from the national units nominally superimposed upon them to make the top of the pyramid. The operating parts of American parties are the state units, for the national chairman, national committee and the national convention do not comprise an independent party machine able to elect candidates to national offices. Candidates for seats in Congress are nominated and elected, presidential preferences are expressed, and campaigns and elections are conducted at the state level and by state party organizations. In the American party system, state organizations are the party.

Although it is not feasible here to examine in detail all structural differences between British and American party systems, certain contrasts justify notice.

PARTY LEADERSHIP

Although an American president and his defeated opponent are their respective party's titular leaders, they often have many rivals and no undisputed claim to primacy. A president has no unified, centralized, cohesive, and disciplined party to lead. Neither has he been chosen specifically for that role. He lacks firm control over policy initiation, and his control of the legislative and budgetary processes is incomplete. His principal bases for leadership are the popular expectation that he will lead because he is president; the power and prestige of his office; his ability to command public attention and manipulate public opinion; his power to control administrative programs; and his ability to bargain, persuade, threaten, reward, and punish. He is separated from congressional party leaders of the House and Senate whose interests are identical neither to his nor to the party's by the separation of powers and by the impact of localized politics on congressional political outlooks. He was elected president, but he was not elected party leader.

On the other side of the ocean, however, a British party leader is elected by his party to be its leader and becomes the apparent successor to the post of prime minister when his party next gains control of the House of Commons. Moreover, the leader is no chosen by a convention of democratically elected delegates but by the members of his party who hold seats in the Commons (the parliamentary party), on whose cohesiveness, discipline, and loyalty rests his and his party's fate.

Once elected, a British party leader is expected to provide continuing, active, effective personal leadership for the party. Reelection to the post is not automatic; the leader has no fixed tenure but may be ousted from his position whenever the group that chose him sees fit to repudiate his leadership. Although Labor party leaders seemingly operate with less freedom than Conservative party leaders, the Conservatives have a longer record for dumping their leaders for lack of confidence in their ability than Labor does. Whereas neither leader is controlled by his party's private members on the back benches of Commons, a leader can ignore back benchers only at his peril.

When his party controls the government, the leader enjoys great power within the executive branch, the legislature, and the party but he is never a party czar. He must take counsel from all quarters of the party organization, particularly from its private members, the whips, and the central executive committee. His is a task of persuasion, compromise, and building support among the disparate elements represented within the party's organs. A Conservative leader is aided by the spirit of deference that runs strong throughout the party. It enhances unified support and backbench acceptance of cabinet policy decisions and control of legislation Yet, more Conservative than Labor leaders have been ousted from their posts.

Labor party leaders are nominally subjected to more internal institutionalized constraints than their Conservative counterparts are, but they are just as powerful when their party makes up the government. Whatever its problems of leadership may be, the British party system affords more effective party control, responsiveness, and accountability by means of centralized party leadership than does the American approximation to party government.

MASS PARTY ASSEMBLIES

American and British parties periodically hold mass meetings of party representatives. The extraparliamentary organizations of both major British parties hold annual conferences. The conferences are thought of as plenary, policy-determining bodies. Delegates to the annual conferences are selected to represent constituency organizations and central party units, plus, for Labor, unions, affiliate cooperatives, and Socialist organizations, so that all sources of party strength and elements of party structure are represented. The Conservative conference is dominated by its leadership, is more staid and orderly than that of Labor, and attends mainly to hearing speeches by the party leader and other top figures. The Labor party conference is run openly and endeavors to assert itself as the plenary policy-making body of the party. It is not dominated by the party leaders and is not content to sit respectfully and hear what its leaders tell it about party policy. Instead, it attempts to influence or make policy by challenging and questioning leaders, adopting resolutions on policy matters and by otherwise asserting itself. Labor MPs are perceived by the extra-parliamentary organization to be functionaries of the labor movement and are not conceded by influentials outside the Parliament to possess power over program and policy or the independence of decision and action that Conservative party MPs are acknowledged to have by that party's nonparliamentary organs. Hence, the Labor conference sees itself as the highest authority in the party. It is not imbued with the Conservatives' spirit of deference. It is more rambunctious and tends to assert itself against the Labor party's formal leadership. That pattern of behavior is stimulated by the heavy domination of Labor conferences by union representatives and by the fact that they and constituency representatives are often more Socialist and radically inclined than are the top party and union leaders and the central party organization.

However, neither party in power can be controlled by its annual conference or be ultimately accountable to it. The government, by constitutional custom, is responsible only to a majority of the Commons, and by constitutional principle it is the "Crown-in-Parliament" that determines the content of policy. Moreover, as a practical matter, no government would leave itself to the vagaries of binding policy decisions made for it by a politically irresponsible conference of party representatives. Nothing prevents an annual conference from binding its party leaders' votes on policy matters when the party is in opposition, however.

The American quadrennial national presidential nominating convention is our closest approximation to a British party's annual conference, but its similarity is far removed. A national convention is intended to be a forum for whipping up party enthusiasm to carry through the coming election campaign. For being an unparalleled rally, a technique for promoting partisan cohesiveness; for conciliating, unifying and stimulating the membership; for motivating candidates and workers; and for building consensus among the diverse segments of the party organization and electorate;[8] the national convention is probably superior to the annual conference of a major British party. The convention is a brief assembly of party officials, influentials, workers, and faithful, mainly from state and local organizations, that brings together in an atmosphere of party good will all the disparate elements of its makeup. In its brief existence, it adopts party rules, approves a national platform, elects a national committee, and nominates national party presidential and vice presidential candidates. No extended or structured debate of party policy occurs on the convention floor. No questioning of leaders and no debate on party policy positions take place. An occasional plank of the platform drafted by the convention's platform committee for adoption may provoke dispute, but the platform is not generally regarded as a binding statement of party principles.

Nevertheless, the platform, like the election manifesto of a British party, does serve to increase party identification and promote cohesion. It recognizes many of the diverse interests within the party. It gives factions and interests an outlet for their ideals and feelings. Its character as a party campaign document is emphasized by the fact that the convention adopts the platform before it nominates its candidates.[9] However, the stamp of the front-running aspirant to the presidential nomination is often clearly impressed on the platform's content, and nothing can obscure the popular understanding that the platform is for the candidates to stand on. But, no matter what uncertainty obscures the nature of an American party platform, a British party's election manifesto states its official positions on questions of national policy to which all of its candidates are committed.

CENTRAL EXECUTIVE COMMITTEES

Each major British party has a central executive committee. It is elected by the annual conference to direct party affairs between conferences. The committees are controlled by the party leaders, and, especially in the case of the Conservative party committee, have acquired strong influence over the bodies that created them. It is in the central executive committees that the principal lines of communication, coordination, and control come together. The party leaders must work constantly, closely, and harmoniously with their central committees, the parties' nerve centers. By doing so, they can remain on top of party business and be informed about and sensitive to the needs and expectations of party components.

Party matters decided by the central committees are carried out by central party offices. Under the direction of the central committee and the control of the party leader, the central offices devise election strategies, carry on research, administer finances, maintain party discipline, prepare candidate lists, endorse constituency choices, keep the leader informed about opinion in all quarters of the party, and carry on external coordinating activities with other units of the organization throughout the country.

The linkage of the Labor party to British unionism is illustrated by the composition of its central executive committee. The committee is dominated by representatives elected by trade unions, but it also contains members from cooperatives, affiliated Socialist organizations, constituency associations, women's groups, and the annual conference. The party leader and whip are also members of this committee, which meets at Transport House, London, headquarters of Britain's largest labor union, the Transport and General Workers Union.

American political parties, of course, maintain national headquarters and permanent operating staffs in Washington, D.C. They perform many of the same functions concerned with planning, information, finances, and other party business as do the British central office staffs, but they are only competent to act for the national chairman, national committee, and national convention.

They supply services for party congressmen and promote intra-party harmony. The difference between the British and American models lies in the fact that the British central party organization —the leader and central executive committee—collectively and cooperatively wield authority over all portions of a national party system. The American party's national units do not. They are essentially powerless.[10] The national committee cannot speak for the party as a whole, for the state party structures are independent. Its influence over party members of Congress, governors, state chairmen and committees may be minimal or nonexistent. It has no authority to direct or command any of them, and the national chairman has no directing, coordinating or policy-making power over any of them.

LEGISLATIVE PARTIES

The Labor and Conservative members of the House of Commons make up the parliamentary party of their respective national parties. Parliamentary parties, especially that of the Labor party (PLP), possess power and influence in the top levels of party authority, but there are differences between the PLP and the Conservative equivalent, the 1922 Committee. Both elect their party leaders, but when his party is out of power the Labor leader must be elected annually, whereas his Conservative opposite number stays in office without term unless he is defeated at the polls, resigns, or is ousted by action of the 1922 Committee. The Labor leader is the head of his party and, at the same time, of the PLP, but the Conservative leader is not. The tradition of deference in the Conservative party characterizes most of the leader's relations with his private members, but it is replaced in Labor ranks by a spirit of egalitarianism so that the Labor leader must work more assiduously to cultivate the PLP's acceptance of his position. The PLP's attitude of independence and challenge toward its leader is reflected in the fact that the leader and ministers, or the shadow cabinet when Labor is out of power, must attend its meetings, explain and defend their policies, and obtain their endorsement by Labor's private members. The Conservative leader and ministers may attend meetings of the 1922 Committee only on invitation. The leadership is informed of committee deliberations by the whip in the House. Although the 1922 Committee cannot make party policy, it serves as a sounding board for policy decisions made elsewhere in the party, and the leaders cannot ignore the backbenchers' views. Nevertheless, the leader remains sufficiently independent of the parliamentary group to choose shadow governments, control the whips, formulate party policy, form and alter cabinets, and discipline recalcitrant members without its approval. However, since the backbenchers can defeat the government's (and party's) legislation, force a resignation or national election, oust the leader, or in other ways jeopardize the party's interests, the leadership must consider their views.

In the houses of Congress, both American parties operate caucuses composed of their respective memberships. They are, however, wholly unlike the PLP and the 1922 Committee in Commons. Their principal function is to meet at the convening of a new Congress to elect a caucus chairman and party candidates for the speakership of the House and president pro tem of the Senate, floor leaders and their aides (whips), and committee chairmen. The Republican groups and the House Democratic caucus are sometimes used to discuss the party's position on a major issue, but Senate Democrats have been so divided among themselves that policy deliberations have been impossible. Hence, that group rarely meets once the Senate is organized to do business. Only the House Democratic rules provide for binding the members to support a party position by a two-thirds caucus vote, but the rule is rarely invoked and does not apply to any issue involving a question of constitutional interpretation or on which a member has made a contrary pledge to his constituency. None of the caucuses try to develop cohesive legislative programs or policies for its party. Those a caucus might discuss have been devised by the leadership in policy planning groups in the chambers. All members know, particularly of the Senate, that most policy-making power rests with the standing legislative committees of each house and that any effort to increase the role of caucuses in that arena would undoubtedly produce open hostilities between them and the committee chairmen.

American legislative party groups have a greatly curtailed usefulness to party leaders. They cannot create party unity and cohesiveness where none but a sharing of party label exists. At best caucuses provide a forum for conducting party business in a chamber, meeting with party leaders, and perhaps reinforcing an already existing consensus; but, in the absence of agreement, meetings of a caucus may only deepen ideological lesions and sharpen interfactional hostilities.

Still, James Anderson states that party loyalty is the single most significant determinant of legislative voting patterns in the American Congress, and, despite weak American legislative parties, party affiliation of members provides the best basis for predicting how representatives will vote. But, he emphasizes, American legislative party coherence does not approximate that of the British parties in Commons, for, although most votes in the House of Commons pit 90 percent of the majority against 90 percent of the opposition party, few votes in the houses of Congress muster that level of party adherence. In recent years only 2 to 8 percent of House roll call votes have done so. In sum, party alignment is a meaningful element in congressional decision making in spite of weak party discipline.[11]

Thus, enough has been said to indicate that party leadership in the houses of Congress is collective and collegial. Many centers of power able to exert power over policy can be found in each house. The occupants of those positions, despite common party affiliation, are individualistic rivals, each of whom has his own resources for helping friends and punishing enemies. At the same time, only weak centripetal forces operate to overcome the divisive effects of localism, individualism, and factionalism. No cohesive majorities are present, no centralized leadership or integrated party legislative program is possible, party discipline is virtually nonexistent, and party platforms lack enacting mechanisms. Party leaders in the houses only incompletely control party units and formal house organizations. Because there are so many semiautonomous centers of power and influence in the party structures and legislative organs, American legislative party leaders must bargain, persuade, and mediate to muster support for a policy; they do so by granting favors and rewards, calling in outstanding debts, and rapping knuckles to influence the fate of measures.

It is probably more accurate to speak of majority coalition

parties in the houses of Congress instead of the more familiar majority party. The numerically greater party is always internally divided, sometimes to the point that leaders fight among themselves and negate even the ability of a two-to-one party preponderance to enact legislation or reverse vetoes of its legislation by an opposition president.

PRESSURE GROUPS

Britain and the United States possess political cultures that emphasize the importance of freedom of association and communication of ideas. Political parties remain the principal agents for aggregating and organizing politically relevant interests of the citizenry, articulating them, transforming them into manageable policy alternatives, and enacting and implementing them through official channels of public power. But, political parties cannot effectively mobilize and express the multiplicity of diverse interests which separate men in modern democratic society, for aggregation of interests necessarily injects distortion into their representation by the parties. The distortion comes about because the aggregation forces moderation of individual diverse interests and their accommodation at an increasingly high level of generality.[12] Therefore, political interest groups are needed to restore specificity to the process of interest articulation within the political system. In the process, the political parties are freed to consider the needs and wants of a broader section of society, if not of the society as a whole. Persons having interests beyond the capability of parties to represent or too insignificant for them to notice often form associations for the purpose of communicating their views to the general public and official decision makers. Many groups do not enter the arena of political activity; many others do become politically active in order to gain official notice for their wants and policy preferences. Those which attempt to influence the formulation, enactment, or implementation of public policy are known as political interest groups to distinguish them from special interest groups that pursue their ends wholly outside the governmental environment.

Politically active special interest organizations play the same roles as agents of interest representation and communication in any open society. They and the parties are not distinct isolated phenomena, but two components in a single mechanism for identifying and transmitting expressions of public needs and wants to decision makers. To the end of more completely realizing the ideals of political liberalism, pressure groups stimulate political participation, raise the level of political awareness, complement the representational capability of parties, operate as agents of opinion formation, aggregate capacity for effective political action, communicate ideas to decision makers about what government should and should not do, function to promote governmental responsibility and responsiveness, supply expert information and empirical and experiential data to decision makers, increase political moderation by promoting compromise and mutual toleration among diverse interests in society, and in numerous other ways function as dynamic elements of the political and governmental processes.

Their presence in a democratic society raises certain tough questions. Ought these nonresponsible unofficial coalitions of power have the capability to influence—sometimes to control—legislative and executive decision making? How can power and influence be equalized among groups having greatly varying numbers, wealth, status, leadership, commitment, cohesiveness, and other attributes that affect success? Who will speak for unorganized interests in the political process? How can weak interests be protected from the domination of strong but hostile ones? Whether these or other questions of like nature be answered, the existence and operation of political interest groups in the United States and Britain raise fundamental issues about the equity, if not the propriety, of their activities. Nevertheless, the alternative to their existence and role fulfillment—close regulation or abolition by government—is an unacceptable remedy worse than the problems that invoked it and, in the United States, would violate the First Amendment guarantees of freedom of communication, of assembly, and of petition for redress of grievances. In Britain, extreme measures of governmental suppression or control would violate norms of political liberalism deeply embedded in and cherished by the political culture. It scarcely need be said, therefore, that in the British and American political-governmental systems, interest groups are accepted as legitimate, play similar roles, and are largely duplicative.

They employ somewhat different strategies appropriate to the constitutional characteristics of the systems in which they respectively operate.

Thus, in Britain and the United States, politically active groups represent interests associated with patriotism, professions and occupations, religions, forms of economic endeavor, and myriad other concerns of human society. No other society in the world is as pluralistically organized or contains the range of voluntary organizations found in the United States. Politically active special-interest organizations abound and are becoming increasingly more numerous in Britain, but they still represent an emerging feature of the political scene; the extent of their activity and the impact of their efforts have not reached the levels attained by American groups in the political process. In fact, some commentators on Congress have observed that interest groups so dominate its legislative processes that it is unable effectively to represent local constituency or national interests; it can only respond to the demands of powerful special interests. Interest groups are politically significant in Britain, although the nature of British cabinet government and the prerequisites of a responsible party system compel them to utilize different points of access to decision makers.

The political cultures of the United States and Britain limit what interest groups can demand and the means by which they can pursue their goals. For a pressure group to violate the political culture of its society can precipitate a negative reaction that makes it impossible for decision makers to recognize the culpable group's interests. Merkl points out that the British political structure hampers all but the largest groups from pressuring individual MPs or the major parties. Lesser groups must focus their attention and efforts on the executive structure.[13] The largest British interest groups, however, are regularly consulted by the cabinet on matters affecting their interests. Because those contacts often involve controversial matters of social and economic policy, lines of negotiation and compromise between groups and government tend to harden into inflexible positions when consultation turns into bargaining, and when that occurs the cabinet on the rare occasions when it has failed to obtain group support will insist upon its policy position over the group's opposition.[14] British administration regards even consultation with smaller groups to be a positive good, albeit their interests will not receive the degree of deference accorded those of the most powerful national interests and will be overruled more frequently. The British political culture is one of the most generous in permitting interests to become involved in policymaking processes.

POLITICAL PARTY AND
INTEREST GROUP DIFFERENTIATION

Political parties are usually differentiated from pressure groups on the grounds that they are broadly inclusive whereas pressure groups possess specialized memberships and narrowly focused outlooks; parties stand for principles, but special groups pursue interests; parties engage only in political activities, but pressure groups often engage in many nonpolitical endeavors.[15] While these points of contrast have merit, the one most commonly cited as the controlling factor in the United States does not apply in Britain with the same assurances its proponents give it here. American students of political dynamics frequently separate the two categories by saying that political parties do, but pressure groups do not, strive to gain control of public offices by electing their candidates. Instead of directly entering the political lists, political interest groups influence party policies, and they generally work through the parties and electoral processes. In addition, they pressure congressmen and committees, the president and administrative officials, utilize the mass media to stimulate public opinion, and litigate in the courts to attain their ends. British interest groups employ some of the same tactics as do American groups, but certain characteristics and practices obscure the neat distinction mentioned above. For example, a Labor candidate for a seat in Commons can be "sponsored" by a union which by law may pay up to 80 percent of his election expenses and in a pro-Labor constituency virtually purchase him a seat.[16] However, the Conservative party does not approve of outside interests paying the election expenses of its candidates. It does not have groups affiliated with it, as the Labor party does, and only rarely is a Conservative candidate "sponsored." Many MPs are closely aligned with groups that identify with the party, however.[17] Hence, the onservative party remains freer from the intrusion of influences that blur its character as a party. The extent of blurring on the Labor side can be brought home by asking whether in the American sense the Labor party is a party or an interest group—British unionism masquerading as a party. The two identities are so merged in the Labor party that Richard Rose characterized it as two-thirds pressure group and one-third party.[18] Unions select all but a small percentage of the annual conference members, hold two-thirds of the seats on the powerful national executive committee, and in some Labor constituencies the union local and the Labor party are synonymous.[19] The party draws all but a handful of its membership from affiliated unions, is heavily backed by them, requires that every Labor candidate be a union member, and clearly gives unions a disproportionately large voice in the decision-making councils of the central party. At the same time, a meaningful distinction exists between the Labor party and the British union movement, so that the merger of identities is not complete.

STRATEGIES OF PRESSURE GROUPS

The strategies and tactics of American and British interest groups share more in common than separates them. They endeavor to achieve their goals by working through the parties and electoral processes outside the national legislatures; by focusing on the members, processes, and internal structures of the legislatures; and by concentrating on the administrative parts of the government. But, whereas special interests throughout American history have used our judicial system to attain their ends by winning favorable rulings on points of law, the British legal culture almost completely cuts British courts off from playing a role in public policy formation. Therefore, British interests are not able to invoke judicial power as American interests so frequently do, so that this examination of their activities will be limited to nonjudicial arenas inside and outside of the legislatures.

THOSE INSIDE LEGISLATURES

Pressure group activities directed at legislatures can be disposed of with some expedition. American interest spokesmen have ready access to policy makers in the houses of Congress. Power in the houses over pending legislation is so fractionated that any one of several members in each chamber can obstruct or defeat its passage. Members of each house have unlimited power to initiate legislation and can readily introduce measures groups desire. Group contacts with individual members can influence their votes and testimony before the specialized standing legislative committees of the House and Senate gives access to key decision-making centers. If a special interest fails to attain its objective in one house, it can start over again by focusing its efforts on control points in the other. Interest groups not only provide members of Congress with ideas for national legislation but also furnish them with fully drafted measures often prepared by experts on their groups' staffs. Legislative agents of special interests supply members with authoritative information related to pending bills, in effect doing the member's policy research for him, though not always with great attention to objectivity and thoroughness. They rally other groups to bring more concerted pressure; they mobilize letter-writing campaigns, and they use the mass media to arouse public opinion favorable to their positions and to persuade legislators that the public wants what they want.

This brief catalog of tactics does not exhaust the subject, but it is sufficient to set the contrast with British pressure group tactics that involve the legislature. Whereas institutional forms increase the accessibility of Congress to pressure groups and make their strategies more effective, the institutional forms of Parliament drastically limit lobbying tactics. Opposition members do not introduce measures; backbenchers on the government side are given only very few opportunities to initiate them and no assurance that they will be enacted, for the introduction of serious measures and the use of legislative time are controlled by the government party leaders. During debate and question hour, private members can champion the interests of groups they support. In fact, some private members come to their seats in Commons publicly aligned with interests and known to be their advocate, sometimes even as an officer in or a consultant to a special interest organization, a relationship that British legislative practice tolerates but does not encourage. Members committed to an interest can support it cause during general debate, question time, adjournment debate, while serving on committees, or when making public speeches outside the House. The opposition, on its part, can only try to elicit concessions from the government that are beneficial to the interests of minority supporters. "Backbenchers," however, are virtually powerless to affect the government's policy, and party discipline compels them to support the party position. Consequently, British interest groups do not make major efforts to influence individual votes of members. The British legislative process affords few access points to special interest spokesmen, with the result that the influence of pleaders for political interest groups over the legislative process is all but nonexistent.

THOSE OUTSIDE LEGISLATURES

American and British pressure groups utilize all possible avenues to success, those outside as well as those inside the chambers, but British groups are compelled by their lack of easy access to Commons, its members, and committees to work almost wholly outside. Interest groups on both sides of the Atlantic try to control the choices of party candidates, but British groups are rarely able to succeed. They render campaign aid to their favorites and oppose their adversaries. The relatively sharp ideological differences between major British political parties make it more difficult for British pressure groups to shift or threaten to shift their support from one party to the other. Most pressure groups interested in social and economic issues can find a comfortable fit with one of them but cannot as snugly lie down with the other. The policy orientations of American political parties are more amorphous. The coalitions of Democratic and Republican members of Congress that form to support pending bills indicate the fluidity of party lines. Consequently, pressure groups can transfer their support from one major American party to the other more easily than they can in Britain. British groups align with the Conservative as well as with the Labor Party, but the linkage of Conservative supporters to the party is not as formal or direct as Labor's is. Unless a group is aligned with a party, its prospect of swaying a British candidate to support its cause is small, for the candidate's party label and election manifesto determine his position on matters of policy. He, the voters, and the pressure group all know he cannot contravene the party's election statement. A candidate in Britain may not only be publicly allied with an interest group, he may be sponsored by one. In either case, if he is elected, he takes his special relationship into the House of Commons with him. His special ties may color his backbench participation, but they will not control his vote except in circumstances of extreme alienation from his party leadership or when he is in opposition and discipline is not as tight as it is when he sits on the government side.

None of these constraints curbs the electoral activity of American interest groups, however. They operate fully and freely except as limited by laws regulating election finances, corrupt and illegal practices, and requiring the filing of registration and disclosure statements.

In addition to activities involving legislatures and the electoral processes, American and British pressure groups also concentrate on the executive part of the governments. They know that policy is made by administrators who possess broad discretion and exercise it to give meaning to ambiguous statutory policies. Bureaucracies formulate, promulgate, and enforce rules and regulations to amplify the meaning and facilitate implementation of vaguely written general policy measures. All bureaucrats function in relative obscurity, protected from close public scrutiny. Especially in the British civil service, they are allegedly above partisanship and dedicated to faithful administration of public policies. In both systems countless detailed administrative decisions each day affect the substance of policies or the manner of their implementation and bear directly on interests served or regulated. Moreover, the British political culture leaves its bureaucracy to function free from public observance and close accountability. All of these conditions promote active relations between administrators and pressure group representatives in British and American agencies. Moreover, the relative strength of the British executive's position in legislative-executive relationships is cemented by party discipline, collective ministerial responsibility, and party regularity. Its stability leaves the cabinet, ministries, ministers, and the top-level bureaucracy freer than their American counterparts to negotiate with spokesmen for special interests without fear that a partisan or personally vindictive legislative inquiry into their administrative behavior will be directed against them. But in each system interest group representatives know well that if they can reach the administrators, they can gain in the administrative agencies what was lost in the houses of the legislature.

British interest groups, unable to function effectively in Parliament, also concentrate heavily on the cabinet. In the cabinet system, all policy proposals must be endorsed by the collective executive, the cabinet under the leadership of the prime minister as party leader. Interest groups may seek to pressure it by stimulating public opinion, to which it is very sensitive, and by arousing in Commons a pro-group attitude, to which the cabinet might also be reactive. In contrast, the American president's cabinet does not figure in pressure politics as an access point because it is advisory only; has little or no sense of party cohesiveness, discipline, or loyalty; and is not bound by traditions of individual and collective responsibility. Pressure groups in both systems are in close and continuing contact with decision-making political heads of departments, subordinates, and career bureaucrats. Pressure group spokesmen seek to influence administrative decisions by supplying facts and arguments favorable to the group's interest. They also serve on administrative liaison, study, and advisory committees involved with policy initiation or implementation; provide expert assistance; evaluate and react to administratively proposed legislation before it goes to the legislature; endeavor to influence appointments to agencies whose programs affect it; and urge their policy proposals on administrators. In the United States, special interest groups lobby administrators as well as legislators, support beneficial programs before legislative and budgetary committees of Congress, pump up administrators' egos, and often employ after they leave office those former administrators who were helpful to them. The sensitivity of an administrative agency to interest groups is particularly acute when the groups represent the clientele that an agency was created to serve or regulate. Groups, individually and in coalitions, form cozy and often lasting reciprocally beneficial relationships with bureaucracies. In the United States this cozy relationship may become a triangular one, with the subcommittee in Congress that deals regularly with the subject areas, the interest groups, and the administrative agencies forming the three component parts. This does not occur in Britain, largely because of the lack of a committee role in shaping policy and because for the most part British legislative committees are not specialized as to subject matter.

The atmosphere in which these relations are carried on differs between the British and American systems. The high traditions of the British civil service put an aura of formality and conformity to expectations of proper conduct into the relations between the pressure groups and the bureaucracies. The cabinet and administration are attuned to public opinion and that of the Commons; they voluntarily consult with and seek the cooperation of interest groups on all aspects of important policies during their formative and implementive phases. These relations are open and above-board because the British political culture legitimates groups having a maximum role to play and opportunity to be heard when governmental action affects them. But a sense of obligation to party and public interest precludes the crasser forms of political activity, even ones that in the United States are accepted, perhaps with a shrug of resignation, as the realities of politics. Scandals involving abuse of public trust are rare in British administrative experience.

But in America, interest group activity is regarded with suspicion and distrust as a violation of the idea that government should serve the interests of all the people idealistically conceived in an abstracted collective form, not as an aggregate of individual and group interests. Whereas the British have virtually co-opted interest group activity and incorporated it into the executive-administrative phases of policy making and governance, Americans see it as a rival and subverting force on the exercise of governmental authority. The centralization of policy decision making which has pre-empted that function for the British cabinet and drained practically all control over it away from Parliament has not occurred in the United States. One result is that the constant bargaining process between the cabinet-administration and interest representation—carried out in Britain in a respectable, moderate, and controlled way—here occurs in all three branches of government as a sort of unconstrained scramble to see which group can get the most for self. Because of the multiplicity of decision-making points in the American system, more groups probably obtain access to some of them than is the case in Britain. Because more gateways exist, more are able to enter. However, once access has been attained, the ability to shape definitively the final decision is less than in Britain simply because power to make policy is so diffused in the United States. Power centers are so numerous and authority is so widely distributed, individualized, and fractionated in the political parts of the American national government that no one can be sure how decisions are made, why they turn out as they do, and who actually responsible for making them. This consequence probably stems in no small degree from the existence of separated powers and from the absence from the American political and governmental ethic of a highly developed principle of accountability made operable by a demanding political culture. In Britain, the principle of accountability functions more effectively because it is more deeply embedded in the constitutional order and supporting political culture. There, too, the processes of democratic policy making by bargaining and compromise are more orderly, overt, legitimate, and institutionalized than they are in the American national government.

SUMMARY

There seems to be no major difference in the British and American attitudes toward the legitimacy and value of political parties and interest groups in democratic political systems. Both accept them as essential organs of communication, activity, and involvement in a democratic society. They are long established elements of both political systems, but in both their presence and involvement raise certain tough questions of a theoretical and practical nature concerning their equitableness, abuse of power, and even of their corruption of the democratic processes. On the whole, the dangers they present have probably caused fewer concerns in British politics than in American, but in both perhaps the greatest problem they generate is raised by the extent to which they operate behind the scenes beyond the searching light of public knowledge.

The foci of their efforts seem to be essentially the same in both systems—administrative organizations, national legislatures, and

the public—although their techniques and points of stress va
somewhat in response to the respective structures and politic
realities of the British and American governmental systems. A
cordingly, their principal efforts in the American system of sep
rated powers are directed at Congress, with a fall-back to th
executive and courts and occasionally to the mass public, where
in Britain their main efforts are directed toward the executiv
their fall-back being to Parliament and, remotely, to publ
opinion.[20]

Whether interest groups in the one system are more effecti
than in the other is a matter of dispute that will doubtless go u
resolved until a scheme of objective measurement can be devise
Samuel Beer has contended that British national interests are mo
effectively organized than American because they are more co
centrated, whereas Americans tend to be divided and represente
by more than one organization. He alleges that British groups ha
greater impact than do American because of the unitary gover
mental structure by means of which policies are made and a
ministered nationwide, in contrast to the multiple policy-maki
centers in American federalism.[21] However, there cannot be muc
dispute over the conclusion that American pressure groups a
more effective on Congress than British groups are on Parliamen
American groups may also have more success with the executiv
for tight government control over finances, personnel, policy, ar
administration in Britain generally diminishes the capacity
British interest groups to persuade or to obstruct the executiv
The looser and larger American bureaucracy lacks the high trad
tions of public service that animate the British routine executiv
American executives possess great discretion to define the publ
interest from diverse administrative viewpoints that can accomm
date group influence, and they may operate under only wea
sporadic, and remote overhead political direction. But, at anoth
place, Beer asserts that British producer groups have develope
access to decision makers that bypasses Parliament and the polit
cal parties and operates directly on, through, and with the exec
tive. Those contacts are so close and enduring, Beer states, th
they take on the character of a separate system of functional repr

sentation apart from but supplemental to the ordinary democratic representation of Parliament and the political parties.[22]

In both systems interest groups operate on and through the political parties, and the parties are built to some extent upon voters that the interest groups aggregate into memberships. These associations between the parties and the interest groups exhibit some notable features. More than the British, contemporary American political parties have become dependent upon organized group support; while British parties have frequently taken on that complexion temporarily, they have more typically been the means for presenting to the British electorate reasonably clearly formulated conceptions of the common good.[23] They have fulfilled that function of political parties in a democratic polity better than American parties have, and they have probably also attained a higher degree of ideological and programmatic differentiation, structural integration, and internal cohesiveness than characterize American parties. They, more than American parties, present to their voters clear alternative conceptions about what constitutes the common good, what policy proposals are appropriate to it, and how the authority and resources of government should be used to achieve it. It is also highly probable that those conceptions of the common good are more than bargained compromises reached by conciliating special interests and patterned to attract, or at least to not alienate, those interests and their voting memberships.[24] That result, if valid, is perhaps the inevitable result of British party government, which demands that its parties play a prominent role as agents of social change. Nevertheless, the distinction between parties and pressure groups in Britain is less sharp than it is in the United States, and British parties always depend to some extent upon the support of organized groups, campaign for certain of them, and are the objects of organized group attention. But, the political parties, administration, and Parliament are by no means subservient to them in Britain. The political culture assures them access to policy decision makers but does not assure them acceptance of their preferences or proposals.

In Britain and the United States, current systemic roles and functions of political parties and pressure groups are undergoing reexamination. The traditionally accepted linkage between them and their representative capacities is being subjected to increasing challenge on the grounds that they are inherently elitist, only selectively responsive to public demands, biased in their allocation of public resources, and, especially in the United States, incapable of defining and serving the common good. The major political parties of both systems may be undergoing realignments; at the very least they are in a period of transition that may stop short of realignment. That seems particularly true of the Democratic and Republican parties in the United States. In Britain, the floating vote, shifting patterns of party support, and marked declines in the constituency party memberships of both major parties, and, in America, the growing proportions of independent voting, abstention, and ticketsplitting testify to the declining significance of parties. In both countries nonpolitical forces—the media, pollsters, communications, advertising and public relations experts, governmental regulations, and, in the United States, public financing of national campaigns and elections increasingly are inducing alterations in established political relationships and techniques, thereby limiting the initiatives and weakening the control available to party leaders and actives. The new politics of intensive media campaigning in the 1974 British elections went far to displace the old politics of constituency party organizations of the type that had evoked criticism in America following the 1972 presidential campaign.[25] Parties in both Britain and the United States are hearing demands for participatory democracy that in the latter have produced various, mainly ill-fated, responses in policy making and implementation. Particularly in Britain, the welfare state has gone far toward displacing individualistic, competitive, pluralistic democracy with a democracy of collectivized cooperativism, and in America idealism has become in recent years an important motive for individual political activism and partisan affiliation, as older materialistic incentives have fallen in some quarters into disfavor.[26]

CHAPTER FOUR

Electoral Activities and Voting Behavior

It is difficult to compare campaign and election processes because they are acccompanied by very dissimilar party systems and structures. Nominations and elections of British candidates are brought about by a more centralized party organization extending from the prime minister to the constituency organizations of the party, but American nominations and elections for national positions are accomplished by localized organizations at either the congressional district or, in the instances of senators and presidential electors, at the state level, both of which necessitate a heavy infusion of localized political influence.

ELECTORAL ACTIVITIES

ELECTION FREQUENCY

British national elections must occur at least once each five years, for the life of a Parliament is set at that length, but American elections occur on a staggered basis, with a partial separation of legislative from executive elections so that the probability of divided party control of the two branches is increased. The British prime minister on his own authority, however, may request the monarch to dissolve Parliament and call a general election whenever in his judgment it is desirable to obtain electoral approval of his party's programs and record. An element of unpredictability attends British elections; they can be held in rapid succession as were those of February and October 1974 or at intervals up to but not longer than the five year statutory life of a Parliament. Most are held before expiration of the statutory limit, however. Unlike American national elections which are geared to a constitutional calendar of set terms of office, prime ministers request dissolutions when they think the political climate is most favorable to their party's electoral good fortunes and endeavor to force electoral stands before the voters on issues that will cast their party in the best light. Of course, the monarch must accede to the dissolution request, for to do otherwise would amount to the monarch's becoming involved in politics and would violate the neutrality of the Crown. Because of the uncertain scheduling surrounding general elections, British, unlike American, political parties must be ready to undertake an election effort on short notice and at uncertain times, whenever the prime minister decides to "go to the country." The frequency of elections is most often controlled by practical considerations. Elections are expensive, inconvenient, unwelcome to backbenchers and constituency organizations, and a demand upon the viability of the democratic process. The decision whether to hold an election or to go the full life of Parliament before doing so is always a political decision.

A major difference between British and American parties grows out of the start and stop nature of periodic American campaigning and the more permanently ongoing character of the British. In Britain, the election campaign is limited to the brief period between the announced dissolution of Parliament and polling day, but astute organization leaders can usually read the signs and anticipate a dissolution well in advance of the fact. Therefore, party preparation never really ceases; concerted efforts begin well ahead of dissolution and may be affected by party decisions made months or years earlier. National party organs must remain in a state of semipreparedness. In anticipation of an election expected sometime between spring and autumn of 1974, for instance, British parties were ready by fall 1973, and in 1974 had to conduct not one but two national campaigns and elections. The parties must also remain semioperational between general elections because, as

Duschinsky reports,[1] 80 percent of British voters have made up their minds how they will vote before the campaign starts. Hence, the parties must continually cultivate the electorate. To that end at the constituency level, agents or constituency organizations between general elections carry on canvassing, social activities, fund raising, organizational, and staffing activities; they also identify prospective parliamentary candidates and complete other measures necessary to maintain constituency readiness and to ease the burdens of campaigning when dissolution comes. Unlike American national party organizations consisting of large numbers of hastily created and manned campaign committees that disappear when the election is over, a British central party structure is a permanent bureaucracy, many of whom are career party officials, approximately two hundred in number, plus outside experts such as pollsters, media experts, public relations specialists, film makers, and the like. It is this permanent bureaucracy that plans and runs the highly political national campaign, but its principal function is to prepare the party's Election Manifesto[2] which declares its national program and by implication the issues on which its leaders hope to fight out the contest.

As was noticed above, the British electoral calendar, unlike the American, is a short one of compact events. Only seventeen to twenty business days normally elapse between the dissolution of Parliament and the date of the election. Because the interval available for nominating and campaigning is so brief, custom requires that the opposition party be given one month's notice of an impending election date to protect it from having elections sprung upon it. In contrast to the accelerated pattern of a British election is the protracted American practice. Instead of one month of electoral activity, the American nomination and election processes may extend well over a year's time measured from the occasion when the first aspirant to a party's nomination declares his desire to be the nominee until the general election is held. By the time a President takes office he may have completed twelve to sixteen months of gruelling campaigning, whereas a prime minister and his government will have spent only three or four weeks on the hustings before assuming office.

CONSTITUENCIES

In a single-member district system, such as is utilized to select members of the American House of Representatives and the British House of Commons, representation is based on a combination of territory and population. It becomes necessary, therefore, periodically to redraw voting district boundaries to reflect changes of population distribution caused by internal migrations. Reapportionment of seats in the American House of Representatives to reflect population shifts among the states precedes realignment of constituency boundaries. An automatic process provided by act of Congress and based on the national decennial census reapportions representatives among the states, but it is the state legislatures that make the necessary changes in the boundaries of congressional districts. The redistricting processes in the separate states are dominated by politics, and the result invariably favors the political party that controls each state legislature. In the absence of any requirement of national law that districts be composed of compact and contiguous territory and contain as nearly as possible equal numbers of people, a certain amount of political manipulation of boundaries by state legislatures is a normal feature of redistricting for congressional elections. Absolute equality of population has not been required by Supreme Court standards protecting the principle of "one man, one vote" in American representational democracy but a high degree of equalization has been attained by means of judicial intervention and supervision of the process.

In Britain the realignment of parliamentary constituency boundaries is performed by four politically impartial permanent boundary commissions, one each for Wales, Scotland, Northern Ireland and England. Boundaries are adjusted every fifteen years, the revisions being submitted to Parliament for adoption. An effort is made to attain a reasonable approximation to an equal number of voters in the constituencies, but boundary commissions may ignore the principle of equality with the result that wide variation in size exists between the largest and smallest constituency. That result, of course, derogates from the principle that everyone's vote in a democratic franchise should count the same.

The task of fixing constituency boundaries is a difficult one acking clear guidelines. Neither the British nor the American process strives to ensure that constituency lines reflect integral social communities instead of merely convenient units of electoral administration. Some of the lost representation, however, is recovered by the impact of localism in the American Congress and, in both systems, by the linkages between representatives, political parties, and constituency electorates.

Although British boundary commissions work in a nonpartisan way, the recommendations they produce have political consequences for electoral fortunes. Those that benefit the government will probably stimulate vigorous resistance from the opposition before being approved. However, adoption of those which benefit the minority usually must await a time when it controls Commons and has the votes at hand to approve them. Major redistributions of seats have generated cries of gerrymandering despite the best efforts of boundary commissioners to accommodate both sound principles of realignment and the practical effects of societal changes without permitting a party to gain a majority of seats from a plurality of popular votes. The results of their efforts are generally applauded. Gerrymandering, Frank Stacey asserts, has been almost totally absent from British constituency making,[3] a result that stands in sharp contrast to American practice.

CAMPAIGNS

British national elections choose both legislature and executive at the same time and are truly national party elections. The campaign is integrated to centralized control more thoroughly than are American presidential and congressional elections and is characterized by a higher degree of issue and procedural uniformity because of that fact. A British general election is a singularly national event, but it is concurrently fought on the national and constituency levels.

American national elections are somewhat more complex than the British for several reasons. First, separate processes for choosing national legislators and an executive are conducted concurrently but entirely independently from one another by largely autonomous and unarticulated units of party organization. Second, although British elections consist of two short but discernible phases separated by the election announcement, they constitute essentially a single period of undifferentiated effort. But American state party practice employs congressional primaries and a distinct, now-dominant pattern of primaries and national nominating conventions of the parties to select presidential candidates. Primary periods constitute the first phase of the electoral process and are followed by the second, and shorter, election campaign phase. Although the Supreme Court has described primaries and elections in the United States as inseparable parts of an integrated process for choosing public officers,[4] the parts lose their individual identities only when viewed at a high level of abstraction. Third, the territorial bases employed to make presidential and congressional choices produce winners whose constituency interests and issue orientations may be diametrically opposed even though they share a common party label. Fourth, American campaigns stress issues less and candidate image more than do British campaigns. American elections, especially congressional elections, are often dominated by candidate image and are only secondarily issue-oriented. Even at the national level, candidate perception strongly influenced the outcomes of the presidential campaigns of Eisenhower, Goldwater, Kennedy, McGovern, Nixon, and Carter. Image is never entirely absent from British elections, but despite the fact that its maximum influence is exerted in by-elections to fill vacant seats in Commons, voters exhibit a high degree of party regularity, even when the fate of the government cannot be affected.

Nevertheless, broad similarities can be discovered in British and American campaigns. For example, the common purposes of the campaigns are to mobilize voters behind party symbols or labels to build or mobilize coalitions of support; to legitimize governance to achieve peaceful transfers of authority; to provide opposition and alternative choices; to provide a mechanism for compromise for levelling ideological differences, and for enforcing accountability; and to fulfill other roles appropriate for political parties in democracies.

Between American presidential and British national electioneering, differences probably exceed similarities. British parties do not need to make partisan appeals to win blocs of voters which may float from party to party (as American national electioneering tends to do). There is no electoral college in Britain operating to affect the places and intensity of campaigning and frequently producing distortions between electoral success and distribution of the popular votes. The British electorate contains few uncommitted voters, and party allegiance in constituencies is usually firm, albeit a swing vote of 5 to 8 percent may occur in closely divided two-party areas. Because Americans hold separate elections for legislative and executive offices that are not electorally interdependent, only presidential contests take on a clean national character, all others being strongly flavored by localism and fractionated efforts. Of course, each presidential candidate tries to help congressional candidates of his party, but these efforts are only incidental. In contrast, the national campaigns of British parties are truly that. British general elections are distinguished by the overwhelming emphasis they give to national issues, to use of nationwide media, and to reliance upon campaigning by national party notables. They put heavy emphasis on making the issues of the party's national election address known locally; nationally known party figures concentrate on contests for winnable seats in strategic, closely divided swing constituencies. It is the press and the electronic media that tie together the national and constituency electioneering efforts of a major British party and unify them to make a single party endeavor out of them.[5] Increased use of regional television by BBC and ITN during their coverage of the 1974 and 1979 campaigns produced no discernible localizing effect on voter attitudes or behavior, and on those occasions all election broadcasts, major interviews of leaders, and election forums put on by the parties were directed at the national electorate.

British general election campaigns increasingly are coming to resemble the presidential style that Americans know. Party leaders dominate the planning and execution and alone speak authoritatively for their parties. Utilization of electronic media is rapidly expanding, issues are more and more presented in generalized form, and mutual criticism of personality and leadership qualities by opponents are becoming central features, more like past American than British style. As party leaders have assumed a campaign role typical of American presidential candidates, personality has tended to become an important factor in party leadership selection and electoral success. The strong position and positive image of Harold Wilson in the largely electronic campaign of 1970 enabled him to dominate that campaign, even though Labor was defeated by the force of other factors. But the criticism generated by the presidential tendencies of electioneering techniques in that instance caused him and his opponent, Conservative party leader Edward Heath, to subordinate their involvements in the elections of 1974 in favor of more collective efforts by party leaders[6] and greater reliance on party broadcasts, opinion polls, constituency appearances and other nonelectronic techniques.[7] Although the lackluster Heath retained enough party support to retain his leadership post after the Tory's loss to Labor in February 1974, he could not survive the second defeat by Labor in October 1974 and lost his position to Mrs. Margaret Thatcher.[8] In May 1979, Mrs. Thatcher, following the most "presidential" campaign ever waged in Britain,[9] became its first lady prime minister. In the 1979 campaign, incumbent Prime Minister Callaghan and Mrs. Thatcher, as Conservative leader, dominated the planning and implementation of their party's respective national campaigns. The Tory victory in that election has been described as a personal one for Mrs. Thatcher.[10]

Hence, for different reasons, both British and American campaigns for national offices are carried on at two fairly distinct levels and, at least in the case of British constituency electioneering, by very different techniques. Constituency activities depend heavily on mailings, posters, door-to-door canvassing, mass rallies, smaller meetings, and preparation and wholesale distribution of the candidate's election address (position statement), but the candidate's positions on policy issues are those of his party; deviation and independent thinking at the local level are not encouraged. It is from the national campaigns waged by the central party organizations that the voters learn the issues on which the contest will be waged and where the parties stand on them. The constituency campaign consists, therefore, almost wholly of undramatic, routine, and nonpolitical activities. Partisan activity largely takes the form of a few meetings which are usually poorly attended unless a national party figure is to be present. Local financial resources are usually limited and are spent on printing, rents, and similar items. Printing the candidate's election address is the biggest expense and may consume as much as half of the funds available to him.[11] Statutory limits on constituency campaign spending are so low that little money is normally available for paid political advertisements in the press. Because in Britain virtually all electronic media are national, constituency candidates do almost no television or radio campaigning. However, in 1974, the fifteen regional independent stations presented more programming designed to reach local voters than ever before.[12]

The national campaign is as intensely political as constituency activities are characteristically mechanical. Preparation, approval, publication, and nationwide distribution of the party's electoral manifesto of policy issues and positions is a major concern. Central party organs help the leaders to plan campaign strategies and tactics. They arrange for daily strategy sessions; plan and organize nationwide television and radio programming; put on press conferences attended by the leader or other principal party spokesmen; conduct research; aid constituency organizations and candidates; contract for private opinion polls, media experts and other campaign support personnel; and in numerous other ways facilitate the leader's national campaign effort. But it is in the constituency campaign that the party's hired election agent fulfills his role.

ELECTION MANAGERS

Election campaigns in open political systems must be carefully planned, organized, directed, staffed, and otherwise managed, but the typical candidate has no time or ability personally to undertake those essential steps. Hence, some form of campaign management must emerge to meet the practical need.

In the United States, candidates for national office must have campaign managers. They are normally individuals selected by the candidates from their close supporters on an ad hoc basis and may be amateurs in politics who may or may not have prior experience. But increased participation in campaign management by professional management firms has followed on the rapid inflation of campaign costs caused by the growing use of sophisticated but expensive technologies. Candidates desire to maximize their returns for each dollar spent, and to that end have increasingly resorted to the services of professionally directed efforts. Candidates who can afford the assistance of a management firm usually receive a "package" which includes public relations, speech writing, polling, computer analyses, research, publicity, fund raising, image refinement, and public relations services essential to a modern political campaign. Expanded use of television and of professional firms have combined to further inflate the costs of campaigning. At the same time, their use has undermined the roles of the political parties, for party influentials must now compete with professional campaign aides in selecting and defining issues or determining and shaping the candidate's image. In other ways as well, the professionals take from the party its traditional roles in campaigns. Although congressional campaigns are still largely conducted with principal emphasis on traditional techniques involving face-to-face contact and direct appeal to voters, presidential campaigns give primary attention to the indirect techniques of media campaigning.

The British parties have also adopted professional campaign assistance, but their campaign managers are increasingly of a different type from the American. Each candidate for a seat in Commons is required to designate an election agent. A candidate may, but rarely does, act as his own agent. Most candidates of Labor and minority parties rely on volunteer personnel to run their campaigns, but better organized and more affluent constituency associations that can afford them usually hire managers to run their local campaigns. Those specialists are known as constituency party agents. Rose indicates that in 1973 the Conservatives maintained 390 agents in constituencies and 133 agents at regional and central offices. Labor had only 125 constituency agents and 96 agents at regional and central headquarters, and the Liberals had only 16 and 22, respectively.[13] In the February 1974 election, the Conservative central office made a special effort to provide full-time agents for the 83 Conservative constituency associations in most marginal constituencies. They were given special instruction on electioneering in closely-divided marginal constituencies and were paid by the central organization. The action embodied a clear deviation from the established practice of locally hiring and paying the party agents, but it also was a tacit admission by the central party organ that local campaigning continues to have value for party success.[14]

Although American campaign managers and British constituency party agents have similar responsibilities for planning, organizing, and directing constituency election efforts, American party organizations do not provide their candidates with professional aides like the agents. Whether they are full-time or part-time, British agents are paid, trained specialists skilled in planning, staffing, directing, and winning campaigns. Where they are hired, they take charge of building organizations; recruiting and directing volunteer workers; managing finances; complying with all legal regulations affecting campaign practices and procedures; planning strategies; arranging for meetings, rallies and other events; and, in general, supervising all phases of the campaign. Agents have professional organizations and can move from poorer to more affluent and better-paying constituencies as they build records of demonstrated ability.

The influence of agents as local party leaders is variable, and Blondel points out that generalizations are unreliable.[15] They are sometimes regarded as outsiders in the constituency organizations; they may attend meetings of the local influentials, but they are not always accepted as members of the inner group. Their inputs, however, may carry added weight locally because they are linked to the central party organs and are knowledgeable about the external affairs of the party. Blondel concludes that Labor agents carry more weight with the constituency party than their Conservative counterparts do because the latter are more commonly perceived as employees rather than as partners of the constituency leadership.[16] Neither party maintains many agents at regional or central party headquarters, and their small numbers and geographic dispersion tend to dissipate their influence at both locations.

PARTY POLICY STATEMENTS

British party manifestos and American party platforms fulfill essentially the same functions. Neither is noted for acuity and explicitness of content; both tend to be on the colorless side. Neither is thought to exert much influence on the outcome of national elections or to make them more issue oriented. They are usually of a soothing partisan nature designed to appeal to as many voters of different persuasions as possible, while alienating as few as possible in the process. Manifestos, like platforms, tend to be couched in terms of broad party principle, avoiding specific solutions to identified problems. Party regulars tend to agree already with what they express, and unpersuaded voters are rarely affected by their content.

It is probable, however, that the national election manifesto of a British party plays a more salient role in a typical general election than does an American national party platform in the United States. The manifestos are the sources from which constituency party candidates derive their policy positions on national questions in the election addresses which they prepare and distribute in large numbers to local electorates. Millions of the national manifestos are prepared and distributed by national parties. They receive extensive media coverage, but they rarely set forth new or innovative policy positions. Manifestos are not thought of as pledges to the voters that the parties will carry out their stated positions if returned in a majority, and because the manifestos are issued quickly after a dissolution is proclaimed and an election set, they do not set forth party stands on issues raised during the short period of the campaign. Instead, they present to the voters general statements on those matters that have been selected by the party leadership which the party believes are important. Recent governments have shown a disposition to take seriously the policy statements of their manifestos. Carter notes that, following its victory in 1970, the Conservative government proceeded almost step by step to transform manifesto statements into legislation.[17] And within six weeks following the election in May 1979, the Thatcher government had proceeded to translate the principles and objectives of its election manifesto into policy proposals to implement what it said it would do if elected. The government's first budget was an unparalleled expression of political candor intended to give explicit content to an uncommonly explicit campaign. Withal, it is the Labor party more than the Conservative that regards success at the polls to be an electoral mandate to transform its manifesto into a program of legislation.

CANDIDATE SELECTION

One of the most significant phases of the democratic process is candidate selection, that is, the process by which a political party determines who among many aspirants will carry the party's label as official candidate in the final election.[18] Its importance, in Britain especially, lies in the fact that it is the principal screen for selecting persons from among whom the party will draw its future leaders, ministers, and deputies; although in the American system legislators who move into the executive arena of government do so through different channels. But, in both systems, candidate selection is virtually synonymous with election in the 60 to 80 percent of the constituencies that are "safe" for one party or the other. In any election, of course, incumbents derive most benefit from one-party control, but some new faces are always chosen for the first time. In one-party areas the group that identifies the party's candidate makes the only meaningful choice the process affords, for the voters in the election merely ratify its selection. In both party systems, candidate selection can have impact, sometimes determinative, on the policy-making process, albeit that impact is more direct and discernible in the British than in the American system. The tendency in recent years for Labor constituency associations to select more radical leftist candidates is reflected in the policy leanings of the party's members in the House of Commons. That, in turn, colored their relations with the more moderate Callaghan government and their attitudes toward its policies. In a more abstract context, candidate selection can also impact on American legislative-executive relations and the policy-making process, but the nature of the American governmental system of divided powers and the absence of party government largely dissipate its influence and obscure its visibility within our system.

Members of British and American political parties may take part in candidate selection, but in Britain few do so. The parties there have not undertaken to democratize the selection process by adopting the direct primary, nominating convention, or other devices designed to involve large numbers of members. On the contrary, Austin Ranney states, British candidate selection takes place almost wholly in private, removed from media coverage and constituency gaze, and controlled by a few actives in the constituency association.[19] By contrast, American congressional candidates are almost all selected by direct primaries held in the congressional districts. Primary contests among aspirants to a nomination may produce as much publicity, sometimes nationwide, as is generated by general election campaigns and may cost as much in time, money, and effort.

A major difference between British and American selection procedures grows out of the matter of residence in the constituencies. A tradition of localism predating the American Constitution was partially responsible for a constitutional requirement that American candidates for the national legislature be inhabitants of the states from which they are selected, and by custom representatives must reside within their congressional districts. This tradition of localism, plus its more explicit forms, assures that candidates for seats in the House of Representatives must also live within the district for which they seek nomination. American practice places heavy emphasis on the local backgrounds, roots, and values of its nominees, for they cannot adequately represent the district unless they embody its spirit and understand its people and their needs. Were one so foolish as to seek it, an American nonresident aspirant to a district's nomination would have to move into it, and even then would have to overcome strong local prejudices against outsider candidates, make a foredoomed effort to obtain the nomination, or simply abandon the objective. No legal or customary requirement of the same nature operates in British constituencies, but most local associations prefer indigenous candidates, albeit a few prefer outsiders.[20] Therefore, British aspirants to a prospective candidature may, and some do, seek party acceptance in a series of constituencies, beginning in one where there is no hope of winning the election but where the neophyte can gain experience and demonstrate vote-getting ability. Later, party endorsement may be gained in a more balanced two-party constituency providing a better chance to win.[21] Strong tradition protects local selection of candidates in Britain, but party rules of the Conservative and Labor parties mandate that all constituency choices must be approved by the central party organs before they can be regarded as even prospective candidates, a full step removed from nomination.[22] That tradition protecting the right to make local selections does not mandate that the selectee must be a local person, however. A British constituency association may endorse an outsider who is unknown to it and unfamiliar with it; but, because its choice is expected to represent a party and its policies, not constituency interests in the American sense, the British do not regard lack of attachment to the constituency as politically significant. The flexibility in candidate selection resulting from that attitude is totally absent from the American pattern and permits British central party organs to move important party figures from doubtful swing constituencies to safe ones where opposition is minimal or lacking. Their future service to the party can thereby be assured, and they can be groomed to assume increasingly important roles in government. Incumbent and former MPs are rarely rejected by constituency associations, but when seats become vacant and new faces are recruited, the local selection process virtually guarantees that a local hopeful, loyal to the party and having a record of party activism, will be chosen. On the Labor side, however, constituency autonomy may produce candidates with more extremist views than are held by Labor Party leaders and produce a wider range of viewpoints among Labor backbenchers than exists among Conservatives in the House. The Conservative party is more centralized and disciplined than Labor, and its associations more readily defer to national leadership and show less tendency toward independence. Intraparty homogeneity is therefore greater.

In the United States, extensive legal regulation of party primaries, organization, ballot forms, voting procedures, finances, and other party matters is contained in statutes, principally of the states; but, in Britain, legal regulation of parties is almost unknown.[23] Hence, American parties enjoy far less flexibility, freedom, and intraparty discretion than do British parties. In both countries, however, eligibility for a candidature and filing of nominating papers are regulated by law.

British selection procedures are controlled mainly by party rules and practice and are markedly different from those used by American parties. Aspirants hoping to become prospective nominees usually present themselves to the constituency association. Some may be brought to local notice by a party's central organs, which maintain lists of approved prospective candidates. Whatever their origin, hopefuls present their availability and credentials to a small constituency committee of party actives which screens them and reduces the number of a half dozen of the most likely looking prospects. A second, much larger committee invites them to address it, answer questions, and, in the process, respond to heckling from the audience. Heckling is a major characteristic of British campaign experience, and candidates must be able to handle it without losing their composure or alienating their crowd. The ability to do so is not possessed by all persons and is especially sought in prospective nominees. When the auditions have been completed the constituency committee selects one aspirant to be the prospective candidate for Commons. The choice is presented in principle to the full membership for adoption, but, once again few members participate.

The national party organs play a role unknown in American congressional nominating practice. Identification of the constituency's prospective nominee is accomplished with participation of a regional agent, and every local choice must be approved by the national party's central committee in London to carry the party's label. The central organs can but infrequently do reject local selections. They can recommend persons for constituency endorsement, but associations have refused to accept such suggestions and have chosen others more to their liking. Although they cannot dictate a choice, the central organs can veto unacceptable ones made by local initiative. In both parties, central approval is contingent upon the prospective candidate's accepting central party doctrine, programs, and discipline. But, whereas the deferential attitudes of Conservative party constituencies toward national organization assure a minimum of friction and formal control between them, the rules of the Labor party exert extensive control over candidate selection by constituency Labor associations.[24] In sum, candidate selection by British associations is not an open democratic process accomplished by wholesale participation of rank-and-file members of constituency parties.

In contrast to British procedure, the nomination of American candidates to be national senators and representatives is accomplished under diverse decentralized conditions by a variety of state-controlled means. An incumbent who desires to seek reelection will not normally encounter opposition for the nomination of his party. He may be unopposed or face only token opposition when he appeals to the rank-and-file members of the party to nominate him in their primary. If the nomination is open, however, the choice of candidates to run for the national House and Senate may be heavily influenced or even controlled by county chairmen, state chairmen, or other local or state party influentials. To be elected, the nominee must build his own local power base out of diverse party and other interests. Candidates for both chambers of Congress normally conduct campaigns separate from one another and from the presidential effort, during which they may receive some financial aid from the congressional or senatorial campaign committees of their parties or, more likely, from the state party organization. Most members of the House and Senate come out of election efforts with their own local power bases and organizations intact and in positions to bargain and to dispense national patronage at state and local levels, but independent of state and local control. They owe little or nothing to national organs of the party, which played no roles in nominating or electing them, so that they emerge as nearly autonomous political actors free of scripted roles in party, legislative, or executive organization and activity.

ACCESS TO THE BALLOT

Access to the ballot is controlled in part by eligibility to become a member of Parliament or Congress, and eligibility, in turn, is controlled by law. Consonant with democratic standards, broad eligibility and freedom to stand for election prevail in both systems. In Britain any citizen twenty-one years of age or older who is not a peer, lunatic, clergyman of the Catholic or established churches, bankrupt, criminal, regular member of the armed forces, policeman, civil servant, or full-time judge may hold a seat in the House of Commons. To take a seat in the American House of Representatives, however, one must be twenty-five years of age, a citizen of the United States for seven years, and an inhabitant of the state for which he is chosen. A senator must be thirty years of age and a citizen for nine years. In each system, therefore, formal qualifications for candidacy are minimal and play little part in undemocratically restricting access to membership in the national lawmaking bodies.

Access to the ballot is also partially controlled by nonlegal considerations. Here, inequality of treatment between the sexes rears its head, for British and American political cultures share a reluctance to nominate women candidates. The houses of both national legislatures contain few women members. That reluctance, especially in Britain, seems to lie at the constituency level. Although the Labor party is more willing than the Conservative to give women access to the Commons, none of the British and American major parties can be regarded as a dedicated champion of female interests and viewpoints in the national legislature.[25]

Voters' perceptions of candidates may also influence access to the ballot. In America, prospective legislators have to overcome two obstacles on their way to office, while British aspirants have but one. In all but a handful of states, they must first win a primary to become nominated and then win an election to gain office. At both stages, the image projected by a candidate is likely to influence the American voter's perception of the candidate and electoral behavior more than do the issue orientations of national parties. Weak party loyalties, localism, and extensive voter independence in the United States encourage voter reaction to nonrational aspects of a candidate: personal appearance, family attractiveness, or even the household dog. Such irrational factors affect election outcomes and, therefore, are politically relevant. American electoral emphasis is mainly on candidates who can *win* a local contest and only secondarily on the agreement with national issue orientations, party discipline, and promised future loyalty that are paramount in Britain. The roles of personal traits and issues in British elections are reversed. The candidate centrality that characterizes American elections is missing from British contests. There the outcomes of constituency elections are mainly determined by forces and factors almost wholly extraneous to the local scene, and issue orientations of national parties override the influence of most voter perceptions of candidate images. Yet, it cannot be denied that to some extent in American as well as in British legislative elections, outcomes are affected by national political trends, by national party records, by issue orientations of national party spokesmen, by incumbency, and by the intraconstituency division of partisan strength.[26]

Still other obstacles to getting on the ballot must be overcome

In Britain, a person selected by a constituency association to be its candidate must file nominating papers with the local returning officer on nominating day. The nominating papers must be signed by two registered voters acting as nominators and by eight others acting as seconders. In the United States, the almost exclusive method for nominating persons to be both senators and representatives is the direct primary, most commonly closed to all but members of the sponsoring party but sometimes open to all voters with the result that those of one party may help nominate candidates for the other. Details of form and procedure are myriad and complex, regulated by state laws, and greatly varied from one state to the next. Because no single day for nominating is set by law in the United States as is set in Britain, the states have staggered their congressional primaries over a long period from March through October, with the consequence that it is almost impossible concurrently to focus voters' attention in the many states on the same matters of national policy. That fact, in turn, further weakens the influence of national party leadership by diminishing policy uniformity and all but destroying internal coherence.

ELECTION DEPOSITS

Another point of contrast arises from the fact that British parties must post an election deposit for each candidate they run. The deposit of £150 is forfeited in every constituency where its candidate fails to receive at least one-eighth of the total vote cast. Posting of the deposit is to discourage frivolous candidacies, but that purpose is not realized in practice, for many deposits are lost in every general election. In 1979 several minor parties lost all election deposits: the National Front forfeited 301; the Ecology party gave up 53; and the Workers' Revolutionary party lost 60. The requirement can be costly and does deter parties without substantial resources from entering all the election races they might wish to contest. To that extent it is clearly incompatible with the ideal of open democratic electoral processes. American state electoral laws do not require election deposits. The American political culture supports the proposition that any candidate who can gain access to the ballot under our state laws, no matter what his cause or chance of success, ought not to be impeded by a requirement that would favor affluent parties or candidates. The tradition of independent and small-party candidates is much stronger in American than in British electoral practice and will not accommodate a money requirement for the privilege of seeking elective public office.

INDEPENDENT CANDIDATES

Independent candidates seeking seats in Congress are far more common than are persons standing for the House of Commons without a party label to back them. They also have a much better chance to be elected. The absence of strong party government in the United States and its democratic political culture allows for independent candidates and encourages them to run, even though they lack party affiliation, financing, and organization. An independent who is elected to the House or Senate will almost certainly find shelter in the organization of a major party. However, a British independent elected to any but a narrowly divided Commons would be a member of a large parliamentary body, tightly controlled by dominant party leadership, in which all business and procedure are managed along party lines. Only if party division were so close that his vote was important to the government would an independent MP be more than a silent figure in the House of Commons. But an independent senator or representative can play an active role as an autonomous member of his chamber, especially if taken into the embrace of a party, admitted to its councils, and given one of its seats on committees.

VOTER QUALIFICATIONS

Democratic nominations and elections count for little unless the suffrage is also democratic. The democratic suffrage should be as broadly based as possible to assure maximum participation in the processes of choosing governors, holding them accountable, and communicating to them popular opinion about the needs and wants of the public. Who, then, can vote in Britain and America?

Treatment of this subject is complicated by the fact that American suffrage eligibility is controlled by the laws of the separate states and is only partly homogenized by national statutes, constitutional amendments, and judicial decisions. In Britain, on the other hand, a single set of national laws governs all major aspects of the matter, although some minor variations exist among the four jurisdictions making up Great Britain. The American and British systems are committed to universal adult suffrage and to equality of the vote. Plural voting has never been known in the American national electorate, but it was only recently abolished in Britain by the Representation of the People Act of 1948 which ended the business premises and university franchises. Women's suffrage equal to that of men's was secured by adoption of the Nineteenth Amendment to the Constitution of the United States; in Britain the same end was achieved by the Representation of the People Act of 1928. Democracy was slower in coming to the British franchise than to the American, and neither system has been fully open to all categories of voters or free from purposive disfranchisement.

Today, the suffrages have been drawn into more similar terms by the common movement toward greater openness and fairness. The voting age is fixed in both countries at eighteen, and the secret ballot is uniformly used. Voters in Northern Ireland and in the United States must be citizens, but in other units voters must be subjects of the Queen. Absentee voting is uniformly available in Britain to categories of voters who might be disfranchised by illness or disability, absence from the country, change of residence, or travel out of the constituency on polling day. Every American state permits absentee voting by members of the armed forces stationed outside the state or the country; all but one extend the same opportunity to civilian employees of the national government; and they variously authorize absentee voting for diverse other reasons.

Certain qualitative criteria also affect who can vote. Some are shared and others are unique to Britain or the United States. Both disfranchise aliens, persons who are mentally defective, and, under varying rules, those who have been convicted of certain crimes although discharged from prison. Persons are disfranchised who have not attained voting age and who are confined to prison; however, persons serving less than one year in Britain may vote by mail, but those in American jails and prisons, even persons awaiting trial, may not vote under the laws of most states. The laws of Britain and of many American states inflict special disqualifications on persons convicted of violating corrupt practices statutes designed to protect the integrity of the electoral process. In Britain, peers of the realm may not vote, and returning officers, one of whom administers the election in each constituency, may not vote in any election for which they are responsible. On the whole, the qualitative restrictions on the suffrage are reasonably successful in accomplishing the goal of protecting the meaningfulness of election results without unduly compromising the ideal of universal adult suffrage. Nevertheless, both British and American electoral law excludes certain categories of persons, such as clerics, discharged felons, and persons held in pretrial detention, whose disfranchisement raises some perplexing questions of compatibility with a democratic franchise.

VOTER REGISTRATION

The ability of qualified voters to vote in Britain and the United States is dependent upon the fact of their registration. In both electoral systems, access to the ballot is limited to voters on official voter registration lists. Voter lists in localities in America are prepared under state law by registration officials or others authorized to act, such as party workers and official candidates for public office. Their purpose is to control fraudulent voting, but they have been widely used nationally by political parties to discriminate against various classes of voters on racial and socioeconomic grounds. Urban registration in the United States is commonly administered on a periodic basis, but, in rural areas with more stable populations and less anonymity among people, registration is generally permanent as long as the voter keeps his registration alive by participating in an election within a stated period of years. No uniformity exists, however, among the laws and practices of the several states, except that all place responsibility to register on the voter who desires to vote. Although becoming more decentralized (even registration by mail is becoming more common), many state registration systems require voters to appear in person at a central place to establish their eligibility for the franchise. American registration systems place the initiative on the individual, who, because of legal and procedural complexities,

convenience, apathy, alienation, ignorance, forgetfulness, or leth-
rgy, may forfeit his vote.

British voters are registered annually by local registration offi-
ers who implement a nationally uniform procedure. Voter regis-
ation is an annual public function conducted by agents of the
egistration officer, who make a door-to-door canvass in the fall
1 an effort to reach all eligible voters at their places of residence.
Each head of household is required to designate every person in
esidence who is eighteen years of age or older and a British sub-
ct or a citizen of Northern Ireland. When a new register has been
repared, it is made available for public inspection for a short time
nd can be examined and challenged. Voters who change residence
fter a register is compiled and cannot establish their eligibility to
ote in their new constituency may vote by mail in their old one.
The system misses some voters, and others neglect to obtain mail
allots following a change of residence, with the result that they
re disfranchised until they gain access to a later register. But rela-
ively few complaints are heard in Britain about the process or the
nanner of its administration, in contrast to the often contemptible
istory of the effort in the United States.

DISPUTED ELECTIONS

Electoral systems must provide some method for resolving chal-
enges brought by losers against winners. Those employed in the
United States and Britain stand in sharp contrast. The houses of
Congress are the judges of the elections, returns, and qualifications
f their respective members. Disputed congressional elections often
irst involve a local recount of ballots, the outcome of which may
e challenged by the loser in the appropriate house. That chal-
enge usually attacks the validity of the certificate of election
ssued by the governor to certify the apparent winner's election.
The dispute may result in the member-elect being sworn in and
ater expelled by vote of the chamber, or he may be asked to stand
side when other members-elect are sworn. In that case, he will
ake his oath when he has won the dispute. If he loses it, his certifi-
ate of election will be cancelled.

When a dispute is brought to a house of Congress it is referred

to the appropriate committee. But such contests are decided alo[n]
strictly partisan lines, so that the outcome is determined by t[he]
party that controls the committee.

American experience with presidential elections is more limite[d]
Only those of 1800 and 1876 produced inconclusive results. T[he]
resolution of both by Congress became ensnarled in interparty co[n]
flict, but despite the best efforts to balance partisan forces [to]
produce a neutral result, the resolution arrived at was dictate[d]
by party votes. Hence, American procedures for resolving dispute[d]
national elections provide no precedent or protection agai[nst]
blatant partisan control and can scarcely be said to be fair, obje[c]
tive, and statesmanlike.

The British need settle only disputed national legislative ele[c]
tions. However, instead of referring them to a committee of t[he]
Commons, they are heard before judges of the high court, one [of]
the superior courts of the judiciary. The judges have authority [to]
declare void the election return issued by the constituency electi[on]
officer if they become satisfied that irregularities contaminated t[he]
election result. By way of contrast, it is pointed out that althoug[h]
American national judges would take jurisdiction over justiciab[le]
questions growing out of a disputed election, the separation [of]
powers doctrine, the "political question" principle, or the san[c]
tity of judicial independence free from involvement in the politic[al]
thicket would doubtless preclude judicial settlement of a dispute[d]
congressional or presidential election.

CAMPAIGN FINANCES

The regulation of money in elections is a major problem in t[he]
American and British election systems. American state and n[a]
tional law sets limits on the amounts that can be raised and e[x]
pended, the sources from which funds can be obtained, the amoun[t]
those sources can contribute, and the purposes for which expend[i]
tures can be made. Regulation strives to assure financial account[a]
bility and honesty by requiring an elaborate system of records a[nd]
reporting. The statutes have been largely cosmetic but have doub[t]
less had a deterrent and cautionary effect against the worst abus[es]
of money in elections. The sieve-like nature of many regulatio[ns]
produces a suspicion that enacting bodies have not wished [to]

create an effective system of constraints in which they will become enmeshed. Those same regulations have had the effect of dispersing internal party control and making it more difficult for parties to coordinate the electoral activities of their many semiautonomous parts. An ancillary effect has been to make successful money raisers independent sources of power and influence within the party organizations.

To make the burden of presidential primary campaign financing more equal, to tighten financial controls over presidential primaries and election campaigns, and to provide public funding for both, Congress enacted the Presidential Election Campaign Act in 1974.[27] That act created a special presidential election campaign fund supplied by voluntary contributions allocated from national personal income tax payments. The fund was first used to finance the 1976 presidential election.

British elections costs are paid entirely out of party monies. No public financing is provided; no limitations on expenditures apply to central party organs engaged in running national campaigns,[28] for those campaigns do not directly elect persons to office. British constraints on party finances are probably as evadable as those in American law, but for the most part there is little discernible tendency to violate their letter or spirit.

British control of constituency election finances is strictly enforced and concentrates mainly on regulating amounts and purposes of expenditures and avoids much of the cumbersomeness that characterizes American efforts. The constituency party agent is responsible for all spending done on his candidate's behalf and for complying with the legal limits set on constituency campaign expenditures. Only those made by the candidate or his agent are legal under the Representation of the People Act of 1949. Expenses incurred before the formal election announcement is issued do not count against the election total. Election expenditures are low by American standards,[29] and financial constraints may severely limit campaign activities. They favor candidates who can bear part of the load out of their own pockets, but, in order to neutralize the inequitable advantage of wealth, Conservative party rules forbid a candidate to contribute more than £100 to his own campaign. British law also imposes heavy penalties on the provision of campaign-related goods and services by nonparty interests whose support of candidates would remove some financial burden from the parties and amount to evasion of the statutory limitations, and the American technique of creating multiple campaign committees, each of which spends to the authorized limit, is illegal in Britain. However, British failure to control expenditures incurred for partisan activity prior to the short formal election campaign favors the more affluent constituency parties.

Money assumes an importance in American political practices that it does not command in similar British arenas. The political culture of the United States generates and validates expectations of reward for political contributions. Successful candidates are expected, and expect, to reward workers and contributors. The necessity to fight nominating and then election campaigns in the face of steadily rising costs strains the financial resources of aspirants and parties. Opportunities for distribution of jobs and other goodies by successful candidates are relatively numerous. Expectation of gain is a major stimulus to political contributors in American politics. By way of contrast, the tight structure of British parties, cabinet control of policy formation and enactment, administrative implementation by a prestigious apolitical civil service, control of nominations by constituency committees, short general election campaigns, and a political culture that encourages advisory participation of government with interests while virtually eliminating patronage and other forms of political reward combine to all but eliminate from current British experiences the troubling influences of money that plague American government and politics.[30]

It is doubtful that British legal constraints achieve their purpose of equalizing opportunity for electoral success any more than American laws have done. But, the corrupting influence of money in American politics has been made a minor one in British national politics and has not been reflected in the substance of their law as it has been in American.

PUBLIC OPINION POLLS

Public opinion polls have become an important part of British and American politics. National polls such as Harris and Gallup operate in both countries along with several others. On a continuing basis, they elicit, usually for newspaper publication, national opinion on issues of the day.

During periods of national campaigning, their use is intensified. British and American parties and many American candidates employ private polls to keep them informed of trends and shifts in voter opinion. Intensive use of polls is made in British national elections by central party organs. In the 1970 Conservative party campaign, Edward Heath, party leader, received the results of three specially commissioned national opinion surveys each day.[31] Despite the poor record compiled by British polls in the 1970 general election, still greater use was made of them in 1974 and 1979. Both parties extensively employed private polls to influence opinion, gauge public reactions to radio and television appeals, for partisan research, and for tactical campaign planning. Their ability to predict the electoral outcome was only partially proved by the final results.[32] Polls are also employed in intraparty factional disputes to repudiate the issue-positions of rival faction leaders by demonstrating their lack of support among party members.[33] Polls are used by British parties to shape propaganda addressed to portions of the electorate, but they are not often utilized as a basis for making party policy, Rose reports.[34] Nevertheless, the parties fully appreciate the potential offered by polls for other partisan purposes and continuously use their results to measure the pulse of the body politic. British pollsters have overcome the initial problems they experienced with polling as have American, and polls are and will remain a major feature of electioneering.

Although there is no evidence that polls have determined the outcome of British elections, their use has raised questions peculiar to that system of government. For instance, prime ministers utilize polls to gauge public reaction to the policies and record of the government to help them determine when to call a national election. It is suggested that if such use produces reliable results, the majority party will be able to put the minority at a greater electoral disadvantage than the system ought to be forced to tolerate. Stacey concludes that the prime minister's use of opinion polls has too greatly reinforced his position and that of his party. The advantage he and his party derive thereby is excessive but might be offset by ending the power of dissolution and substituting a fixed term for Commons in its place.[35] In a system of party government built on a presumed close relationship between electoral opinion and government policy initiatives, there is also a question of how closely government ought adhere to revealed electoral opinion, whether constant or shifting. Is the government bound to adjust to a policy preference expressed through poll results when it believes that preference to be ill-conceived? Ought it abandon a policy believed to be well-founded because poll results show that the public is indifferent or hostile to it? Despite uncertainties surrounding the use of polls in British electoral politics, no substantial sentiment exists to ban them.[36]

MEDIA CAMPAIGNING

Electioneering in Britain and the United States has become heavily dependent upon the use of electronic media, and in both radio and television are indispensable for waging national campaigns. That is particularly true of British national, but not local, electioneering, and in this country applies especially to campaigns for national legislative and executive positions. Television is the principal electronic media, and in Britain, it has been mainly responsible for making the electorate more aware of and informed about general policy issues.

Major print and all broadcast media in Britain are centered in London, where the government and parties are based, and they are national in scope. Seven major British newspapers can be read throughout most of Britain on the date of publication and are supplemented by many regional and local papers.[37] Radio and television are dominated by the British Broadcasting Corporation (BBC), stateowned but governed by an independent, nongovernmentally controlled board, and by the Independent Television Authority (ITA), a private commercial company that operates on a modified American model. Both the BBC and ITA operate through regional outlets that provide British audiences with regional programing and give them their only media attention to local matters. British programing is not sponsored. BBC and ITA must maintain complete political neutrality and may not sell political advertising to parties, candidates, or other purchasers.[38]

By contrast, in America, almost all media of mass communica-
on are in the private sector and are operated for profit. The sole
ception to this statement is the Corporation for Public Broad-
sting, established by Congress but financed, operated, and
verned wholly outside of the governmental system. Local control
air time is extensive so that use of electronic media in statewide
d local campaigns is a common feature of American, but not of
itish, politics. The American press is also regional and local for
e most part; only a few papers have been able to build up any-
ing like national circulations.

Other differences important to democratic political processes
ist between the two countries. The short British campaign period
oduces a more intensive outpouring of media response than does
e much longer American effort, except that American parties
nd to concentrate their use of electronic media toward the end
the period, so that intensity accelerates as the campaign draws
a close. Whereas the British must develop their messages to the
ters, try new techniques, and perfect old ones within a period of
om three to four weeks, American candidates can experiment in
imaries, and they and the parties can elaborate on and continue
develop their techniques during the general election campaigns.
oreover, partisan campaigning and use of mass communication
edia in Britain are almost wholly the function of national party
gans and employ national media that reach nationwide audi-
ces. Almost no media, especially electronic ones, are used by
nstituency associations or agents, in part because local television
d radio are not readily available, and in part because local cam-
ign finances are usually inadequate to meet the necessary ex-
nse. American national campaigns make heavy use of electronic
edia, and the availability of local programing also permits their
tensive use by candidates for seats in Congress. Use of national
edia in British general elections imparts a high degree of homo-
niety to them throughout most of Britain, but American elec-
ns still comprise more a cacophony of localized appeals than
ey do coordinated national party efforts.

Newsworthiness does not play the same role in British and
merican media, particularly the broadcast media. American
edia are influenced in their choices of such mattters as coverage

and program format by nonpolitical considerations. Audience ra
ings, sponsor preferences, and a desire for profits affect the abili
of candidates to get air time. Air time is sold at commercial
profitable rates to candidates and parties who can afford it, so th
the market economy heavily affects the role of the media in Amer
can elections. But, British media, especially the electronic agenci
of mass communication, give a preferred status to politically rel
vant information, regardless of its newsworthiness, by featuring
on daily news broadcasts and on public affairs programs and 1
covering party campaign activities as news events. Each allocate
party broadcast is aired on all channels at the same time to exclu
all other viewer options except turning off the set.[39]

Practices controlling access to air time provide yet another d
ference between British and American campaigning. Marketpla
controls operate in the United States subject to some judici
statutory, and administrative regulation. They make access to a
time for electioneering depend upon the ability of a party or cand
date to buy it. In this case, "Them that has, gets," and small pa
ties and poor candidates are at a distinct disadvantage compar
to wealthier ones that can "buy" their ways into public office. Co
trary to American philosophy and practice, however, time
British radio and television is allocated without cost by a co
mittee representing the two electronic media and the three maj
parties. For the 1974 general election campaign the Labor ar
Conservative parties received time for five major broadcasts of t
minutes each and the Liberals three. Minor parties running at le
fifty candidates each received a total of five minutes of televisi
air time. The committee also allotted to the parties an equal nu
ber of eight-minute radio spots in the same ratios. The British te
vision authority can program additional coverage of special ca
paign activities, debates between candidates, or other featur
subject to party approval of format.[40] In these ways the Briti
strive to counteract some of the advantages that money gives
possessors in elections, because adaptation of the new technolog
to campaigning has greatly increased the costs of reaching vot
in England and the United States. In 1971, Congress respond
to the rising costs of electronic media in American national ele
tions by limiting broadcast media costs to not more than 60 pe

cent of total campaign expenditures,[41] but in 1974, it repealed that limitation when it imposed ceilings on the total amounts that can be spent by candidates seeking national offices.[42]

VOTING BEHAVIOR

What considerations cause voters to vote as they do? The idea once widely held that each voter in a democratic polity ought to make a rational judgment about how to cast his ballot after comprehensively researching and analyzing all available alternatives is now recognized as an expression of classical democratic idealism. The polling behavior of British and American voters fails to live up to the classical theory largely because it was formulated for a polity lacking a mass suffrage, party organization and allegiances, and the cross pressures of contemporary political life. That voters are not influenced solely by the record of the government in office, by the promises of candidates seeking votes, or by the rational bases of decision making is established beyond dispute. Instead, voting behavior is the product of myriad influences, some internal and some external to each elector, but all working on him to cause him to shift party allegiance or to remain firm, to be apathetic or committed, and to vote regularly, sporadically, or never.

To compare the voting behavior of British and American electorates is not an easy undertaking. Differences of electoral composition, varying incidences of class consciousness and its impacts, differences of political cultures and their continuing effects, and the dissimilar schemes of party organization and roles and of elections cause systematic comparisons to be both difficult and, in an inquiry of this nature and scope, limited to high levels of generality.

SYSTEMIC INSTABILITY

Comparisons between British and American electoral behavior are made unusually difficult by the impact of recent unsettling events on the British and American political scenes. Internal population migration has shifted old patterns. Millions of Americans have redistributed voting strength by moving from the South to the North and West and from all parts of the United States to the West Coast and Southwest. Also, political assassinations, civil unrest, racial tensions, riots, societal restructuring, technological changes, and recent atypical presidential candidacies have tended to realign American political forces, and the parties seem to have adapted poorly to their consequences. Higher rates of political independence and split-ticket voting and growing numbers of abstainers reflect the declining sense of party allegiance felt by millions of American voters. Symptomatic of the new situation is President Carter's 1976 election victory, which brought back into the Democratic fold 90 percent of the members who deserted McGovern for Nixon in 1972[43] and was based on a new coalition of electoral groups. But that new alignment did not hold together to reelect incumbent Carter in the 1980 election. Hence, conclusions about the electoral behavior of American voters may be too old to reflect recent and continuing transitions or too new to be reliably indicative of contemporary patterns.

The British political scene is also changing. Party conflict has intensified under the pressure of severe economic dislocations that have focused renewed emphasis on differences of party ideology and proposed solutions for societal problems. Class ties are weakening.

In the last decade voter behavior in both party systems has undergone striking shifts. Unpredictable departures from customary patterns of party support have increased as party regularity and solidarity have suffered attrition. Parties on both sides of the Atlantic have experienced what Samuel Beer, writing about British parties, has referred to as "party decomposition."[44] Beer identifies several symptoms of the decomposition, including a sharp decline in constituency party memberships, a reduction of class-based party support in favor of noticeably heightened tendencies toward voter individualism (especially among Labor party supporters), increased numbers of voters who identify with no party, a weakening of traditional middle-class support for the Conservative party, falling participation rates in national elections, a marked increase in voter volatility, and a willingness of voters to shift support from one party to another over a short span of time.[45]

GENERAL POINTS OF COMPARISON

In spite of the uncertainties confronting the venture, an attempt will be made here to draw some comparisons between selected features of American and British voting behavior. Some general points of comparison will make clearer the framework of voter behavior patterns.

In both systems, party identification is a more important and enduring determinant of voting than are such factors as age, sex, and education. Although perceptions of class status are not widely or clearly held by American voters, class is the determinant of British electoral behavior that is felt to be most reliably and persistently significant. But, since British class membership tends to be defined by occupation, and because both British and American voters tend to align behind party labels according to occupational category, differences of class consciousness between the two electorates provides only an apparent basis for contrast.

It is probable that many voters in both systems associate parties with images, so that, pro or con, the American Republican party is seen as the party of big business and the British Labor party is the party of the working class. Of course, such stereotypes are inaccurate but are nevertheless widely held among the respective voters. Issues are less often the basis of party identification and attachment than are emotionally charged perceptions of party image grounded in family attachments and prejudices as well as in issue orientations viewed against differing voter perceptions of society.

Neither British nor American voters act primarily from knowledge of candidates, parties, and issues. The average American voter knows virtually nothing about the qualifications of candidates, their issue stances, or the issues, per se. Voters in both systems commonly align with parties and cast their votes according to perceived self-interest, and in Britain, a change of party allegiance, even when done for scarcely disguised economic reasons, evokes little censure. Neither the British nor American electorate exhibits much variation in party allegiance from one election to another. In Britain since 1950, the average vote shift between parties in general elections has been only 2.5 percent of the poll,[46] but major shifts of votes do come about in both systems when numerous voters permanently realign their party preferences, as black voters seem to have done recently in America. The emergence of the Labor party as a major party in Britain and the decline of the Liberal party to minor party status reflected massive shifts of political allegiances that occurred when nonconformist voters abandoned the Liberals after the fight for religious toleration was won, when the electoral appeal of the Laborites became known; candidates then drew support more from class interest and less from religious beliefs.[47] Nevertheless, party identification remains one of the most stable grounds of voting behavior for most members of both electorates.

In both the British and American party systems and electorates, party membership and loyal support of party label serve voters as substitutes for information and as cues for legitimate political behavior. The character of British parties enables the British voter to rely on party label with greater assurance than Americans probably feel in that it will afford him a reliable candidate-issue orientation. American party labels are little more than political compass needles pointing toward possible future policy stances on specific issues. American parties play the role of reference points for voter identification and aggregation more than for enforcing political accountability and control of national decision makers.

British voters, probably more than American voters, believe confidently and understandingly that their party system is the means for choosing a government that will transform partisan issue orientations into appropriate policies. They believe in the efficacy of political accountability implemented through party control, and they confidently expect that a change of party government will be followed by a meaningful reorientation of policy. But like American voters, British voters are more divided among themselves on policy issues within their parties than they are by the main party division.

POLITICAL INVOLVEMENT

British and American voters are not highly motivated politically. It was formerly thought that, in contrast to the uninformed, generally distinterested American voter, British voters were induced by the unpredictable occurrence of general elections to maintain a high level of political alertness and of information about national issues. The British voters' presumed accentuated partisan involvement was contrasted to the Americans' alleged apathy. More re

ent research indicates, however, that systemic party and governmental differences of the two countries do not affect the levels of
partisan awareness and political involvement of their respective
electorates. Political awareness is at only a moderate level in
Britain.[48] Despite the fact that they are skeptical of campaign
propaganda and generally lack interest in national politics, there
is a strong cultural pressure in British voters to vote in national
elections[49] but almost none in the United States. Brennan suggests that the high turnout in national elections is attributable to
an accompanying atmosphere of heightened expectation and
competition, like that of the national test matches, that stimulates
an impulse to participate.[50] They are not well informed on policy
issues, and, like American voters, they participate on the policy
level to influence the general outcome only. Political activity is no
more central to the life of a British voter than it is to that of an
American. Both political parties have definite identities in the
minds of many voters, due at least in part to the average citizen's
lack of involvement in the affairs of government.[51]

Voters of both electorates participate in national elections in
reasonable numbers, but participation rates fall off sharply as elections become more local (congressional) or off-calendar (British
by-elections). Participation of voters in by-elections has never
exceeded 50 percent of the total electorate,[52] and in American
congressional off-year elections between 1954 and 1974, participation averaged 42.7 percent. Shallow issue orientations and preoccupation with private affairs are inadequate bases on which to
build interest in partisan politics into a central feature of individual
lives.

Nor do British voters engage in more political activity than
Americans do; only a very small percentage of either group does
more than vote. Only a small number of persons in either electorate are political actives, and the electorates' paucity of knowledge about governmental forms, processes, and issues parallels
their lack of involvement.[53] But, the incidence of party irregu-
larity in local elections is higher among Americans than it is among
British voters. Butler and Stokes report that British voters are
little concerned with local politics, and, when they vote in local

elections, they adhere to their party allegiances to an overwhelmin
degree,[54] whereas ticket-splitting and other evidence of wea
party loyalty are features of American voting behavior.

PARTY IMAGES

Neither American nor British voters see the political parties c
their country as ideologized and rigid. All, in fact, are characte.
ized by notable degrees of pragmatic flexibility. Voters in the re
spective systems perceive parties as presenting noticeably differer
policy orientations. Although party label probably figures mor
prominently in British than in American mass voter behavior,
voter's candidate perception and issue orientation may nevertheles
influence what a British voter does. That possibility is especial
real when, as in recent national elections, policy matters hav
tended to be overshadowed by party personality or obscured t
overgeneralization. Moreover, Blondel asserts that for much of th
time issue orientations are not determinants of voting behavior fe
many supporters of either major British party.[55] Albeit cand
date perception and irrational bases of party support operate a
strong influences on some British voting (as well as on America
voting behavior), most British voters adhere on principle to the
chosen party. It is the American voter who is most apt to vote a
cording to his favorable perception of a candidate and perm
candidate image to dominate or distort his perception of the cand
date's or party's policy stand. His candidate orientation can als
be strong enough to override disagreements on policy questions b
tween himself and an opposition party candidate whose image l
likes. Despite major differences of issue orientation, millions
Republicans deserted the ultraconservative Goldwater to suppo
the very liberal Democrat Lyndon Johnson in 1964; similarl
large numbers of Democrats, scared away from McGovern by h
image of runaway liberalism, voted for Nixon in 1972.

VOTER INDEPENDENCE

The outcomes of national elections in the United States ar
Britain are made uncertain by unpredictable voting behavior. Th
is a manifestation of voter independence. What constitutes ind
pendence is difficult to define. In many voters it is a reflection

rtisan noncommitment varying in degree from participation and
olitical activity apart from party identification to total alienation
om and nonparticipation in the system. In between are degrees
  party attachment and support representing such factors as
sillusionment, transitional party orientations, and incomplete
rty commitments. In the United States, an increasing proportion
' the electorate—approximately 35 percent—acknowledge no
rty tie, although many persons think of themselves as "inde-
ndent" Republicans or Democrats. Independent voters tend to
 under thirty years of age and college educated and to possess
gh incomes and socio-economic status, but they increasingly are
und on all rungs of the socio-economic ladder. Because national
ections in the United States and Britain are frequently deter-
ined by small margins of the total popular vote, the shifting vote
ay be the most important factor in the balance of contending
rty fortunes. The floating voters and those of weak party com-
itment who may be induced to join them in any election bring
out many shifts of power from one party to another. All major
rties go after the volatile vote and struggle to control it. To the
tent they are successful, systemic stability is enhanced; to the ex-
nt they are not, American presidential elections may produce
urality or minority presidents or even be thrown into the House
' Representatives for decision according to constitutional pro-
dures. On their side, British governments may have to operate
ith reduced margins of strength in the Commons or, as with the
re-1979 Labor government under Prime Minister Callaghan, de-
nd upon a coalition of support to stay in office.

British political language does not know the independent voter.
he narrow margins of electoral victory given British parties, vary-
g from 0.8 percent in 1951 to 6.0 percent in 1966,[56] are at-
ibutable to floating voters who move their support among the
abor, Conservative, and Liberal candidates from one election to
other. But the British floating vote is by no means as large a
ortion of the total electorate as is the American independent vote.
londel reports that 85 percent of the voting electorate has re-
ained true to its party attachments since 1950.[57] The British
ating vote, like the American independent Republican and
emocratic vote, exhibits weak party allegiance and often includes

among its numbers the least informed and least knowledgeab
members of the electorate. But Gallup reported in 1966 that on
3 percent of British voters consider themselves to be independe
of party attachment as that term is used in the American politic
vocabulary.[58]

SPLIT-TICKET VOTING

Split-ticket voting is a phenomenon of American voting b
havior that is unknown to British general elections. The growi
practice of American voters to support the presidential candida
of one party and one or more congressional candidates of the oth
has steadily increased in our national elections. But British vote
are presented with only one choice in a general election, so th
while they may shift candidate support or even realign party a
legiance, they cannot divide their votes between parties. Henc
a prime minister never has to contend, as American (especial
Republican) presidents sometimes do, with a legislature controll
in whole or in part by the opposition party because his supporte
failed to vote for the legislative candidates of his party. That fa
befell presidents Eisenhower (except for the 1953-1955 years
Nixon, Ford, and now Reagan, despite their party's efforts to secu
a contrary result. In that way, split-ticket voting may exascerba
legislative-executive friction generated by the separation of powe
and further complicate policy formulation, legitimation, and ir
plementation. It also works to loosen further the partisan attac
ments of the American voters and may contribute to the rise
numbers of independents.

Some evidence suggests that even though split-ticket voting
prevalent among them, the party identification of American vote
is more enduring than that of the British and is more able to a
sorb deviations from party regularity without precipitating chang
of party allegiance, perhaps because the Americans' party identi
cation is looser than is the British. Butler and Stokes conjectu
that the reason lies in the fact that American voters must exerci
electoral options among candidates for a variety of positions ran
ing across several levels of government. The American voter
thereby presented with numerous options he can take in diver
circumstances without incurring a feeling of party disloyalty. T

British voter, on the other hand, opts for a single candidate in a general election. When he deserts his party's candidate his action will probably result from a sense of serious dissatisfaction with his former allegiance and will register directly upon him without any chance that partial support of the ticket, as in America, can assuage his conscience for his partial deviation. Hence, the dissatisfaction that causes him to desert his party's candidate may also be sufficiently aggravated to change his party alignment.[59] American voters in presidential elections who abandon their party's candidate usually do not permanently shift party loyalty. Most will return to the fold four years later.

NONVOTING

American and British voting behavior share the phenomenon of the nonvoter. Both systems know the disinterested or alienated voter who never votes, the occasional voter who responds only to candidates or issues of particular elections and votes randomly and infrequently, and the excluded voter who, for example, is unregistered, ill, or away from his voting place on election day. In the United States, voter turnout in presidential elections from 1956 through 1976 has averaged only 60.1 percent. In 1972, an estimated thirty-three million Americans of voting age failed to register; approximately twelve million who were registered failed to go to the polls in that year, so that a total of forty-five million potential voters failed to exercise their franchise.

Participation rates in American presidential elections compare somewhat unfavorably with those of British national elections. The figures in Table 4-1 show that American rates have consistently lagged by significant margins behind the British. They show that the average participation rates were 59.5 percent for the American electorate and 78 percent for the British, so that the nonvoting rate in American presidential races was 40.5 percent while that in Britain for approximately the same period was less than 30 percent.

Out of the total picture other features emerge. Omitting those voters who were prevented from voting by the intervention of insurmountable obstacles, voluntary nonvoters in both countries exhibit similar group characteristics. Highest nonvoting rates are

Table 4-1

Percent of Voting-Age Population Participating in National Elections

American		British	
1980	52.3	1979	76.0
1976	53.8	1974	78.7
1972	55.7	1970	72.0
1968	60.9	1966	75.8
1964	61.8	1964	77.1
1960	62.8	1959	78.7
1956	59.3	1955	76.8
1952	61.6	1951	82.6
		1950	83.9

American data were derived from *Statistical Abstract of the United States, 1974* (Washington, D.C.: Government Printing Office, 1975), p. 437; G. Pomper, *The Election of 1976,* p. 172; *Facts on File,* Vol. 40, p. 838 (Nov. 7, 1980).

British data came from R. M. Scammon, "The Election and the Future of British Electoral Reform," in H. R. Penniman, *Britain at the Polls,* p. 164, and British Broadcasting Corporation's News Information Service.

found among young (eighteen to twenty-one) and elderly (over sixty-five) voters, women, low-middle and working classes, poor, and less well-educated electors. The consequences of nonvoting, fluid party support, and voter rejection of party control add to the problem of declining party strength in American and British party systems. Unreliable voters in both contribute to the inability of parties to control electoral outcomes and compel parties to cultivate apathetic and uncertain voters, especially when so many results are determined by narrow margins of the votes cast. Those conditions force some measure of compromise on issue intensity, blur and soften ideological and programmatic differences between parties, and foster moderation and responsibility.

INFLUENCE OF PERSONAL AND SOCIAL FACTORS

Patterns of political behavior in both electorates coincide with such personal characteristics of voters as age and sex and with social considerations such as occupation, status, religion, and education. The pattern and impact of these factors on the American voter agree more than they disagree with their influence and effect in British electoral behavior, but these comparisons are very general and are therefore bound to incorporate inaccuracies and distortions of a complex subject. Recourse to the abundant studies of American and British voter behavior will enable the interested student to acquire more detailed knowledge and understanding. A brief look at each of several influences follows.

Age

The younger American voter, like his British counterpart, tends to be more liberally oriented than are older categories of electors. In the respective systems they support the Democratic and Labor parties. Candidate orientation appears to be more influential than party allegiance among younger voters. Voting stability is less among younger voters, but, as age increases, the electorates tend to become more conservative and stable in party choice and to vote with less volatility. Blondel reports that every voter age group in Britain favors the Labor party, but a 15 percent margin of support among young voters narrows to a mere 3 percent among those over sixty-five.[60] The elderly, however, seemingly vote according to their perception of how the parties view the issue of pensions, disregarding virtually all other issues. Their vote is volatile, shifting from one party to the other, normally giving only a small margin of preference to the party of the moment.[61] Between 1952 and 1976, younger American voters deserted the Democratic presidential candidate only twice, to vote for Eisenhower in 1956 and Nixon in 1972, while the over-fifty voters left only Republicans Goldwater in 1964 and Ford in 1976.

Sex

A British Gallup poll study has shown that women voters in Britain tend to vote less than male voters do and to be more con-

servatively oriented than the men. They are more likely to suppo
Conservative party candidates, whereas male voters show a consi
tent preference for the Labor party.[62] Data indicate that in t
elections from 1945 through October 1974, except for the Febr
ary 1974 contest when the male vote divided almost evenly b
tween the major parties, men favored Labor Candidates. Exce
for the elections of 1951 and 1966 women voters favored Co
servatives, but the margins of preference by both groups we
minor.[63] The Gallup study concludes that age and sex of Briti
voters are worth little as reliable indicators of voting behavior b
cause the thin margins of support ostensibly attributable to tho
factors can be explained equally well by other influences. Milbra
and Goel report that politicization levels in both electorates a
high, and that in both, men show higher levels than women and a
more likely to be psychologically attuned to operating in a politic
environment than are women.[64] American women voters also vo
less than men and tend toward conservatism. They have given su
stantial margins (16–24 percent) to Republican presidential cand
dates Eisenhower (1952 and 1956) and Nixon (1972). They pr
ferred Nixon to Kennedy (1960) and Ford to Carter (1976)
2 and 3 percent respectively, but in 1965 they turned away fro
the Republican Goldwater and his image of "shoot from the hi
reaction, and in 1968 they preferred Humphrey to Nixon by
percent of their votes. American male voters differed from fema
voters in 1960 by supporting Kennedy; in 1968, when th
counterbalanced the female vote by giving a 2 percent edge
Nixon; and in 1976, when Carter was their choice over For
Nevertheless, as with the British voters, sex does not seem to
a clear determinant of voter preference or behavior in the Amer
can electorate.

Education

Certain correlations between education and voting behavior a
discernible in the voting patterns of British and American ele
torates. Nonvoting, for example, is highest among the least ed
cated elements of the electorates and declines as educational a
tainment grows. Educational levels, more than any other vot
characteristic, correlate to differences in voter participation in t

Jnited States and Britain. Less educated American voters are iumerous among political apathetics as well as nonvoters. In presilential elections from 1952 to 1976, only one deviation can be ound (1964) in a pattern of voting behavior that consistently saw ollege graduates support Republican candidates by margins of ireference that exceeded in every instance the percentages of naional votes received by the respective candidates. The same condiions prevailed in the allocation of support by voters with gradechool educations, who preferred Democratic candidates except n 1972, when large numbers abandoned McGovern for Nixon. But in every instance of Democratic fidelity, their margin of supiort exceeded the percentages of national votes that went to their :andidates. Other evidence of the correlation between education und voting behavior can be found in the fact that in 1968 and 1972, 75 percent of the voters having four or more years of colege voted in both elections, and only 6 percent of the same group voted in neither. Only 30 percent of those voters who had fewer han four years of college voted in both, and 45 percent participated in neither. Higher percentages of voters with advanced :ducation vote; however, increased levels of education in the United States have not produced corresponding growth in the rates of national voting. Nevertheless, education seems to be one of the nost important stimulants of voter participation, perhaps because political activism increases as political information becomes more accessible and understandable—results reasonably associated with the benefits of education.

In Britain, it is difficult to distinguish the influence of education on voting behavior because education, along with occupation and income, is a principal determinant of class, and class is probably the most important factor that can be correlated to political attitudes and voting behavior. Educational attainment is still a potent conditioner of an individual's prospects in life—his future income level and the type of occupation open to him. Moreover, his access to university preparatory education, and hence to university education, for entry into professional, executive, high administrative, and managerial positions in the private sector and for high elective and nonelective government positions, remains significantly correlated in practice to the social status of one's parents. Richard

Rose has suggested that the educational system socializes pupils into expectations of political roles and social achievement appropriate to their class status. Children of upper-class families overwhelmingly attend grammar and public schools, and the latter, especially, teach them to anticipate a life of success and of public activity. Children of lower-class families are far more likely to attend secondary modern or comprehensive schools, where they will be socialized to expectations of lower social achievement, commonplace occupations, and political inactivity. The influence of education on party affiliation, political activity, and voting behavior is inseparable from the influence of class.[65]

Social class

The sense of social class is much more deeply set in British political culture than it is in American, where no strong consciousness or tradition of class exists. American egalitarianism decries the notion of class, and, although many Americans identify in a superficial way with a "working" or a "middle" class, neither a subjective nor an objective class identification is translated into party allegiance or voting behavior.

Studies of British electoral behavior indicate that there is a direct correlation between objectively determined class status of voters and party support, although that correlation is not equally strong for all social categories.[66] The British voter exhibits a greater and more stable degree of party support by class than American voters do by occupation and income.[67] A steady relationship has existed between social class and voting behavior in every general election from 1945 through October 1974.[68] Class is generally accepted as the most reliable indicator of voting behavior in Britain.

The influence of British class on voting behavior is most pronounced among members of the upper and middle classes, who give consistently strong support to the Conservative party but comprise only a small part of the total electorate (15 percent). Lower middle-class support (22 percent) also goes by safe margins of 35 to 45 percent to Conservative over Labor candidates, but working-class and poor voters (63 percent of the electorate) favor Labor by margins of from 10 to 28 percent. There are deviations from these patterns of party identification and allegiance, however. Labor has been successful in attracting support from middle-class professionals, who now provide most of its constituency leaders and candidates. Moreover, the Conservative party's survival is dependent upon the support of "working-class Tories," approximately 30 percent of the union members' vote[69] that amounts to 50 percent of the Conservatives' total poll. At the leadership levels the class differences between Labor and Conservatives are disappearing, according to Butler and Stokes.[70] Traditional grounds of party identification are continually being supplemented by new and more complex ones, so that class, while still dominant, is tending to become but one among a large number of factors, more like the situation typifying voter-party alignment in America, where class has never exerted the influence it has in Britain.

The class basis of British politics varies with class and party. Party loyalty to the Conservatives is more steadfast among middle-class voters than Labor's is among working-class and poor voters. But, because there are almost twice as many working-class and poor voters as there are voters in the middle classes, Labor derives 75 percent from its larger base of support whereas the Conservatives receive 50 percent of their vote from a much smaller middle class.[71] D. Kavanagh suggests that working-class Tory support of Conservatives is more due to the socializing influence of parents than it is to programmatic commitment.[72] The remainder of Conservative party support comes from the upper class, which is too small (1 percent of the electorate) to be politically significant, and from the workers. Were it not for the working-class Tories the Conservative party would be hopelessly outvoted and in a permanent minority position. The ability of the Conservatives to draw support from all portions of the socio-economic spectrum prevents that from happening. Labor, on the other hand, is clearly the party of the working class but is unable to hold their solid allegiance, which it must share with the conservatives.[73]

Although consciousness of class does not lie in the forefront of most Americans' awareness, party allegiance and voting behavior also reflect the influences of socio-economic factors that in British society are associated with class membership. Such factors as income, occupation, and education are thought of as determinants of social class, but, for Americans, the chief of them is perhaps income, although all are closely related.

Political stratification in American society has neither the importance nor the permanence it has in British politics. The leveling of extremes of income, education, and status among many groups of Americans has done much to blur the lines and diminish their political significance. Except for the votes of ethnic groups that remain cohesively in support of Democratic candidates, neither of the major American political parties can count on near-monopoly support from any cohort of voters. Nevertheless, the 1976 presidential vote divided according to social class,[74] the most clearly operative determination being income level. The bulk of Carter's strength came from lower-income voters, and, as income increased, his strength directly declined. Since the days of the New Deal, the Democratic candidates have received heavy support from the least economically well-off portions of the electorate. The Carter victory brought back into the Democratic column margins of strong support from low-income, blue-collar, manual workers who had deserted McGovern in 1972. He also recaptured and built up Democratic support from professional, business, and white-collar voters to exceed 1968 levels received by Humphrey. The 1976 results therefore suggest that lines of socio-economic differences between Republican and Democratic support may have been reestablished, but they also indicate that Democratic inroads into the higher status vote may signify a blurring of heretofore sharp socio-economic influences on American voter behavior. The result may be an outcome of the facts that large segments of American society are upwardly mobile and that income levels continue to rise, as does educational achievement, so that parties in America must endeavor to win the support of an electorate that is increasingly middle class, comfortable, informed, educated, and affluent. But, such voters are inclined to be more independent than their forebears, less tied to old party loyalties, and less seriously disadvantaged by fluctuations in national economic well-being. Moreover, American parties are almost totally devoid of ideological commitments that can be transformed into bases of class support, and American voters are pluralistically organized and cross-pressured that traditional patterns of group-party allegiance survive only as pale reflections of socio-economic status. Any tendency that might be felt in American party circles to make class-based electoral appeals will most certainly be opposed by the practical necessity to attract votes from all quarters. All that can be safely said, therefore, is that high-income, educated professional and business voters are more likely to support the Republican than the Democratic party and that they will probably be joined by considerable numbers of white-collar workers and farmers and much smaller numbers of blue-collar voters. On the other side, the ranks of Democratic supporters include millionaires; increasing numbers of business and professional, higher income and college educated voters; and a growing proportion of strength from farmers and rural voters. But, the bulk of the party's votes comes from white-collar, lower income, and less well-educated manual and unskilled workers. Nevertheless, substantial portions of any reference group may behave unpredictably in a particular presidential election, and none is held to party allegiance by a sense of class membership comparable to the strength of that identification existing among British voters.

Religion

Although religion has markedly influenced voting behavior in earlier days in Britain and the United States, its contemporary effect is benign but discernible. Its influence today is largely overshadowed by socio-economic factors associated with income and occupation. Thus, in Britain, upper-class, upper-middle-class, and middle-class voters are most likely to be Conservatives and Church of England worshippers, but the working-class Tory vote might be more likely to come from Catholics, nonconformists, or Anglicans. In fact, more Anglican and Church of Scotland worshippers, along with most nonconformists and Catholics, vote Labor than vote Conservative. In Wales and Northern Ireland, religion plays a more prominent role in determining voter behavior than it does in other parts of Britain,[75] but Catholic and nonconformist Conservatives are found throughout the electorate. But, religion is so inter-mixed with class and occupation that to separate its effect on vot-

ing from theirs is virtually impossible. The links between party ar
religion in the modern British electorate are clearly vestiges of pa
relationships.[76]

In the United States religion in presidential elections has unt
recently been a force to contend with. Anti-Catholic sentime
defeated Al Smith in 1928 and thereafter prevented the nomina
tion of Catholic candidates until John F. Kennedy in 1960 wa
able to break the barrier of organized Protestant resistance. Neve
theless, while Kennedy attracted 78 percent of the Catholic vot
(which Democratic candidates normally receive), his religion co
many lost Protestant and independent votes. Protestant voter
apart from anti-Catholic sentiment, have shown a distinct prefe
ence for the Republican party in presidential elections from 195
to 1976. Carter received 46 percent of the protestant vote, an i
crease of 16 percent over McGovern's share in 1972, but the trad
tionally Democratic Catholic vote gave the fundamentalist South
ern Baptist only a disappointing 55 percent. In sum, it is probab
not possible to demonstrate that religion plays a more decisive rol
in American presidential politics than it does in British nationa
elections, but religion in American electoral politics seems to b
a more primary influence that produces clearly isolable impact
than it is in Britain.

Ethnicity

Polls and voting behavior studies in the United States have lon
substantiated the importance of ethnicity as a determinant of vot
ing behavior. Concentrations of voters in American cities havin
Slavic, Polish, Italian, Irish, Jewish, or other ethnic background
have influenced local campaign tactics, nominations of candidate
and other party decisions. Nationally, ethnic blocs have generall
favored the Democratic party, but Nixon received substantial sup
port from ethnic voters in 1972 when they joined most othe
groups in abandoning McGovern.

Two ethnic blocs are particularly important to the Democrats
The Jewish vote has regularly rallied strongly to the support of it
candidates and gave even the Catholic Kennedy 80 percent of i
ballots. It held to McGovern, giving him 63 percent, and increase
its support of Carter to 68 percent. The second major bloc is th

black vote. Since the days of the New Deal, it has formed cohesively behind Democratic presidential candidates, giving them
in the 1952–1976 elections an average level of 79.8 percent support. They joined the Jewish bloc and gave McGovern 87 percent
of their votes. Black voters now seem to have turned their backs
on the Republican party of Abraham Lincoln and to have become
attached to the national Democratic party without regard to socio-
economic differences within their population. The black vote was
so important to Carter's victory that Pomper concluded it is unlikely Carter would have carried any region of the nation without
it.[77]

In Britain, ethnicity appears to be absent from the list of forces
that influence electoral behavior, unless recent heightened mani-
festations of Welsh, Scottish, and Irish nationalism be counted as
demands for recognition of ethnic identity. The homogeneity of the
British peoples has not heretofore been fractured by the presence
of politically significant ethnic differences (apart from the nationalist question), until the arrival of large numbers of Commonwealth immigrants after World War II and before 1962, when im-
position of restrictions began. But ethnicity has not thus far
emerged as a force producing bloc voting. The immigrants have
settled in the poorer sections of large cities. They have not been
welcome or assimilated; they are competitors for jobs; they are different in appearance, language, religions, cultures, and allegiances
from indigenous Britains. Working-class voters view them with
suspicion and hostility. Black portions of the new arrivals are
particularly regarded by traditional white elements as outside the
established political community. They do not share its heritage or
understand its institutions. In general, the immigrants are perceived as retaining primary allegiance to their countries of origin,
whereas the British citizenry have not divided their loyalty for
many generations.[78]

Since their arrival, the presence of the immigrants has precipitated spirited debate over immigration policy and led to enactment
of the Commonwealth Immigration Act of 1962 with amendments
in 1968. Numerous ugly racial incidents have occurred, and racism
has entered politics and national consciousness to an unprece-
dented degree. Racial hostility has erupted as a continuing political

problem, and extremist racist parties have won heavily in local elections and gained almost 10 percent of the popular vote in some by-elections. Both major parties oppose racism, and although mass popular disturbances have not broken out, Parliament has been increasingly occupied with enacting antidiscrimination legislation. The British political culture has thus far not proven strong enough to preclude local racial conflict and racism, but it has, for the most part, structured it and confined it to culturally acceptable methods and arenas.[79]

CHAPTER FIVE

LEGISLATURES

Legislatures, or representative assemblies, have been typically looked upon as the sine qua non of democratic government. In most cases, they have been constitutionally delegated the general role of lawmaking, with the executive charged with carrying out the laws. In addition, many legislatures are entrusted with control over the executive actions and in some cases with the power to create and to dismiss the executive. The constitutional assignment of these functions to legislatures stemmed originally from a view of assemblies as the principal representative bodies in political systems. From time to time, the representative nature of the executive or of other political officials may be discussed, but it is primarily legislatures that are perceived to be representative of the population.

In the face of the growth of the powers and functions of the executive, especially in national public policy making, legislative bodies are often criticized for failing to carry out their lawmaking and executive-controlling roles. A closer look at the workings of the legislatures in Great Britain and the United States—both their strengths and their weaknesses—is necessary for a clear understanding of the functions that they can and do perform in their respective political systems.

THE LEGISLATIVE FUNCTIONS

There are important similarities between the British and the American legislative institutions and processes because both are based in fundamental liberal democratic political values that call for government to be limited and accountable as well as representative and responsive. However, major differences between the legislatures in the two countries are apparent. Many of the differences stem from the presence of party government in Britain and its absence in America. The British political parties shape the legislative proceedings, clearly dividing the members of the House of Commons into the two opposing forces of government and opposition. The parties also pattern the relationships between the cabinet and the House of Commons within the parliamentary setting.

In comparison, the political parties in the United States have less direct and continuous impact on the activities of the legislature. Although the internal organization of the Senate and the House of Representatives is patterned along party lines, parties do not structure the actual proceedings or the votes as tightly as is the case in Britain. Coalitions of support for and against policy measures often cross party lines, making a clear-cut and organized opposition of the British type an impossibility.

In addition to the contrasting natures of the party systems, another major factor which underlies differences in the legislative processes in the two countries is the distinction between the parliamentary and the presidential institutional framework. The presence of the cabinet within the legislature itself, the cabinet consisting of the leaders of the majority political party, and the accountability of the cabinet to the whole House of Commons create a legislative milieu far different from that found in the American Congress. The legislators in the United States are functionally separated from the executive. The American Constitution has placed these two branches of government in a relationship that is basically adversary. This obtains even when both the legislature and the executive are controlled by members of the same political party. As former Prime Minister Harold Wilson has observed, the major political confrontation in America is that between the legislative and executive parts of the constitutional system, whereas in Great Britain it is a confrontation between the major political parties in Parliament, a continuing competition between government and opposition, the "ins" and the "outs."[1]

Although there are also similarities in the functions performed by the legislatures in both Great Britain and the United States, the fundamental fact that the American legislature was established to be a policy-making and policy-initiating body, whereas the modern Parliament was never intended to be, makes it clear that there are basic differences between the functions performed by the two legislatures.

LAW MAKING

Statutory law is formally enacted by the British and American legislatures. In Britain, most public bills that are introduced into the legislature come from the cabinet. Once a government bill has been introduced into the House of Commons, its passage is virtually assured because the government's majority party in Commons will vote in favor of it so long as the party members retain confidence in the government. Because the government controls the amendment procedures and handles most of the actual drafting of important legislation, the cabinet bills are voted on promptly and passed in the basic form desired.

The legislative agenda and order of general business in Commons are arranged on the basis of regular consultation between the government and opposition, particularly with respect to the time allotted for debate on major policy issues. Since both government and opposition acknowledge the right of the government to govern so long as it maintains its majority of support, and the right of the opposition to criticize and to set forth its own alternatives in an effort to build its own electoral majority, the agreement about procedures and timing for debate is normally smoothly obtained. On matters that cannot be readily agreed upon, methods for limiting or curtailing debate are available. It is largely the prerogative of the impartial speaker of the House of Commons to apply the rules in order to curb obstruction tactics. In so doing, his major aim is to insure that the rights of the minority party are not abridged.

The main impact that the British legislators have on the general principles of the laws comes in the formative stages, before the full public commitment of the cabinet to the policy. The effect of the legislators generally is made by means of the consultations that take place between the majority party leaders and their parliamentary backbenchers, and from the pressure to take carefully into account the anticipated reactions from the opposition. With the rise of party unity and discipline, the chief lawmaking function of Parliament is that of informing the government about probable consequences of its policy proposals. Debate is rarely the prelude to decisions either to accept or to reject the cabinet bills, but is rather part of an ongoing process during which the House of Commons as a whole questions the government, scrutinizes its policies, and keeps it informed of probable reactions to its policies and programs.[2] Once the government is firmly and publicly committed to a bill, the legislature's role is largely confined to debate and question, leading to ultimate approval, with the possibility of slight amendment.

While Parliament has complete freedom to pass a law on any subject that it chooses, the American legislature does not have such liberty. The subjects on which it may legislate are regulated by provisions in the constitutional document. All other matters for legislation are reserved to the states.[3] Within this somewhat more restricted area, however, congressional members and committees take a more active initiative in policy making through legislation. Each of the houses of Congress controls its own legislative calendar. This contrasts with thesituation in Britain in which the cabinet determines what is to be done in Parliament. The president, unlike the prime minister, has no assurance that the bills he has introduced will pass or even be voted on. If his bills do survive in some form, they may come back to him for signature greatly altered. Although most of the public bills acted upon come from the executive branch, they cannot be introduced into the legislature directly by an executive official because none is a member of the legislature. The administration must persuade a like-minded legislator to introduce a bill, unless it is sent by means of an executive communication.[4] Harold Wilson has pointed out that whereas the prime minister has the constitutional capacity effectively to lead the Parliament, the president's lack of a similar leadership capacity means that he must manage Congress. In order to accomlish this management and to obtain legislative support for administrative measures, he must establish a liaison between the executive and the legislature and barter for support with patronage and favors, which the prime minister does not need to do.[5] In addition, bills may be originated and initiated directly by legislators, perhaps in defiance of presidential preference either for his own version or for no legislative action on a particular issue. This competition from the legislature does not occur in Britain.

The legislative obstruction tactics that are so familiar in the American Congress are absent in Parliament. Nothing approaching a Senate filibuster can occur, and committees never assume absolute jurisdiction over bills. In their comparative study of Congress and Parliament, Bradshaw and Pring suggest that while the legislature's role in lawmaking can be said to be creative and emergent in the United States, it is best described as processional and predictable in Great Britain. This is true because in the United States an inquiring approach to legislation is followed, and the nature of a bill will not be known until it has been shaped by the committee to which it has been referred. However, in Britain a debating approach to the policy substance in a bill is taken.[6]

In both countries under study, the last step in the passage of a piece of legislation is normally assent by a chief executive. But whereas the American president may elect to veto legislation, even though that veto may be overridden by a two-thirds affirmative vote in Congress, the approval by the British monarch that is required for all bills is only a formality and is automatically forthcoming. This is further evidence that there is no adversary relationship between legislature and executive in Britain, but there is an ongoing, constitutionally established confrontation between the two in America. This basic contrast is also present in the crucial area of financial control.

CONTROL OVER FINANCE

One of the historic means by which democratic legislatures control executives is through the power of the purse. Hence, formal control over public finance belongs to the legislatures in Britain and the United States, but in practice the financial measures approved by the treasury and the cabinet in Britain are almost certain

to be passed. When a budget proposal is presented by the treasury
it is debated at length in the House of Commons. However, al
though approximately one-third of the time in each parliamentar
session is devoted to financial matters, little changes as a result o
the debate and deliberation, and a majority of the legislators wi
cast favorable votes on the budget. All financial bills must b
introduced first into Commons, and only those recommended b
the cabinet may be considered. The hereditary, nonaccountabl
House of Lords may only delay passage of a financial measure fo
a period of one month. The constitution prohibits any increase i
the sum recommended by the cabinet, and political realities pre
vent the success of attempts at reduction by legislators. Thus th
"pork barrel" squandering of public funds which sometimes occur
in the United States Congress is precluded in Parliament. At th
end of the process, the treasury estimates are embodied in th
annual appropriations act.

Parliamentary procedures for handling taxation, or ways an
means, do provide for a somewhat greater degree of supervisior
Proposals for taxes come from the executive, and once they hav
been presented Commons immediately passes tax resolution
authorizing the government to collect the new taxes. The ensuin
debate that precedes passage of the full finance bill involves close
scrutiny than does debate on supply, and the power of Common
to amend the details of the taxation proposals is greater than it
ability to change supply proposals. However, even here, change
are limited to detail rather than general taxation policy. By con
trast, scrutiny over both taxation and appropriations is muc
closer in the American Congress, and the legislature in that coun
try can be truly said to hold the national purse strings. Congres
can, and often does, finally vote more or less money than th
amount the president requests. In addition, while committee advic
counter to government proposals in Great Britain is not followe
in Commons when the vote actually takes place, in the Unite
States, committee advice is normally followed by the full houses.

In contrast to the procedures in Britain, which forge links be
tween bills involving expenditures and those concerning appropria
tions, different committees handle the authorization procedures fo
each in America. Under the rules of the House of Representatives

no funds can be appropriated for a purpose not already authorized by legislation, and no authorization bill can appropriate funds. Thus, a conflict can arise between the legislative functions of approving policy and of authorizing funding to carry it out in the United States. In Britain such a conflict cannot occur because a bill involving expenditure must be covered by a money resolution which only the government can initiate.[7]

In both countries, the executive may carefully prepare a budget and submit it to the legislature, but, whereas in Britain the budget will be approved largely intact, in the United States the legislature is basically its own master in budgetary matters. Once the president's financial proposals have been set adrift on the legislative sea, they are at the mercy of the winds of congressional prejudice and the myriad special interests represented there. The result is that unpopular taxes may be cut, special expenditures demanded by pressure groups may be added, and appropriations for some executive departments may be reduced drastically.[8] By contrast, the strong party discipline in the British House of Commons virtually negates any parliamentary power to alter financial proposals once made by the government. This does not mean that the British executive is unchecked in financial matters; the checking and controlling in this area are accomplished at the formulation stage, largely through the intraparty processes of compromise and the anticipation of attacks that the opposition will mount.

SURVEILLANCE OF THE EXECUTIVE

At the heart of the parliamentary system of government is the surveillance of the executive by the legislature inherent in its functions of supplying, sustaining, or defeating the cabinet. The resignation of the cabinet or dissolution of the legislature which normally follows a negative parliamentary vote on a major policy measure has already been discussed. Because of the tight party discipline and the support in the population for responsible party government, when a political party holds a majority of the seats in the lower house of the legislature, affirmative votes on major cabinet policy proposals are normally assured. Yet, the fact that majority party backbenchers do hold the threat of a negative vote or of abstention acts as a form of prior restraint on the cabinet as it formulates its policy, programs, and actions. At the same time, however, the backbenchers are restrained from using their power lest they topple their own party from office. The contrast of this role of Parliament in maintaining the executive in office with the inability of the American Congress to remove the popularly elected president from office except by impeachment processes has led former Prime Minister Wilson to observe that the prime minister lives far more dangerously than the president. However, although the prime minister can be ousted from office abruptly if he loses control of Parliament, he has great assurance that while parliamentary confidence persists, he can get most of his legislation carried through. By contrast, the president, who is virtually secure from all possible removal, may be continually frustrated by his inability to get his legislation through a hostile Congress.[9]

In addition to its constitutional functions of supplying, sustaining, or defeating the executive, the House of Commons also performs the important functions of directly criticizing the government and questioning the individual ministers. The role of the opposition party is crucial in these functions. The House of Commons extracts the information about government plans and actions necessary to evaluate and criticize the executive. Special times each week are set aside for question periods when members of Commons, especially those in the opposition party, put questions to ministers. Questions may be put to the prime minister directly twice a week. Unlike the case with some American presidents in their press conferences, follow-up questions are usually permitted during question period after a minister's answer in order to prevent skirting the subject at issue. A drawback to the effectiveness of the question period as a useful critical tool is the relatively short amount of time allotted for it.

Question period is preeminently a testing time for a minister; he must know thoroughly the background information on the question put to him. If he makes a good showing at question period, he gains the respect of the House, but if he does not he loses much of it. He can refuse to answer questions, but rarely does so because this is construed as a weakness in his ability. The cut and thrust of the supplementary questions and answers give the question period its dramatic quality and often great news value. Press coverage puts the ministers in the limelight as they are subjected to a barrage of questions and thus helps prevent high-handed action or maladministration in the various departments.[10] There is no question time in the United States, but some of the same role is filled by the appearances of administrators before congressional committees for interrogation.

The congressional committees in America do not have across-the-board, regular interrogation functions, but it is in the standing committees and select committees that members of the executive branch are most often questioned. The president does not undergo legislative interrogation similar to the prime minister's biweekly appearance at question period because of the coequal constitutional status of the two branches of government in the American separation of powers framework. The surveillance function takes place more indirectly, through the procedures for receiving testimony from members of the executive branch in committee and the general congressional oversight functions.

Congress' power of the purse gives it a monitoring function. Hearings and investigations conducted in order to monitor spending serve a broader function of directing attention to specific policy issues. Congressional investigations, and especially the threat or mere possibility of one, undertaken to obtain detailed information to enable Congress to take action in particular areas, are constantly in the forefront of administrative planning and serve to check or supervise administrative action. In addition, congressional involvement in both staffing and structuring parts of the executive branch gives the legislature influence over the operation of that branch.

In addition to these procedures, which give the American legislature opportunities to scrutinize executive action, presidential press conferences are often cited as the closest counterpart to the parliamentary questioning of the cabinet. What makes the press conference different, however, is the control that the president can exercise over it—control of timing, of responses to questions, and of permission for follow-up interrogation. The prime minister and other cabinet ministers are less able to control the questions put to them in Parliament. Perhaps the most important difference between the question period and the presidential press conference is that the former takes place within Parliament whereas the latter does not involve the legislature at all. Thus, the press conference does not involve one group of elected and politically responsible officials calling another to account; rather, it is a media event.

The British question period is the most publicly noticed and closely followed procedure for calling the British executive to account, but other opportunities for criticizing the government abound. The debate on adjournment is a half-hour period at the end of the parliamentary day during which a member may raise a point on which he was not satisfied during the earlier questioning. The debate on the policies and programs of the government which are presented in the Queen's Speech at the opening session of a new Parliament may be lengthy, lasting perhaps five or six days. Twenty-nine days scattered throughout a parliamentary session are designated as "supply days." Debate on supply, led by the opposition, has come to be debate on policies and programs in general rather than on the particular financial measures before the legislature. This provides an opportunity for the opposition to scrutinize and criticize, as well as to publicize, departmental programs and policies, at the same time making public and defending its own alternative positions. The government in turn takes this occasion to explain and defend its proposals. Such debate will not normally change the outcome of the vote on the particular financial measure in question, but it does permit the public to evaluate the positions of both parties and to hold the government party accountable for its actions. Thus the debate affects the outcome of the next general election. Another, less frequent, procedure for criticism at the disposal of the opposition is the somewhat drastic motion of censure, debate on which gives the minority party an opportunity to criticize the government and affords the cabinet a chance to defend itself. The government always yields time to the opposition for a motion of censure, and the opposition, as previously noted, criticizes government policy continually in general debate.

Because the relationship between the executive and the legislature is so different in the United States and in Great Britain, the oversight function in each country has different purposes and takes divergent forms. The constitutional arrangements in Britain are rimarily designed to insure that Parliament and the government work along the same lines. By contrast, in the United States, the Constitution provides for useful coexistence of the executive and the legislature without accord between them. A major factor which makes the processes of scrutinizing and checking the executive in the United States different from those in Great Britain is the separation between the personnel in the legislative and executive branches of government and their independent, fixed terms of office. "Oversight" in Britain is designed to keep Parliament informed of what the ministers are doing, allowing scope to consider whether or not they should continue to be supported. Since the cabinet needs the confidence of Parliament, this oversight function provides Parliament with the opportunity to judge whether or not the cabinet is worthy of that confidence. Because the issue of confidence never arises in the United States, oversight has become an expression of the rivalry between the executive and the legislature, not rivalry between two political parties, as is the case in Britain. In comparison with the routinized, ongoing surveillance of the executive in the British House of Commons, the occasions on which a member of the executive branch in America is questioned in the legislature do not provide the same type of regularized, continuing scrutiny. The nature of the British political process makes Parliament the political information center of the country in a way that Congress is not.[11] Parliament cannot expect to defeat the policies and programs of the executive in light of the nature of British party government, but it does scrutinize and criticize them in a public forum, keeping the electorate informed and the cabinet attuned to changes in party opinion and in public opinion in general. Thus it serves as an important check on executive discretion. Because this checking is carried out by a body that is representative of the population, it is a vital part of achieving limited, accountable government.

REPRESENTATION OF CONSTITUENTS

Representing constituents in a legislative assembly is a key function to be performed in liberal-democratic political systems. The members of the British House of Commons and of the American House of Representatives and Senate are expected to perform this representative function. However, both the proper focus and the proper role for a representative is conceptualized differently in each of the two countries.

The focus of representation refers to the entity, or interest, which is to be represented. A basic distinction can be made between a national interest orientation and a local interest representation. Both the expectations and the actual reality of representation in Britain highlight the national interest as the unit represented. History and tradition combined with the development of the British party system to bring about this orientation. In late medieval times, the monarch was considered the representative of the whole community and Parliament the representative of the component parts. In line with the localism of parliamentary representation, an individual member of Parliament (MP) lived in his constituency, represented his constituents' interests, and was paid a salary by his constituency. By the end of the seventeenth century, however, the king had lost active representative function, and the MPs had become representatives of the whole community as well as of the component parts. No longer was an MP bound by instructions from his constituents, nor paid by them, but instead was expected to subordinate particular interests to the general interest of the whole. The concept of Parliament as the collective representative of the whole nation was linked to the supremacy of Parliament over the monarch.[12] With the rise and growth of the party system, the national orientation was furthered. Party government is possible only in circumstances in which the principal representative focus is on national interests. Hence, the shift of focus to national rather than local interests furthered the development of responsible political parties, and, in return, the nationally organized parties contributed to the disposition to take a national orientation toward political issues.

Today, the members of Parliament are not required to reside in the districts they represent, although they do maintain centers there. Their first responsibility is to their political party, and indeed the electorate votes more for the political party than for an individual representative. Hence, the British legislator can and does think primarily in terms of the national interest, as conceived by his political party, but also makes strong efforts on behalf of the particular needs of his district. On general policy goals, the broad public interest is the principal focus; more local and particular interests are largely seen as fulfilled by private members' bills and specific actions undertaken by the individual MPs for their constituency's benefit.

In the United States, a much less compact and homogeneous political unit than is Britain, the old concept of localism in representation took root and flourished. The president, similar to the Tudor kings, represents the interests of the national community as a whole, and the individual legislator's main loyalty is to the district.[13] Local residence requirements remain in effect. Consistent with the pervasive localism is the assumption that the American representative will have close ties to his home district and to its local interests. He is expected to carry these local interests to the national legislature and to bring them to bear on his issue positions and on his vote. Local pressures on individual congressmen are strong, and Congress is largely a patchwork of local interests, with a brokerage function performed to combine them on specific issues to reach decisions. Prewitt and Verba point out that although members of the House of Representatives are serving in national office, they are tightly tied to their local districts and to the mix of interests there, first because, in contrast to the British MPs, they are ordinarily longtime residents of the locality and have probably received their education in local educational institutions. Also, they have usually served in local and state-level political offices. Continuing in national legislative office in the United States also contributes to the closeness of the local ties; campaigns for reelection every two years in the home districts reinforce close contact with local interests and local party and campaign organizations.[14]

The American Congress is much more easily penetrated directly during the policy-making process by well-organized and well-funded interests from all levels than are the British institutions. The effect of party discipline and the collective character of cabinet responsibility in the British system minimize the pressures that might effectively be exerted on the individual members of Parliament by particular interests.[15]

In addition to the focus of the representative, the role he is expected to fill differs from Great Britain to the United States. A contrast exists between the representative role of trustee and that of free agent. The distinction refers to the extent to which a legislator is expected to register as accurately as he can the constituent opinion on policy issues or is free to arrive at his own position. Whereas, in the United States, representatives are generally expected to be responsive primarily to constituent opinion, the British MP is more free from particular constituent opinion, but is expected to follow closely his party's position. Carter quotes Samuel Beer to the effect that the emphasis in Britain is less on demanding responsiveness to constituency opinion than on deferring to the MPs judgment and then holding him responsible through the party vote in the next election.[16] The extent to which an MP has supported his party's position in Parliament is likely to be a major factor in the election decision. However, this role expectation does not completely eliminate any responsiveness to constituency opinion. The MP must be reelected by his constituents and continue to be selected as the candidate by the local party organization when there are many applicants to the local party for the seat he fills. He is also an important link between the constituency opinion and his party's leaders in Parliament. In the mix of roles to be filled, however, that of party agent predominates in the British concept of representation.

Despite the emphasis on adhering to the policy positions of the parties, British legislators shape those positions by bringing to bear on them their own and their constituents' opinions on political issues. The representatives, in addition to being party members, are individuals with varied backgrounds. The discussion now turns to an examination of the backgrounds of British legislators, especially with respect to their occupations and education, and a comparison with the backgrounds of representatives in the United States. This should shed some light on the legislative function of representing constituents, as it is performed in the two countries.

BACKGROUNDS OF THE LEGISLATORS

One concept of representation includes the belief that the legislators as a group are representative of the citizenry insofar as they mirror, in rough proportion to the whole population, key characteristics, such as age, sex, and social, economic, and ethnic backgrounds. According to this view, the degree of representativeness is correlated with the extent to which the representatives are similar to those whom they represent. As a yardstick for measuring representation, this correlation is somewhat problematic, particularly because it is not at all clear that the sharing of certain demographic characteristics is a factor relevant to either the degree to which a representative is able to bring the views of his constituents to bear on policy decisions or his ability to arrive at policy positions in the course of legislative debate and discussion.

In both Britain and the United States, legislators as a group are older than the average citizen of the country. Also, there are few women in the legislative houses in either country. In fact, when Margaret Thatcher became the first woman prime minister of Britain following the May 1979 general election, fewer women were sent to the House of Commons than had held seats there prior to that election.

Differences between the legislators in the two countries can be seen in their occupations and in their educational backgrounds.

OCCUPATIONS

Insofar as likeness between legislators and constituents may have some importance for the process of representation, the British House of Commons ranks higher than the American Congress in terms of occupational similarity between the members and their constituents. Although Parliament is not at all a mirror of the occupational breakdown of Great Britain, it contains members of a greater number of different occupational types than does the American Congress. The largest number of the Conservative party members of Parliament after the 1974 election were company directors and brokers. Barristers and solicitors, business officials, managers, and executives, journalists, and farmers follow in order of numbers in the ranks of Conservative party MPs. Thus the vast majority of Conservative MPs as of 1974 had middle-class or upper-class occupational backgrounds, although within those categories a variety of occupations is present.[17]

The Labor party originally introduced into the British legislature

MPs from working-class occupations. The number of actual working-class legislators has declined in recent years in favor of a growing percentage of educators, lawyers, and trade union officials, as well as businessmen and professionals. In the period 1951–1970, the general occupational backgrounds of Labor party members in Parliament underwent a change, while that of the Conservative party MPs remained relatively constant. In that period the number of Labor MPs from working-class occupations decreased by 7 percent, while the business or professional occupations directly represented increased by 10 percent.[18] The result of the 1974 election was a Labor party in Parliament of which only one-fifth of the members were connected to the Labor interest, either as workers, trade union officials, or officials of the political party.[19] Even with this change, the Labor party in Parliament remains a more heterogeneous group with respect to occupational backgrounds than is the Conservative party in Parliament, in which businessmen as a group predominate.

Jean Blondel has noted correlations between Labor party MPs' occupational backgrounds and their political attitudes. Labor party members who belong to the more established professions and who are also members of the middle class are more conservative on most issues than the rest of the MPs. They are unlikely to be strong partisans of nationalization and likely to be moderate on most social issues. But, members of the newer professions such as journalism and school teaching are often to the left of these members of the older professions. Finally, manual workers, forming the third important Labor MP group, are likely to be more concerned with the details of implementing social reforms. On the other hand, they are usually to the right of the members of the older professions on matters concerning foreign affairs and civil liberties. These differences do not derive from class conflicts, but from different political attitudes, and the attitudes are closely associated with occupational groups.[20]

Traditionally, British legislators have been viewed not as professional politicians, but as amateurs in politics, serving out of a sense of public duty. Members of the House of Commons have been encouraged to retain their outside interests and paying jobs. In re-

ent years the salaries for the MPs have been increased and are
udged sufficient for a sole income without need for outside supple-
nent. However, they are well below the salaries of American
epresentatives and senators.[21] There is a growing perception of
he need for full-time commitment to legislative duties on the part
of British MPs, but not to the extent that this has been true in the
United States. In addition, many MPs are members of special inerest groups such as the Socialist cooperatives or the British
Medical Association. This contrasts with the tendency in America
or congressmen to form links of interest with such groups, but not
o be members of the groups themselves. Recent legislation limits
harply the amount of outside income which an American con-
gressman may earn. At the same time, a large salary increase was
granted to senators and representatives. The combination of increased salary and limited outside income was largely the result of
attempts to lay the groundwork for a higher ethical standard to
guide the activities of the legislators. However, it also illustrates
he extent to which serving as a national legislator is seen as a full-
ime occupation.

Less than one-fifth of the British MPs are lawyers, but 57 per-
ent of American congressmen are members of that profession.
Congress contains few manual workers, trade union officials, or
armers. The difference between the two countries in the occupa-
ional backgrounds of representatives seems to stem in part from
he tendency for British parties to select members of a variety of
occupations to run for Parliament, while in the United States the
custom of linking lawyers with Congress and lawmaking has per-
isted.[22] This is consistent with the American perception of Congress as a policy-making body and the British view of Parliament
is a body to debate and to deliberate, but not to initiate policy.
Part of the difference also stems from the presence of sponsored
andidates in Britain, who are financially supported in their elec-
oral expenses by trade unions, and their absence from the Ameri-
an scene. Besides lawyers, businessmen and bankers form the
ext most numerous group in Congress, followed in numbers by
ducators.[23] Thus an upper-class and middle-class occupational
predominance exists in the American legislature, as well as in the

British, but it exists in America without the counterbalance of working-class occupations that still obtains in the House of Commons.

EDUCATION

Both Britain and the United States staff their legislatures with an educational elite. By far the greatest diversity of educational, as well as occupational, backgrounds is found in the representatives of the British Labor party. About one-fifth of the Labor MPs in the House of Commons in 1970 had not progressed beyond the elementary level of formal education. Of those who had attended a university, most had studied at one of the newer "Redbrick" universities, not at the most prestigious of the country's colleges in Oxford or Cambridge.[24] The changing pattern of the Labor party's representatives' educational backgrounds is worth noting. Between 1951 and 1970, the percentage of those with a university education rose from 41 percent to 59 percent. It appears that the educational background of the two parties' MPs is growing closer together. The Conservative MPs, however, continue to come largely from the more elite educational institutions. Most have had a public school education, and over half have attended other universities. In contrast to the 20 percent of the Labor MPs in 1970 who had only elementary level educaton, fewer than 1 percent of the Conservative party representatives had not studied beyond this level.[25]

In the United States there is a greater diversity within the educational backgrounds of the legislators from one perspective, but less from another. There is no American tradition of elite preparation for public office at schools comparable to the prestigious British public schools such as Eton and Harrow. Although the Ivy League colleges may provide a rough American equivalent to the "Oxbridge" tradition in England, a great diversity of educational backgrounds prepares American legislators. On the other hand, there is much less diversity in the level of formal education reached by American legislators than is the case in Britain. Nine out of every ten American legislators have attended a university. Since the great majority of American congressmen and senators are lawyers, law school attendance is obviously the norm. Yet, even in this category, greater variety of different law schools has prepared the Americans for their legislative service than is the case in Great Britain.[26]

ORGANIZATION OF THE LEGISLATURE

BICAMERALISM

Both the British and the American legislatures are formally bicameral, that is, composed of two houses. In Britain, the House of Commons is the lower house, to which 635 representatives are elected directly by popular vote from single-member districts. According to the constitutional statute, elections for Members of Parliament must be held at least once every five years. The terms of office are not fixed by law beyond this requirement, however. Elections may be called for prior to the five year limit, either because the majority party perceives it to be an opportune time to increase its amount of support in the legislature, or because the cabinet has lost its legislative support as a result of losing seats in by-elections or of party dissension and defection on key policy votes in Commons. This contrasts with the two legislative houses in the United States which have memberships elected for fixed terms of office.

Whereas the United States Senate has co-equal power with the lower house of the legislature, the upper house in Britain has almost no direct control over policymaking. The difference in status in the upper houses in the two countries stems from the diversity in the procedures for obtaining seats in each. The senators are elected to their seats by popular vote in the states, but the members of the House of Lords are not elected. This upper house is composed of about a thousand potential members, most of whom hold their seats on the basis of an inherited peerage. Other members of Lords include those who receive honorary appointments for life or belong to the body by virtue of their positions as law lords, hold the office of lord chancellor, or are officials of the Church of England. In an age of widespread liberal-democratic political values, such a body stands as a political anachronism. Since its members are not elected to office, they are neither responsive nor accountable to public opinion and organized interests. Thus, major government officials are not readily selected to their cabinet posts from the House of Lords but rather from the lower house, and the government is responsible only to the House of Commons. For these reasons Lords has lost most of its direct power over public policymaking. A procedure has consequently been developed to permit those who are Lords through inheritance to resign their peerages in order to seek positions of major political influence through membership in the House of Commons. Thus far, one such former lord has risen through the ranks of the House of Commons to become prime minister, Sir Alec Douglas-Home.

The undemocratic character of the Lords has been offset by making them politically impotent. The power of that body over policy has been reduced to delay power only. Bills that are passed by the House of Commons may be delayed by a veto in the House of Lords for a period of one year, if the measures are nonfinancial, and for one month if they deal with either supply or ways and means. The upper house may oppose, and thus delay for further deliberation, policies for which it appears that the government has no electoral mandate. For bills about which there is much controversy, the delay power which Lords can exercise may prevent hasty and ill-considered passage and may allow public opinion to crystallize and shed light on the issues involved.

The House of Lords does contribute directly to the British legislative process, even beyond this delay power. The body fills an important role in revising details, although not substance, in legislation already passed in the House of Commons, and in originating private bills and public bills of a more technical than politically significant nature. Thus it eases the massive burden of work before the lower house. In addition, Lords engages in debate of often very high calibre on financial legislation and on important policy topics for which time does not permit full discussion in the House of Commons. The life peers have brought an added depth of knowledge and experience to these debates in Lords. The other major contribution of the debate in the upper house lies in its ability to focus on topics and issues that are not before the House of Commons. Many of these debates deal with highly controversial subject areas, for example, abortion, capital punishment, and treatment of homosexuals. Lords, freed from the need to work for reelection and from the exigencies of strong political party cohesion, debates subjects such as these which the lower house rarely touches and may reach a level which partisan MPs cannot attain. Such debates inform the government and public opinion, and may sound out the public responses to such issues. It is largely because the House of Lords has such a high level of prestige and contains many well-educated persons with long public experience that its debates make contributions to the quality of British legislation.

Because both houses of the legislature in the United States have full decision-making power, bills must run successfully the committee and floor gamut in each before becoming law. In addition, they may have to be reworked in a conference committee composed of members of both houses in order to obtain a version of a bill which is fully acceptable to both. In Britain, however, only one house of the legislature has life or death power over a bill. This illustrates the differences between the American obstacle course, check-and-balance approach to policymaking and the British approach which facilitates party policymaking processes.

PARTY ORGANIZATION: GOVERNMENT AND OPPOSITION

Parties structure the membership of the House of Commons into clear-cut camps of government and opposition. Coincidentally, the physical arrangements of the interior of the House of Commons chamber make this political reality highly visible. Benches run along both sides of the chamber, separated by the center aisle. The members of the majority party occupy the benches on the side to the right of the speaker. On the benches across the center aisle, facing the government benches, sit the members of the minority party, the opposition. By custom, representatives of the minor parties—Liberal, Scottish, and Welsh Nationalist, for example— sit on the back benches of the government side of the House. Voting may take place by means of a division whenever this is specifically requested. The MPs divide, with the "Ayes" filing into one lobby and the "Nays" into the other to give their votes to the teller in each lobby. Should members of one party choose to vote with the other party, they must cross the aisle to do so, making their party defection highly visible and prominent. It is interesting to note the contrast in the physical arrangements in the American legislative chambers. The legislature in the United States is not clearly divided internally by political parties into government and opposition. The structure of the chambers appears to reflect this; instead of a seating arrangement which physically establishes two opposing camps, the seats in Congress are arrayed in a semicircle, with no clear-cut physical divisions.

Under some circumstances, the minor parties which have some representatives in Commons may be able to exert an impact there out of proportion to their relatively small numbers. If neither of the two major parties has a majority of the parliamentary seats, but only a plurality, then the party which receives the voting support of the minor parties will be able to govern. Once it is decided that, at least temporarily, the third party representatives will support a government, it is not likely that their support will be lightly withdrawn, thus toppling the government. Such an event takes these parties, along with the major parties, back to the polls for reelection. Given their small numbers in the best of circumstances, they are not likely to be willing to jeopardize their position. By contributing their voting support to a major party, they derive great leverage on policy, more than their minority status would otherwise give them on their best day.

The high degree of cohesion and discipline in the government party helps to stimulate in response a relatively cohesive and organized opposition to confront it. Inevitably, a legislative party in opposition will be somewhat less cohesive than it is when it is the majority party. The immediate consequences of a failure to support the leadership on an issue are less serious because, unlike the case in the majority party, the backbenchers do not fear toppling their party from power. This lesser cohesion in opposition is true in both British parties, but more marked and obvious in the Labor party. In opposition, the formal authority reverts to the parliamentary Labor party as a whole, while it remains with the leader in the Conservative party in opposition. Nevertheless, the opposition has a front bench organization, the shadow cabinet, led by the leader of the opposition, with constant opportunities to attack and criticize the government and to present its alternative proposals.

Much of the battle between the parties in Commons is directed to the public in general. In modern times, it is rare that the opposition can hope to unseat the government from its position by means of a negative vote in the legislature. The ongoing party legislative conflict is now, in effect, a continuous election campaign, carried on in the House of Commons. The principal aim of the opposition in these circumstances is to build public support for its programs and policies, while eroding that for the government, with an eye to the outcome of the next general election. The influence that the opposition exerts on the government is thus to induce it to anticipate potential electoral gains for the other party's programs, adjusting its own policy proposals in order to maintain and increase its own electoral support. At the same time, the opposition party tends to adjust to the popular government proposals. Hence, it is not only the alternation of the parties in power that brings about policy changes; changes in policy also take place as each of the two parties adjusts to the other. This helps explain the lack of abrupt swings in policy direction when one party replaces the other in power. Samuel Beer suggests that today, in fact, the key source of the influence of the opposition on the government is found not in changed votes, but in the anticipatory reactions on the part of the ministers. In turn, this attunes the performance of the legislators somewhat more finely to the anticipated reactions of the public.[27]

Whereas there is no position for the losing presidential candidate in the United States and no clear designation of any leader of opposition forces, the leader of Her Majesty's opposition in Parliament has an official title and receives a salary, ultimately from the taxpayers' pockets. This seems to indicate two important features about political opposition in Britain: the leader of the opposition heads an institution dignified by the title "Her Majesty's," as is the government; and the institution is deemed so important to the proper working of the governmental system that Parliament considers it fitting to pay the opposition leader from public revenue. It is thus an official, public duty of the leader of the opposition to guide the shadow cabinet in carrying on a unified, systematic, and prolonged attack on government policy, while at the same time keeping its alternative program and policy proposals before the public.[28] What the opposition chiefly contributes to political accountability is the regularized public focus it provides in Britain for debates on broad national policy directions.

Political opposition in the American political system is symbolized, by contrast, almost entirely by party name and the electoral process. In the first place, the lack of a leader of the opposition that would be a counterpart to that leader in Britain precludes any organized, focused countering to the administration in office. The party losing the presidential race has no acknowledged leader once the election is over; in fact, the losing candidate may well have no position within the government at all. Within Congress, although each party has some official leaders, the actual party leadership roles are diffused to the two legislative houses and within each house among floor and committee leaders. In the next presidential election, the out party may select as its candidate someone from Congress, from a state governorship, or elsewhere. In any case, opposition is not clearly centered in Congress. Largely due to the American constitutional structure which separates the executive from the legislature, no clear-cut opposition within Congress can emerge in response to government, because there is no government within Congress as there is in the British Parliament.[29] Hence, political opposition and competition between the two parties takes place partly within Congress, partly between the legislative and the executive branches, and finally within the electorate. Since decision-making power is spread out to numerous political points rather than concentrated in the government, as it is in Britain, opposition in America is decentralized almost to the point of nonexistence.

In the same way that the sharp distinction between government and opposition forces in Parliament contrasts with the blurring of any such lines in the United States Congress, the intra-party differences between leaders and followers are clearer in Britain than they are in the United States. The discussion now turns to this divergence in the patterns of relationships between party leadership and rank-and-file members in the legislatures of the two countries.

PARTY ORGANIZATION:
LEADERS AND FOLLOWERS

At the beginning of each legislative session in the United States and in Grat Britain, the party members in the legislature, acting as caucuses, meet to select legislative leaders from among themselves. In the United States, the majority party chooses the speaker of the House of Representatives and the Senate president pro tem, along with majority floor leaders, whips, and committee chairmen. The party in the minority also selects its floor leaders, whips, and ranking committee members. This legislative party leadership, distinct and separate from the executive, further contributes to the general diffusion of American party leadership and organization. However, it fills a vacuum that exists because the executive is not present within the legislature to lead the party there, as it is in Britain. In Congress, the party caucus or conference also selects a secretary, chairman, and committee members to formulate party policy for each bill and to recommend the party course of action.

For the majority party in Britain, the parliamentary leaders selected are usually the prime minister's lieutenants in the legislature. The prime minister designates a cabinet member to serve as leader of the house, aided by a chief whip, deputy, and junior whips. Because the party must vote together to support the government's continuation in office, the roles and functions of these party leaders are especially crucial. While similar leaders perform important functions in the American legislature, the tenure of neither the executive nor the members of Congress depends upon them. In Britain, it is the task of the legislative party leaders to arrange the government's agenda in the House of Commons. Leaders from both the majority party and the opposition consult together to determine the details of carrying on the smooth flow of the business of Parliament, including the timing of debate and whether or not to debate particular provisions of a bill. The other principal duty of the whips of both parties is that of informing leaders and rank-and-file members of the policy opinions and positions of each. This is especially important for the majority party. Majority whips act as two-way communication agents, informing the government of what the MPs in the party will or will not support and apprising the MPs about what the government expects from them in support for its policies and programs. Through the vital whip network, all segments of opinion within the party are kept in touch. The party whips in the United States Congress also attempt to round up party members to be present for key votes and are responsible for knowing how many party members can be expected to support particular pieces of legislation. Since party cohesion and discipline is so much weaker in the United States than it is in Britain, the role of the American party whip is comparatively less crucial to the functioning of the legislature.

In Great Britain, a clear and visible distinction between back-benchers and party leaders constitutes part of the party organization within Commons. The backbenchers are the rank-and-file members in Parliament, those who do not hold cabinet, shadow cabinet, or other parliamentary leadership posts. They sit literally behind the government on one side and the opposition leaders on the other side, leaving the front benches to be occupied by the leading members of the two major parties. Former cabinet ministers agree that these backbenchers receive constant, anxious, and even deferential attention from the government. Recollections of the late R. H. S. Crossman, a former Labor cabinet minister, point up the constant preoccupation with any possibility of trouble on the Labor back benches. There are numerous examples of overt activity on the part of backbenchers which have succeeded in bringing about withdrawal or modification of government policy proposals. Yet another type of backbench influence is probably of much greater importance, though more difficult to detect and measure: the pressure of anticipated reactions. During the course of developing policy proposals within the cabinet, leaders respond to opinions of backbenchers by attempting to anticipate their probable reactions.[30]

The British party leadership has resources with which it can exert pressure on the rank-and-file members, but in the final analysis the leaders can go only where the backbenchers are willing to follow. Although the backbenchers' main influence comes about through lobbying within the party in advance of public debates, it is possible for them to speak against the leaders in debate. However, they are expected to support the leadership in the final vote unless the party whip has indicated that on a particular issue a "free vote" is in order. This allows the back-bencher freely to vote according to individual conscience. The time of debate on the motion for adjournment each day is a special opportunity for backbenchers to raise issues that concern them, as has been noted. In addition, early day motions are backbench-sponsored resolutions, not to be discussed on the floor but signed by supporting MPs to record their views on various subjects of political importance. The major functions of the backbenchers are to represent constituent opinion and to support and restrain their party's leaders. In line with this, their opportunities for policy initiative are quite limited when compared to the unlimited initiative available to senators and representatives in the United States. Yet, while they do not initiate policy, they give it much of its final shape.

In marked contrast to the clear-cut distinction between leaders and followers within the parliamentary parties in Britain, the diffusion of legislative party leadership, the lack of party cohesion, and the absence of the executive from the legislature make the relationship between the legislative party leaders and the rank-and-file members in America more subject to variation. Randall Ripley suggests that several different alternative patterns of leadership can be distinguished in the American legislature. Which is in effect at a particular time depends largely on whether or not the president's political party has a majority in Congress, and, if it does, whether the president seeks actively to lead Congress or lets the legislature set many of its own priorities. Further, the leadership pattern will be different depending on the extent to which a president whose party has a legislative majority seeks only partisan support for his policies or attempts to build bipartisan support. In general, the principal task of majority party leaders in Congress is that of mediating between the legislative posture of the president and that of the members of Congress. Since neither the president nor his party colleagues in Congress depend on the other for continuing in office, the legislative leadership is far less likely to be able to hold together all factions of the party in Congress across issues than is the case in Britain.[31]

In addition to the striking differences in the party organization in the legislatures of the United States and Britain which were discussed above briefly, Parliament and Congress diverge in the roles and functions of the formal organizational units within them. Both the presiding officers and the legislative committees, which we will now examine, are markedly different in their natures and roles in each country despite being called by the same names.

INTERNAL FORMAL ORGANIZATION

Both the British and American legislatures are formally organized, with speakers to preside and with some committee structure. In the United States, the party with a majority of members in the House of Representatives selects the speaker from among its members, and he is then confirmed by the whole body. He fulfills two roles at one time, that of a presiding officer keeping order and furthering the smooth operation of the House, and that of a major party leader. He is closely involved in all phases of the body's activities—for example, recognizing members on the floor to speak, designating members of conference committees, and influencing the timing of the consideration of bills.

By contrast, the British speaker of the House of Commons, although originally elected to the lower house as a party representative, leaves that role completely behind in order to preside in a strictly nonpartisan manner. In recognition of the severance of his party ties, another MP in his party takes over his constituency duties for him. The selection of the speaker by a vote of the whole House of Commons is based on his moderation and his committee service, not on his partisanship or debate skill. Unlike the case in the United States, there is usually no contest over his reappointment no matter which party has a majority in the legislature. Both government and opposition parties consult ahead of time on the selection. This neutral and impartial speaker has great authority in applying the rules of the House of Commons, in maintaining order there, and in presiding over debates and votes. Since he is so strictly nonpartisan, he has authority over such matters as the acceptance or rejection of cloture motions and urgency motions, selection of amendments for debate, and limitation on supplementary questions during the question period.

Upper houses in both countries have presiding officers not selected by those bodies for their positions. The vice president in the United States has the constitutional duty to preside over the Senate; in his absence a president pro tem, chosen by the senators, takes over these duties. The vice president is not a member of the Senate; he therefore takes no part in debate and votes only to break a tie. Even when he has been a powerful senator previously, once he returns to the upper house as vice president, he is regarded largely as a member of the executive branch, at remove from the Senate itself. The lord chancellor in Great Britain presides over the House of Lords and, like the vice president, is in a somewhat special position. He is appointed by the prime minister to his post, and, in addition to his function as Lords' presiding officer, he is a member of the cabinet. As such, he serves as the government's chief legal officer. This places him in both the legislative and the executive, and a third role carries him into the judicial branch of the British government; he is also head of the judiciary and presides over the House of Lords when it sits as the country's highest court of appeal. Unlike the speaker of the House of Commons, he is openly partisan in his legislative and executive roles; he has much power as a cabinet member and a political leader, but, as the presiding officer of the upper house, he has little more than a figurehead role.

LEGISLATIVE COMMITTEES

The legislative committees' structure, nature, and functions in each of the two countries under study clearly reflect the differences in the roles of both the executive and the parties within the legislatures. Mayer and Burnett suggest that the growth of specialized and complex knowledge as the basis for any comprehensive, coherent political action has been responded to in some legislatures by making functionally specific committees the basis of most of their activities. The advantage is that, at least theoretically, functionally specific committees can take advantage of the principle of division of labor and specialize in the acquisition of technical expertise. The disadvantage, however, is that insofar as the committees then acquire specialized information or expertise which is not also shared by the members of the body as a whole, the committees tend to become autonomous. Thus the formal lines of accountability are confused.[32]

In the United States, where legislative committees which are functionally specific have become increasingly numerous and relatively autonomous, it is in committee that a bill's future is often determined. Largely independent and powerful committees and subcommittees are used extensively in both houses. Most have

been established by law, are specialized as to subject matter, and
are organized to parallel the structure of the executive branch. On
these three key points, the British committees in Parliament differ
completely from the American. Also, British committees do no
play a role in setting the agenda of the full houses, whereas it is th
standing committees that effectively determine the agenda fo
Congress. Since the committee stage of a bill in Congress precede
any floor vote on the bill, and since the committees themselves hav
such a high degree of power, many bills either do not survive th
committee stage or emerge in drastically altered form. The othe
side of this coin is the high level of success that committees hav
in getting their approved bills accepted by the house as a whole.

To diminish the somewhat undemocratic power of America
congressional committees, bills may be forced out of committee b
means of a discharge petition with the required number of signa
tures, but this mechanism is rarely used. Legislators are reluctan
to move against the committees in this way and are especially war
lest the same device be turned on their own committees in th
future.

Membership on the more important committees is avidly sought
Legislators remain on them for long periods of time, building u
expertise in the special area over which the committee has juris
diction, accruing seniority on the committee, and developing clos
ties with the key interest groups concerned with the subject matte
within the committee's purview. Senior members and party leader
are the most influential in making committee assignments. For
long time committee chairman positions were achieved almos
solely on the basis of seniority. This is still an important factor, bu
beginning in the early 1970s and continuing to the present, th
parties in Congress have departed from the seniority rule in severa
important instances, unseating longtime chairmen and replacing
them with less senior members. Nevertheless, the position of chair
man remains a strong one within a committee, depending some
what on the individual's ability to use the power resources at hi
disposal. By setting committee agenda, the chairman determine
what bills are considered and in what order. He builds politica
capital as he appoints members of subcommittees and their chair

men. Insofar as the seniority system remains a factor, even in attenuated form, the amount of time and energy devoted to committee matters, and the expertise and skill developed by the chairman increase his leadership position.

If American committees and subcommittees, under their powerful chairmen, wield great power over the bills assigned to them, the opposite is true of the British legislative committees. The content of bills has been approved in principle on the floor of Parliament and they are sent to committee only for detailed consideration. British standing committees differ in general from those in America in that they are not functionally specific, but are designated by a letter of the alphabet and are constituted specially for each bill which they consider. Usually a few members are chosen because of their specialized knowledge of the subject matter to be considered, but the rest are chosen principally to achieve the right balance between political parties. Chairmen preside on an impartial basis, and a minister leads the government majority on the committee. The committees in Britain are set up to be useful to the whole house, but not to be decisive. They may amend a bill to some extent, but they will never kill it.

In recent years, the British have made two changes in the committee procedures. First, they have begun a trend toward increasing the number of formal stages of legislative procedures to be taken care of in committee. The principal aim is to cut down on the number of decisions to be taken by the whole house, leaving the body more time to engage in policy debates, discussion of principles, airing of grievances and criticisms, and consideration of new ideas. The second trend of change has been toward some use of specialized committees. The aim underlying this development is to build up experience in special areas and build the level of expertise among members of Parliament in the hope of strengthening the parliamentary scrutiny of the government. However, because the government is itself a part of Parliament and performs the major leadership role there, and because the strong, cohesive and disciplined political parties structure the vote on major issues, the impact of committees on general policy direction will remain slight. Committees in the United States fill a vacuum of power which would not exist if the executive were part of the legislature and if the parties resembled the British legislative parties in cohesion and discipline.

SUMMARY

Jean Blondel points out that in modern, complex political systems, legislatures do not actually make the laws in the fullest sense.[33] Although these bodies do enact statutes in both Britain and the United States, the policy initiative has passed largely to the executive branch of government in both countries. The executive is the main source at which most public policy is conceived, drafted, and finally submitted to the legislature. Even in the United States, where the legislative and executive branches are constitutionally separated and made co-equal, and where Congress can and does initiate public bills and thwart those desired by the executive, the president has come to be called the "chief legislator." This title indicates recognition of the primary role which he plays in initiating policy. Both Congress and the president, with his executive branch agents, share in the policy-making process, but the president's share has increased relative to that of Congress.

The greatest contributions that the legislatures in the United States and in Great Britain make to the democratic political processes and to political accountability within their respective countries appear to lie in their supervising, criticizing, and checking executive policymaking. Concomitant to this, they also bring into the political system the opinions, interests, and demands of the electorates.[34] As the legislators communicate these interests by the various means available, they bring them to bear on the actions of the executives. What chiefly differentiates these legislative functions in Great Britain and in the United States is the means by which they are performed in each of the countries. In Great Britain, the lines of accountability run directly from the voters, through the relatively cohesive and disciplined political parties, and into the lower house of the legislature, where the public debate between the government and the opposition is ongoing. Lines of political accountability extend to the executive—cabinet, and prime minister—because they are part of that continuing debate. The legislative arena is a major forum for calling to account the leaders both within the majority party and between the government and opposition parties. It is often suggested that, in addition to the other important governmental functions of Parliament, a continuous electoral campaign is one of the House of Commons' major activities.

By contrast, in the United States, the lines of political accountability are much less direct and less clearly focused. Political responsibility is diffused—to the executive and to both houses of Congress, and, within those bodies, to several sets of leaders and to committees. Thus, the national political parties cannot function as the key vehicles for exercising political accountability within the legislative arena as they can and do in Britain. The American legislature is not a single major forum for public debate between political leadership groups as is the Parliament in Britain, but is one among many.

CHAPTER SIX

Executives

Alexander Hamilton wrote in *Federalist* Number 70 that "energy in the executive is a leading character in the definition of good government." The head of the executive branch of a government is today the central focal point of that government. Studies indicate that the chief executive is normally the first political official of whom a nation's children become aware; in the United States and Great Britain, children know of the president and the monarch before they can name any other political figure. Such leaders are usually held in awe and respect in early life. This attitude of respect and the tendency to focus attention on the chief executive, the most highly visible political figure, persist to some extent into later life.[1]

THE EXECUTIVE FUNCTIONS

The chief executive is the energizer and coordinator for the whole political system. He is the key source of policy initiative. Energy in the form of initiative and central coordination is supplied to the governmental processes by the executive. A major problem inherent in modern democratic political systems is that of striking a workable and acceptable balance between the sources and uses of energizing powers by the executive and the curbs and restraints on executive power use that will permit holding the executive responsible and accountable for his actions. We will now examine the chief executives in Great Britain and the United States in order to analyze the sources of power and the processes for holding the executives accountable in each system.

CEREMONIAL EXECUTIVE FUNCTIONS

Two types of executive functions can be differentiated. First, there are the ceremonial functions which form the role of "chief of state." Such functions are principally symbolic in nature, imparting a sense of unity to the nation and legitimacy to the acts of the government. Distinct from this figurehead role is that of the working head of government. It is largely in carrying out this role that political decision making and governmental coordination take place.

In the British parliamentary system, these two roles are filled by separate individuals, whereas in the United States the president fills both at once. The British monarch, to whom there is no direct American counterpart, serves as the ceremonial chief of state, while a prime minister actually performs the working executive functions. In Britain, the Crown is the personification of the nation itself, a unifying, symbolic chief of state. As such, the king or queen is essentially the personalized symbol of national unity and also serves as the only link tying together the commonwealth countries. The monarch signifies the persistence of the common national tradition and of historic British values, forming the major point of continuity with the British past.[2]

Although lacking the majesty, ancient symbolism, and link with tradition supplied to the British nation by the monarch, the American president fills the similar role of ceremonial chief of state in his country. As such, the president symbolizes the unity of the nation and performs legitimizing functions. These range from awarding medals of honor to lighting the nation's Christmas tree, much like the monarch's activities of conferring titles and honors and addressing the nation at Christmas.

Clinton Rossiter observes that the American president is the one-man distillation of the American citizens, just as surely as the monarch is of the British people. However, unlike the monarch, he is also the working head of government. The combination of roles in the presidency can add to the demands upon the time of the resident enormously. Yet the president has the opportunity, enied to either the monarch or the prime minister as they divide the executive roles, to parlay the combination of the two roles filled simultaneously into much greater sources of political power and authority than either alone can provide. When senators are invited to the White House for breakfast with the president in order that he might persuade them to support his energy policy, or example, or when he meets with disputants in a labor-management controversy, all are keenly aware that he is much more than just a working executive; he is also the symbolic embodiment of the sovereignty of the American people.[3] In contrast to the position of the president, that of the monarch, embodying the state sovereignty of Britain, lacks any real policy-making power while that of the prime minister, the principal policy-making leader, lacks the ceremonial element.

In Great Britain, all governmental actions are formally actions of the Crown; this fiction provides legitimacy to such major governmental events as the appointment or dismissal of governments, the dissolving and convening of Parliament, and the official promulgation of laws. Although the monarch lacks any power to make policy, the monarchy serves as the formal channel through which power is passed from one government to another in an orderly, peaceful fashion, preserving unity and continuity when governments change. Because the chief political figure in America serves also as the ceremonial symbol of unity, no such link persists through changes in administration. The only element which might fill part of this function is the American constitutional document.

In a more active role, the British monarch has the constitutional right "to be consulted, to encourage, and to warn." He or she is kept well informed, receiving copies of all cabinet minutes and by tradition being consulted and informed personally by the prime minister and the senior cabinet ministers from time to time. The royal secretariat is a great source of strength to the monarch, providing advice and information and serving as a link between the monarch and the government and opposition leaders. Hence, the possibility of the monarch's advice receiving close attention from political leaders and influencing their decisions is a real one. Whatever degree of influence a monarch will actually exert over the

cabinet will inevitably vary according to the personality, abili**
and experience of the monarch.[4] No such source of nonpartis**
advice is available to the American president. Instead, he m**
usually rely upon either partisan or personal advisers, who norma**
have their own political objectives to consider as they counsel t**
president.

In two relatively rare instances, the monarch may perform**
important role as a political umpire in a ministerial crisis. Th**
power is rarely tapped because of the dominance of the Briti**
two-party system, but it does exist and it is thus important that t**
monarch maintain strict neutrality and impartiality.[5] In the eve**
that no one political party receives a clear majority of seats in t**
House of Commons following an election, the monarch may ta**
an active part in the selection of the leader of one of the two maj**
parties to form a government. In such an instance, however, t**
choice the monarch makes is not a free one; it is constrained **
the need to select a leader who can command and maintain **
majority of parliamentary support.

In the past, it has happened that the party receiving a cle**
majority of seats in Commons in an election is unable to agr**
clearly on the choice of party leader. When this happens t**
monarch must designate one of several contenders for the post **
prime minister. Again, the choice is not one made freely; the prim**
minister must be able to command the support of his party **
Parliament in order to govern. On a few occasions the Conserv**
tive party failed to designate a leader, partly because the party h**
not developed specified mechanisms for a clear-cut selection **
leader, holding to the fiction that leaders are not chosen but rath**
emerge. However, that party has now adopted methods for leade**
ship selection, so that the likelihood of a similar deadlock o**
curring again is slim. Finally, between general elections, if a prim**
minister's party should lose its parliamentary majority—for e**
ample, through party losses in by-elections to fill vacant seats **
because of defection of needed support from a minority party—**
the monarch may become the mediator between the parties in **
attempt to reach a solution to the parliamentary deadlock. At su**
a time, the political system is affected greatly by the monarch**
skill at mediation.[6]

One of the most important contributions which the monarch makes to the stability of the British political system is that, standing above partisan differences and internal conflicts between groups in the population, she and the royal family as a whole serve as a focal point for public attention. They provide color and pageantry and receive respect and devotion from the British subjects. The modern monarchy attracts much of the deep, nonrational feeling toward authority figures which could lead to political problems if directed toward partisan figures such as the American president or toward charismatic leaders.[7] It is probable that Americans as a whole are culturally less inclined to stand in awe of authority figures and to seek a personification of tradition and pageantry than are the British. However, all people seem to focus some degree of interest and attention on prominent political leaders, and to the extent that this need is present in the American culture, the president and the first family are the recipients of the public's interest and emotional attachments. As the monarch provides an image of authority, so the president stands to some extent as a "father figure" for the American people.

The two roles filled by the president can become intermingled and confused, though of course they cannot in Britain, since they are separated. There the prime minister and his cabinet can be embroiled as preeminently partisan figures in fierce political battles, while the monarch stands apart from and above any partisan conflict and continues to symbolize the national unity in spite of political division. In Britain it is possible and not uncommon to condemn the government of the day and at the same time to praise the monarch. In the United States the two hats which the president wears cannot be separated so neatly.[8] On the one hand, his lofty position as chief of state may become eroded because of unpopular partisanship or policy positions. More dangerous, perhaps, is the other possibility, that the emotional attachments of the populace to the chief of state may carry over to his working, partisan role, freeing him from some of the healthy restraints imposed by holding him politically accountable for his actions. The combination of the two roles in one official may contribute to a tendency to confuse the office of the presidency with the particular individual who is serving temporarily as president. When this happens, there may result either an erosion of respect and support for the office itself, or blind support for an individual president, whatever his actions, because of the legitimacy attached to the office he fills.

EFFICIENT FUNCTIONS

In the British parliamentary system, unlike the directly elected American president, the prime minister is chosen by the legislature to be the working head of the government. Along with his cabinet, he governs so long as he continues to be able to command the support of a majority of the legislators in the House of Commons. As executive branch leaders, he and the cabinet of which he is a member have the responsibility for coordinating the formulation of policies and programs within the executive branch of the government, a function similar to that carried out by the American president in his role as chief executive. Since a British cabinet is composed of the leadership of the party chosen by the voters to govern, its working role is to bring about the implementation of the programs and policies on which the party ran for office. In a sense, this puts the British cabinet and prime minister one step ahead of the American president. The president formulates policy and program proposals, but he is constitutionally set at odds against the legislature, which may or may not enact them.

The major duties of the British executive are those of policy making and legislation drafting, although, in addition, most of the members of the cabinet have administrative and supervisory duties within their respective ministries. In contrast to cabinet officials in America, who are responsible only to the president, each ministry head in Britain is individually responsible to Parliament for the work of his ministry, according to the convention of ministerial responsibility. There is both legal responsibility on the part of the British ministers for the actions of the ministries, which can be enforced in the courts, and political responsibility to the House of Commons for the policy decisions of the individual ministries.

The members of the British cabinet, led by the prime minister, conceive, draft, and then introduce the important public bills into Parliament, defending the policies in the ensuing debate and guiding the progress of the bills through the various parliamentary stages. This direct executive supervision of bills in their progress through Parliament contrasts with the process in the United States, in which executive proposals to Congress are set loose on the legislative seas with little executive supervision of their progress. The most that the president can reasonably hope for once he has turned a proposal over to the legislature is indirect supervision with the aid of friendly or acquiescent congressmen.

Although the prime minister has achieved a clearly preeminent position within the cabinet in the whole policy-making process, so that he is much more than "first among equals," he is still an integral part of what is both formally and politically a collegial working executive, unlike the American president who stands alone. The president is the nation's sole executive leader in formulating and initiating policies and programs and, if the legislature enacts them, in their implementation by the executive branch of government. In performing these functions, he has a large measure of autonomy since he is not restrained by a cabinet of which he is a member or by the need to retain a majority of his party's legislative support to remain in his post. The president's fixed term bolsters his independence from the legislature, but he lacks the advantage of the assured legislative support which the British cabinet normally receives for its legislative proposals. Part of the difference between the roles of the prime minister and of the president stems from crucial differences between the political parties in the two countries and from the corresponding differences in the chief executives' roles as party leaders.

In the following discussion of the roles and functions of the chief executives in Great Britain and the United States, it will become clear that while both presidents and prime ministers have somewhat similar jobs as they lead their countries, there are great differences in the resources and advantages available to each and in the obstacles that each faces. It is largely because of these differences that although both countries have as guiding political values the democratic goals of limited government and popular accountability of political executives, the means by which these goals are pursued differ in each of the countries.

FORMATION AND STRUCTURE OF THE EXECUTIVES

The British and American executive branches of government consist of two basic categories of officials. In the top positions are those elected to office or chosen by elected officials. Serving these are permanent professionals, selected on the basis of merit to enter the civil services. Since the latter occupy nonpartisan positions, they remain in their posts despite changes in the partisan executive offices. Restrictions placed by law on their partisan political activities aid in insulating them from party politics. In Britain, these career civil servants advance to positions nearer the top than do those in the United States. Conversely, the newly inaugurated president appoints political officials to positions in cabinet departments and agencies that are several steps down into the hierarchy. On the one hand, this enables the president to penetrate further into these bodies with his political choices than can the prime minister. This may lead to a greater degree of control and direction over the executive branch policy-making processes. On the other hand, it may tend to create a buffer zone between the civil servants, who have longevity and expertise, and the new president, making it difficult for him to make much impact on the internal workings of the executive branch.

In the category of politically appointed officials, there is an important difference between the British and the American practices. Whenever the president changes, even if the new president belongs to the same political party as his predecessor, most political appointees are usually replaced. If a prime minister is succeeded by another member of his own party, some cabinet and ministerial appointments may change, but there is generally a high degree of continuity in these posts. More likely than replacement within the cabinet is some rearrangement of officials among specific posts in the cabinet. Even in the event that the opposition party comes to power, it will have a shadow cabinet prepared when it forms a government, and many of its new cabinet ministers have had previous cabinet or shadow cabinet experience. Therefore, whereas in Britain there is a marked degree of continuity in high executive posts, in the United States there is a great deal of shifting in and out of high level positions.

FORMATION OF THE EXECUTIVE

Both the British prime minister and the American president are elected officials, but the American executive is elected directly to that post, while the prime minister has been specifically elected only to a seat in the House of Commons. From among the members of Parliament, the monarch appoints a prime minister. The choice is governed by several conventions and facts of political life, so that the selection is usually very simple. If one party has a clear majority of seats in the House of Commons, the monarch names the person whom the members of Commons belonging to that party have chosen as leader, according to procedures defined by party rules. If the election produces no clear majority for one party, or if the majority party is unable to agree on a leader, the monarch must then ascertain through consultations with party members who have considerable authority but who are not themselves candidates for the office, who has the best chance of commanding support from a majority in Commons.[9] Normally the party leader is clearly identified well before elections take place, holding the post either of incumbent prime minister or of leader of the opposition.

Because the executive in Britain is selected by the legislature, not by popular vote filtered through the electoral college, as is the American president, his power depends on the legislature's support, in particular that of his own party members within that body.[10] Unlike the president, the prime minister cannot derive his power from his election by the people as a whole. This ties him firmly to his party and to the legislature, in contrast to the relative freedom which the president enjoys from each. However, this in no way implies that the prime minister is constrained politically, whereas the president is not. Although the president achieves his position of power independent from the legislators, this does not result in the free exercise of that power. To the extent that both the executive and the legislature are elected independently, do not rely on the support of each other for remaining in office, and hold office in constitutionally coequal branches of the government, the exercise of power by each is limited by the other. The British prime minister's selection for leadership by a legislatively cohesive majority party in Parliament constrains his actions, but it also provides him with the important resource of party and legislative backing, virtually guaranteeing enactment of his policy proposals into law.

In sum, the presidential selection process is primarily a popular one, only partly structured by the political parties, and is one in which the legislature has no role. By contrast the choice of the British prime minister is principally a legislative choice, structured and controlled by party politics.[11] It is only indirectly a popular choice, filtered through the party vote in the general election. The result of the differences in the selection processes is that, whereas the president can attempt to draw upon the popular support that put him into office for further support for his policies and programs, he can count on little political party support and may have remarkably little legislative support, a prime minister's chief resource is the support of his political party, sustained within Parliament.

STRUCTURE OF THE EXECUTIVE

There are two major structural differences between the British executive and the American executive:

1. A British prime minister is part of a collegial executive whereas the American president is not.
2. The president has a personal staff far greater than that of the prime minister, in spite of the recent growth in the size of the staff available to the prime minister and cabinet.

Although the executive branch in America does include a cabinet, that body is clearly subordinate to the president, both constitutionally and politically. The cabinet in the United States has no formal constitutional standing; the body is not mentioned as such in the constitutional document. Nor can the cabinet, as a group or each official independently, take political action which in any way binds the president.

The collegial executive in Great Britain includes the prime minister and other cabinet ministers with their subordinates—ministers not included within the cabinet, junior ministers, and parliamentary private secretaries. Most ministers are either secretaries of state, usually heading large and important departments such as the Foreign Office, or ministers heading other departments or ministries. Some hold historical, nondepartmental posts, either in addition to heading a department, or free from such specific functions to perform more general governmental functions. Among these are the prime minister's post as first lord of the treasury and the post of lord privy seal. Some are legal officers, and others head no department, but have specific tasks assigned to them, such as responsibility for Common Market negotiations. Within each ministry, directly below the top appointed officials, are the senior civil servants in the administrative class.

Thus, the British structure provides a contrast to that in the United States executive, where there are few members of the cabinet who do not head cabinet departments, but the cabinet is only that group from which the executive chooses to elicit advice. In Great Britain, however, the cabinet as the executive has prior and independent existence from any particular posts which might be included within it. The British cabinet can be likened roughly to a pyramid, with the prime minister at the apex.[12] This contrasts with the structural dimensions of the executive branch of government in the United States, in which the president stands alone at the top, with the cabinet as a body clearly below him in the power structure. Indeed, unlike the British case, the cabinet in America does not include the chief executive as a member.

With each new administration, the president selects new heads of cabinet departments, subject to senatorial concurrence. He also chooses heads of agencies and bureaus, as well as his advisers and personal aides. Stephen Monsma suggests that the structure can be thought of as consisting of ten concentric rings, each farther from the president and less influential in the process of presidential decision making. Closest to the president is an inner ring of advisers, which has grown in size and importance, forming a sort of "palace guard" of loyal presidential supporters who may insulate the president from other political officials and from conflicting viewpoints and controversy.[13] By contrast, the prime minister is not surrounded by the same type of political buffer. However, recent increases in the size and importance of his personal staff have tended to give him a further political edge over the other cabinet ministers.[14] But, so long as he continues to function politically within the cabinet and parliamentary settings, he is very limited in the extent to which he can insulate himself from political controversy and criticism. Because he must include other party leaders in his cabinet, some of whom lead factions or wings of backbenchers and have followings within the party at large, and because he has regular, ongoing contact with them in both cabinet and parliamentary settings, he is constantly exposed to their positions on policy issues. He must also mediate disputes which arise, because the cabinet must reach a unified position on major issues in order to present a united front in the House of Commons.

Since the president is largely free to pick his closest advisers without regard for their party leadership positions, he is very likely to choose those who are most in agreement with him on major issues and policies. They work completely apart from any cabinet constraints and are structurally separated from the legislature. Whereas the prime minister works in constant contact with the cabinet and legislature, the division between the executive and the legislature in the United States tends to insulate the president from regular, direct contact with members of either his own party or the opposition in the legislature.

With this understanding of the differences in the ways in which the two executives are formed, and in their general structural outlines, we can now turn to an examination of the roles of prime ministers and presidents within their political and governmental settings.

PRIME MINISTERS AND PRESIDENTS

Throughout the political systems of the world, there has been a rise in the preeminence of the chief executive. Both presidents and prime ministers have grown in importance within America and Britain. Since the executive is normally the directing, energizing, coordinating center of the government, by necessity the policy initiative of the executive has also increased with the expanding role and scope of government involvement in social and economic life. The growing complexity of government business and the increasing expertise needed to plan and execute it requires that the executive branch, the nerve center of a government, grow accordingly. At the same time, the heightened impact of the mass media focuses public attention largely on chief executives, contributing greatly to their overall prominence.

GENERAL POSITIONS OF CHIEF EXECUTIVES

Because the official popular electoral base of the prime minister is only his House of Commons constituency, in a formal sense he has no greater popular backing than does any of the other 634 members of the House of Commons. However, in recent years, the campaigns preceding the general elections to Commons have focused increasingly on the leaders of the major rival parties. The mass media highlight their campaigns across the country on behalf of their parties, and polls indicate that the identity of the party leaders increasingly influences decisions by the voters. This increased attention on the individual party leaders in Great Britain does not approach the level of attention trained on the American presidential candidates, however.

The prime minister does have a second constituency which the American president lacks: the members of his own political party in Parliament. He depends on them for continued support because he lacks a fixed term of office. Thus, he is tied to his party in Parliament and to his cabinet in a way that a popularly elected leader is not. The president does not depend upon the legislature or cabinet to stay in office; he is less directly dependent on party support for policy-making success because he has his own base of support within the population at large. This popular support is largely independent of the rest of his party. He may find his popular base to be good leverage to influence Congress indirectly.

Because of this direct link with the public and the relative freedom which the president has from political party constraints, the office of the presidency is more susceptible to shaping by individuals who fill it than is that of the prime minister. While it is true that the personality and style of individual prime ministers make important differences in the conduct of that office, there is less room for individual impact than is true of the presidency, partly because the prime minister is part of a cabinet. Also, the British people are less fascinated by personal details about the prime minister's life than are Americans about the president and first family, since the British have the monarch and royal family to concentrate on, and their political interest is focused more on overall party image than on the personality of the leader. Since there is no American counterpart to the monarch, whatever color, glamor, and pageantry exists in the political realm is supplied by the first family. Each administration supplies a different tone and style to the national political scene, often affecting general popular tastes in such matters as entertainment, dress, and food.

Lacking a unified party and facing an often recalcitrant legislature, a president must frequently rely on the prestige of the office and its preeminence in the public eye to bolster his powers of persuasion. When the president does "go to the people" over the heads of the legislators, more often than not the public sides with him in a controversy. The prime minister has strong resources in the party, cabinet, and legislative support, but these may be withdrawn from him. If this should occur, he might resign, but a more likely response would be a request from him to the monarch to dissolve the House of Commons and call for new elections. Thus, whatever the nature of the controversy occasioning such a political crisis, it is at least theoretically, "taken to the country" for resolution by the electorate. The prime minister's lack of a fixed term of office and lack of a direct popular base for his executive post is a source of both strength and weakness. He lacks a measure of the political independence from party and legislature which the American president enjoys. The mere possibility that party support might be withdrawn, without it actually occurring, limits the prime minister's political actions. But the asset which his dependency presents him lies in the keen awareness on the part of both his cabinet and party colleagues in the House of Commons that withdrawing their support may result in toppling the government and them with it. Thus, it is clear that the prime minister is in a unique position to influence his cabinet and other party members, for example through his patronage power, but they restrain him because he depends upon their continued backing. His membership in Parliament keeps him in constant interaction with the legislature, so that his influence over that body and its restraints upon him are mutual and ongoing.

The American president is not a member of the legislature, and he faces constitutional barriers in his interaction with Congress that do not confront the British executive. In spite of his links to

he electorate and his security in office, the constitutional provision
or separation between executive and legislative branches limits the
president's ability to insure enactment of his policies. Both the
separation of powers and federalism have contributed to the fragmentation of American political parties. The president cannot enjoy the kind of legislative party support which the prime minister
will normally have. Even his fixed terms of office may become
barriers to his ability to influence. Because a president is constitutionally limited to two terms, in contrast to the prime minister's
almost unlimited eligibility for renewal in office, late in his second
administration he may become a "lame duck" and find that his
political powers have drastically weakened.

PARTY POSITIONS OF THE CHIEF EXECUTIVES

The prime minister is almost always the leader of the majority
party in the House of Commons, but the American president may
face a legislature dominated by the opposition party. Even if the
president's party does control the legislature, the party is neither
unified nor cohesive in its voting, and the president is only
nominally its leader. However, the prime minister heads a cohesive, disciplined legislative party, and he draws most of his
political strength and power from its backing. Yet there are wings
and factions within the British political parties, many with leaders
in Parliament and followers on the backbenches. In order to keep
his party unified, the prime minister must take these carefully into
account, often including leaders of rival party wings in important
cabinet posts. As party leader, his powers of patronage, his authority to appoint and dismiss from cabinet and ministerial posts and
to decide which posts will be included within the cabinet, and his
ability to decide when to ask the monarch for dissolution of the
lower house of the legislature all give him great influence over his
party in Parliament and the rest of the party leadership. As party
leader, he is the principal focal point for party loyalty throughout
the country, generally serving as chief party spokesman and in
particular as the main agent articulating party policy and the party
electoral platform. However, since he is the leader of a party which
best succeeds at the polls if it remains unified, disciplined, and
cohesive, he can only go only where his party will follow him.

This constraint on his party leadership applies especially strongl
to his relationship to the party in Parliament. To continue to lea
the parliamentary majority and hence to govern, he must continu
to take his party's members of Parliament with him.

For both major British political parties, distinctions must b
made between the parties in Parliament, led by the prime ministe
or leader of the opposition, and the extraparliamentary partie
including their national organizations, constituency organization
and parties in the electorate. The prime minister's influence ove
the party outside Parliament is great, stronger than is that of th
leader of the opposition. However, even for the prime minister, th
strength of leadership fluctuates according to the personality of th
particular individual and the circumstances that develop during th
life of a government. Richard Rose suggests that while the leade
of a newly established government can claim popular backing fo
his authority and is thus in a position of strength vis-à-vis the re
of the party, there is a tendency for the government to become les
popular midway in the life of a Parliament. The prime ministe
may cease to appear primarily as the leader who brought the par
to victory and seem instead to be the one who is likely to lead
to defeat in the next election if he is not replaced.[15]

In theory the extraparliamentary Labor party has a higher de
gree of control over their prime minister than does the Conserva
tive party. The greater deference to leadership within the Co
servative party reinforces the historical tendency for its party i
Parliament to guide the rest of the members. The mass membe
ship principle which shapes the organization of the Labor par
contains a philosophical commitment to mass control of leade
ship. However, now that the party has become the other majo
party in a two-party system, the exigencies of governing have a
tered the practice. While the formal relationships between th
Labor party in Parliament and the extraparliamentary party diffe
from those which obtain for the Conservative party, there is littl
practical difference when the party is in the majority. A prim
minister inevitably has greater resources at his disposal than doe
any other group within his party. Thus, the prime minister is th
major party leader, but can lead only in directions generally ac
ceptable to the party in the country.

Although the American president also fills the formal role of party leader, he can draw little political strength over an extended period of time from this role. Because of the fragmented, decentralized nature of the parties and the localism that characterizes both their organizations and general political outlook, a president is less able to exercise real political leadership over his party than is the prime minister. The opposition party in the United States may hold a majority of the seats in one or both houses of the legislature. Even if the president's party controls both, the legislative and executive wings of one party, as well as the different state party groupings, are often not in accord on policy stands. Each of the wings and groupings has its own leadership, as is the case in the British parties, but the factors keeping parties together in Britain do not exist in the United States. Rather, the American parties are pulled apart by forces in the environment. Thus, the president cannot derive as much political strength from his post of party leader as a prime minister who has mastered the role of party leadership will normally enjoy. At the same time, however, the president is freer of party constraints. Since he does not truly lead a unified party, he is not limited to pursuing only those policy directions which the party as a whole can be persuaded to follow. Indeed, he can pick up support from the public in general and from the opposition party as well, at times ignoring key factions and leaders within his own party.

In sum, it is basically the differences between the British and the American political parties which largely account for the marked differences in the roles of party leadership available to the prime minister and to the president. In the case of the prime minister, his greatest political strengths and, conversely, his major political limitations stem from his party leadership post. For the American president, neither strengths nor weaknesses of similar magnitude inhere in his role as party leader.

PATTERNS OF RECRUITMENT TO EXECUTIVE LEADERSHIP

In Great Britain, the selection of an individual as prime minister is the culmination of a long intraparty process in which the current party leadership identifies promising backbenchers, grooming them for future leadership posts. It is the party in Parliament which chooses the prime minister, bearing in mind the need for support from both rank-and-file members and the national electorate. The selection is thus above all a party selection, unlike the case in America in which choice by party leadership is only one factor which goes into the final selection of a presidential candidate. In the United States, the formal selection of a party's presidential candidate is made by the national party convention, but the vote of convention delegates is only one of several factors in the candidate selection. Presidential primaries held in various states single out from the host of hopefuls a few strong candidates. Primaries are rising in use and in their impact on the final selection. This means of introducing a popular element into the candidate selection process has never been used in Britain because the party organization is the controlling factor there, and no popular demand for primaries has arisen. Strength in public opinion polls also contributes to the process in the United States more than it does in Britain. In the presidential election itself, the popular vote often deviates from avowed party support. Even in the course of the campaign, the American party candidates tend to rely more on their own personal organizations than on the party organization, which is the opposite of the case in Britain. Thus, it is clear that party control over the executive selection process is much stronger in Britain than it is in the United States.

The two major British parties differ in the procedures they use for selecting a leader. Until 1965, the Conservative party eschewed intraparty democratic methods of selection. In theory, the party in Parliament, Conservative peers, prospective parliamentary candidates, and members of the executive committee of the National Union of Conservative and Unionist Associations formally acknowledged the choice of the leader which had already been decided by negotiation, behind the scenes, carried on by the most powerful elements of the party. Because they felt that such a method prevented open party fights and factionalism, thus giving the appearance of a party united behind a newly selected leader, the Conservatives preferred avoiding an open contest for leadership. In the face of growing criticism of the informal selection method, however, the party adopted a method of selection similar to that used by the Labor party—secret ballots cast by the Conservative members of Parliament. Different from the Labor method is the final ratification of the candidate chosen by secret ballot by a meeting of Conservative members of Commons, Conservative peers, prospective candidates, and the executive committee of the National Union.[16]

The route to the top executive post in Great Britain is very clearly defined by tradition, with carefully prescribed steps up the ladder, unlike the American process of presidential recruitment. Candidates for the presidency in the United States run for that office from a number of different posts both in and out of the government. But, the rise to the prime ministership is through both the legislative and executive branches of government, from increasing prominence in Parliament accompanied by movement from lower to higher ministerial posts. In essence, a rather lengthy apprenticeship is served simultaneously in legislative and executive positions. This is accompanied by concurrent rise in party leadership ranks generally. Such an ascent to the top is accomplished in one of two ways: either by being singled out by the existing party leadership and raised up by them or by creating and building a backbench and country following into a challenge to the established party leaders so strong that it cannot be ignored. As Samuel Beer points out, if the House of Commons no longer has the power to make or break governments, it does create or destroy reputations. It is still the main arena for leadership selection, and the key characteristic needed for rising to the top is to be a good House of Commons man.[17]

Thus the British prime minister has served a long apprenticeship period, with much legislative and executive experience behind him. The process of recruitment tends to ensure a thorough and deep socialization into the ways of the British parliamentary and cabinet government. Such lengthy socialization during an apprenticeship is absent in the United States. With each new administration, there is a fairly thorough sweeping out of old executive officials and bringing in of a new group.

The average length of national level executive experience for prime ministers at the time of their entering that post was fifteen years, during the period 1945–1976. For the same period the average national level executive experience for all American presidents entering office was four years. The prior executive branch experience for Americans was in the post of vice president, which provides less training for the presidency than a cabinet post in Britain provides for the office of prime minister. For British prime ministers, twenty-nine years is the average length of legislative experience prior to becoming chief executive, while for all presidents during that period thirteen and one-half years, on average, had been spent in the national legislature.[18]

In the United States, the route to the presidency is much less clearly prescribed. National level governmental experience is usually much less and in some cases is nonexistent, and it is rarely in both the legislature and the executive branch. Unlike the case in Britain, experience in both branches cannot be obtained simultaneously. Lateral entry into the presidency—from the armed forces, judicial posts, or state level positions, for example—is possible in the United States, but not in Britain. Presidents thus tend to be less directly socialized or patterned into the traditional ways of doing things in political offices at the national level. In America, there is a bettter chance for the infusion of new blood into the top executive office than is the case in Britain, where the same old faces may remain for long periods, but there is also less ability to draw on the great amount of political background and experience which a prime minister has.

This evidence of the differences in recruitment patterns in Great Britain and the United States does not necessarily imply that the American aspirants for the presidency are any less politically capable on the whole than are those who aspire to the prime ministership. What it does indicate is that their experience is not of the same kind. Given the current recruitment trends in the United States, including the trend away from cabinet posts as presidential stepping stones, it is unlikely that the president will have had prior national executive experience at all, unless in the vice presidency. It indicates also that the incumbent chief executive in the United States holds and conducts his office relatively far removed from those who are major aspirants or rivals for his own office. In recent years, most of the leading party candidates for the presidential nomination have been either senators or state governors. Neither of these is in direct, continuing contact with the president in policy formulation. Instead, the framework of separation of powers and the pattern of presidential recruitment which has developed within it peculiarly insulate the American chief executive from those next in line for his position. On the other hand, in Britain, the next prime minister is either on the opposition side of Parliament, constantly calling the current chief executive to account for his policy directions in debate in the House of Commons, or is with him in the cabinet. A key characteristic of the parliamentary setting in Britain is that it places the prime minister in a direct and unavoidable relationship with those who most want and can most hope to get his post. On this count, at least, he has less freedom in selecting policy alternatives and directions than has the president, because he must accommodate policy to the positions of his rivals, lest they unseat him. In addition, he is less likely than is the president to be cut off from conflicting opinions and alternative viewpoints.

EXECUTIVE POLICY
COORDINATION AND CONTROL

In both the United States and Great Britain, much of the policy-making initiative has devolved upon the executive. In America, the expansion of the country, widening of suffrage, and major social and economic changes all worked to transform the presidency into the major focal point for national unity for varied and heterogeneous groups. Simultaneously, the Congress was falling more and more under the forces of sectional fragmentation.[19] In each country, the large increase in the staff and the special expertise of the executive branch gave it ability to coordinate the complex facets of policies and programs and the capacity to engage in long-range and comprehensive planning beyond that possessed by the legislatures. These factors are combined in both countries with an increase in the popular base for the offices. In the United States, the conversion of the electoral college into a formality in essence makes the presidency a directly elected position. The increase in attention by the British voters to the identity of the party leaders in the general election gives the prime ministership a greater measure of direct popular backing than it had in the past, but not equal to that of the president.

POLICY INITIATIVE AND DIRECTION

The legislative initiative of the British cabinet is inherent in the modern parliamentary-cabinet relationship. Since the party which controls both the legislature and cabinet is expected by the electorate to govern, that is, to put the programs and policies on which they campaigned into effect, it is presumed that the cabinet will take the legislative lead. Much of the legislation that will be introduced by the cabinet into Parliament is presented formally on the opening day in the official speech by the monarch. In reality, of course, the speech has been written by the cabinet. During its tenure in office, the cabinet, headed by the prime minister, develops programs and policies and designs legislation. One of the key cabinet jobs is to conceive, draft, and introduce all major bills into the legislature. In consultation with the opposition leadership the government allocates parliamentary time, distributes business throughout the session, and controls the agenda (subject to the constraints of parliamentary customs).

The government bills are almost certain to be passed. Unless the party whips have been authorized by the cabinet to indicate to the rank and file party members of Parliament that a particular issue is left for a "free vote," it has become more and more common to view parliamentary votes on most matters of major policy substance as essentially votes of confidence. Defeat on any of these measures would then normally lead to government resignation or dissolution of the House of Commons and to a call for new elections. Because of the party cohesion and the consequences of a defeat, the prime minister is much more likely to secure intact his program as presented to the legislature than is the American president, whose legislative party is not cohesive and for whom a defeat on a policy measure will not bring downfall. With his cohesive party behind him and his deference to its views, the prime minister, who is himself a member of the legislature as well as the head of the government, can truly be called the chief legislator in Great Britain. The prime minister is initially constrained by cabinet, party, and legislative forces in shaping policy, but, once formed, the policy is virtually sure to pass.

In the United States also, much of the policy initiative for future legislation has passed to the president. Thus, in describing his position, the role of chief legislator is usually included. At the very least, the president must annually address Congress on the state of the union and present an annual budget. He and other members of the executive branch have constitutional authority to send bills in an executive communication addressed to the speaker of the House of Representatives and to the president of the Senate. Most of the major bills have been drafted in the executive branch, then cleared by the executive Office of Management and Budget, which attempts to insure that the proposed bill conforms to the president's legislative and budgetary policy in general and that it is submitted in the proper form, with accurate drafting. Often these bills are introduced and guided through the legislative procedures by the president's allies in the House and in the Senate. If approved, they are finally signed into law by the president. Although the president is much more autonomous than is the prime minister in shaping initial policy proposals, after that point he has much greater obstacles to overcome in order to insure their passage. In contrast to the case in Great Britain, much policy does originate in the American legislature itself. Legislative initiative of policy may occur either in competition with proposals from the president and his executive officials, or in the absence of any presidential initiative in an area. In his policy-making role, the president's main resources are his ability to persuade, ability to bargain with rewards and punishments, his veto power, and his ability to appeal directly to the voters through major addresses and press conferences.[20] So long as the prime minister retains his ability to lead his party, he rarely has to rely on any other power resources.

It is perhaps in the area of persuasion and use of rewards that the individual personality, characteristics, and style of each president interact with the legal and political outlines of the office and the circumstances of the times in ways that make each administration unique. Personal strengths and weaknesses and the incumbent's views of the presidential role within the political system combine to shape the overall presidency of one incumbent so that it is markedly different from that of another. Without the same type of unified and cohesive party backing that a prime minister can usually call upon and set at odds against the legislature by the checks and balances which the Constitution establishes, a president must draw upon more informal power sources, the use of which depends largely upon his own abilities. Activist presidents such as Abraham Lincoln and Theodore Roosevelt present sharp contrast to more passive presidents with more limited views of the powers and scope of the office such as Buchanan, Taft, Harding, and Hoover. A recent study analyzes the impact of personality types on the conduct of the office and postulates that such characteristics as positive and negative outlooks and active and passive dispositions combine in particular presidents to make their terms in office unique.[21]

Similarly, the formal powers of prime ministers change little, but the office varies according to the leader's view of the position and role, his own style, and the political circumstances he faces. The self-denying role of an individual such as Clement Atlee, the foreign policy focus of Winston Churchill, and the administrations of Anthony Eden and Harold MacMillan, for example, each shaped the office in notably different ways.[22] However, because of the collective cabinet setting, the strength and prominence of the political parties, and the lack of a direct popular base, the office of the prime minister appears to be somewhat less susceptible to the impact of the individual filling it than is the case with the American presidency.

CONTROL OVER FINANCE

The impact which the chief executive is able to exert over the budget has strong bearing on both the amount of internal control he can exercise over his administration and the extent to which he can influence or control the fate of his policies in the legislature. In Britain, the treasury is the dominant force in financial matters. Coordination and control of the budget by the treasury is exercised at all stages of the budgetry process. Every department minister must develop a good working relationship with the chancellor of the exchequer, who heads the treasury. He serves as final arbiter of each department's financial position. However, his position is not impregnable; other ministers may wear him down, especially if several form an alliance to do so. He is, of course, part of the cabinet himself.[23]

Internal Executive Control

No ministry may make a proposal involving expenditures or present a financial estimate to the cabinet without first receiving treasury authorization. Through his post as first lord of the treasury, the prime minister exercises a high degree of control over financial matters and thus over the entire administrative sector. Treasury control of expenditures comes primarily from its annual review of all department estimates and the need for treasury approval of all major projects. In addition, the financial resolutions which must accompany all bills involving expenditures and all cabinet memoranda sent to the rest of the cabinet must be examined and approved by the treasury ministers.[24] Thus, the attention of the cabinet ministers is focused on any financial implications of proposed policies. The total of expenditures in a department is a matter of high administration policy, and major decisions will be fought out at ministry or even cabinet level. The more specific and detailed control exercised by the treasury in financial matters is supplemented by the specific departmental controls and by the general supervision and control coming from the collective responsibility for all policies, financial and otherwise, that binds all members of the government.

However, the British cabinet members generally find that their control over the general financial policy is imperfect. As Samuel Beer points out, the processes by which taxation and other revenue decisions are reached are highly criticized. These decisions are made by the chancellor of the exchequer, who reveals them to the cabinet, which must support them, only a day or two before they are introduced to the legislature in his budget speech. Although he consults in advance with the ministers about those areas which affect them and their ministries specifically, he has often consulted with only the prime minister about the budget as a whole. This tends to preclude any real collective decision making within the cabinet on financial policy[25] Throughout his discussions of his cabinet experience as a Labor minister, Richard Crossman confirms this. For example, in his diary entry concerning a particular budget for 1966, Crossman states his concern about the constitutional issue involved in the existing budget procedures. To him, it seemed to make a mockery of cabinet government and cabinet responsibility to introduce the budget to the cabinet as a last minute surprise, when it was too late for anyone to do anything about it.[26] Thus, in the financial area the prime minister, along with his chancellor of the exchequer, appears to have a great measure of control, far beyond that of the cabinet as a collective group.

By statute, the president must prepare an annual budget to submit to Congress. Within the administration, the purpose of the executive budget, which reflects the president's program priorities and preferences, is to coordinate federal expenditures in order to promote governmental economy, efficiency, and the president's programs. The Office of Management and Budget is the president's central coordinating agency in the budget area. The chief executive's control of his budget within his administration is imperfect, however. Because of the role that Congress plays in financial legislation, both Congress and the clientele groups of the various departments and agencies are sources of strength for executive officials in the budget struggle. Department bureaucrats may be successful in appealing to congressional committees for more funds than the president had allocated. Those clientele groups linked to agencies by virtue of their common interest area will also lobby legislative committees for increases. If these efforts succeed, then a department within the executive branch will have a measure of independence from the president's control.[27] Although it has been seen that cabinet collective decision making is not a complete reality in the British budgetary process, coordination in financial planning is not as difficult to obtain there as it is in the United States because the cabinet collective setting in which final approval is reached brings a high degree of coordination to the process. Only the American president, with his Office of Management and Budget, can achieve coordination in financial planning in the American executive branch, and, to the extent that agencies and bureaus achieve some independence, some degree of coordination is lost.

Influence on the Legislature

In the matter of executive-legislative relations in the budget process, the theory in Britain is departed from in practice. Theoretically, the ministers of the Crown initiate all proposals for taxation, known as ways and means, and expenditures, known as supply. Then, the House of Commons approves or denies the executive proposals. In actuality, most of the control over all aspects of financial legislation lies with the cabinet, especially within the treasury. By a standing order of the House of Commons, all expenditure proposals must come solely from the executive. It is the task of the chancellor of the exchequer to present the annual budget to the legislature.[28] The presumption that it will be accepted intact is so strong that it immediately goes into effect without any specific action being taken by the legislature. Commons has the constitutional right later to rescind or amend the budget, but if this happens it would almost without doubt be interpreted as an indication of a lack of confidence.[29] Thus, while pressure in advance from individual ministers and anticipation of reactions from Parliament (the government's own backbenchers as well as the opposition) may persuade the government to modify its financial proposals at the formulation stage, once the financial statement and requests have been drafted and presented by the executive, Commons cannot openly force any major revisions without coming close to, if not actually, toppling the government. This permits unified responsibility for public expenditures and a coherent financial program, expeditiously enacted, but sharply limits any marked degree of legislative control over public finance.

In the United States, as in Great Britain, proposals for the budget come from the executive, but any close resemblance between the processes in the different countries ends there. Beyond the point of introduction, a process of bargaining and negotiation begins in America. The president's coordination and control over finance decisions in the legislature is markedly less than the prime minister's in Commons because the processes in the House of Representatives and the Senate are much more decentralized. The legislature plays a more decisive role in financial decisions than is the case in Britain, and both houses of Congress take part; in Britain, only Commons is effectively involved. Appropriations committees in both House and Senate have many chances to exercise oversight through the appropriations process. Unlike the House of Commons, Congress may approve more funds for some areas and less for others than are called for by provisions in the president's budget. In spite of its greater autonomy in budget matters when compared to Commons, Congress felt the need to decrease its dependence upon the president's budget proposals and enacted the 1974 Congressional Budget Reform Act. This created a standing budget committee for each chamber and established a congressional budget office. The aim of these measures is to develop a comprehensive and coordinated system of congressional budgetary processes. Whether or not the desired coordination will result remains to be seen.

In spite of the decentralized processes by which it operates, Congress does play a major role in setting governmental priorities through the appropriations it authorizes, as well as by the changes it makes in the president's tax requests. The outcome in financial legislation is usually a compromise between the priorities of the president and those of the legislators. For this reason, responsibility for the final product is diffused and difficult to pinpoint definitively. In Britain, it clearly lies with the cabinet and the majority party.

CONTROL OVER FOREIGN POLICY

The position of a chief executive at the apex of the executive branch of government makes him a country's principal spokesman in international affairs. The nature of international relations in the modern world has tended to concentrate foreign policy-making power in the hands of the chief executive and of his close advisers much more than is the case in domestic affairs. In both Britain and the United States, a tendency toward bipartisan support in foreign matters, both in the general population as well as among party officials, has lessened party conflict in such issues.

The American president's foreign policy-making power is augmented by several factors: his role as chief of state; the constitutional provisions and congressional statutes giving him more desion-making power in this area than is the case in domestic matters; his position as commander-in-chief of the armed forces; he disposition of courts to uphold the use of presidential power n foreign matters; and the general support of the public for presiential supremacy in this area. The president can enter into execuive agreements that have the force of treaties but which do not equire Senate agreement, and the number of executive agreements ntered into far exceeds the number of treaties ratified.

Congress and the general public are generally more disposed to ive the president latitude in the international arena than they are oward deferring to him in domestic matters. To some extent, this s a result of a greater degree of public attention to domestic issues because of the impact they have on daily life and of a patriotic eeling that support for the nation, personified in the president, in he international realm is necessary and proper.

Since the reaction against the Viet Nam War, some changes of ttitude have taken place on the part of the public and of the Congress. Demonstrations, criticism, and heightened public inerest in foreign affairs, at least with respect to military intervention in the third world have all combined with congressional iction to limit the president's powers to wage wars. Even so, the arlier trend toward giving the president much more latitude in oreign than in domestic affairs seems to be resurfacing. He is still *he* foreign policymaker for the United States. The cabinet role which an American president most often assumes himself in practice, in spite of the existence of the secretary of state, is that of hief foreign policy drafter.

R. M. Punnett suggests that the chief executive is also preminent in the foreign policy sector in the British political system. Normally, the prime minister involves himself heavily in foreign policy matters, sometimes to the exclusion of the foreign secretary. The need for rapid military decisions in an age of nuclear weapons, and the style of modern diplomacy, with summit meetings of chief executives and their top advisers, have combined to make the prime minister's foreign policy involvement direct and personal. The exigencies of two world wars in this century resulted in a conentration of the power to conduct foreign affairs in the chief executive which has lasted into more peaceful times.[30] There is in Britain, as in the United States, a tradition of bipartisanship in foreign affairs, so that party identity makes for less difference then than it does in domestic matters. Agreement between the two parliamentary front benches is not unusual.

It is interesting to note in this connection the tendency for retired prime ministers to emphasize in their memoirs the time spent on foreign affairs. The prime minister receives Foreign Office papers as a matter of course, which is not the case with all papers concerning domestic affairs. The immediacy of many foreign affairs issues, demanding quick decisions on short notice, makes them relatively unsuitable for full cabinet discussions.

Rose suggests that, in Britain, it is only in foreign policy areas that the decision-making process follows a "ruling clique" model. By this he means that the prime minister, with the Foreign Office and the Ministry of Defense, makes decisions in relative isolation from outside. However, this gives the prime minister slightly less foreign policy authority on his own than that which the American president enjoys. There may be policy disagreement and conflict between the prime minister and defense and foreign ministers. Major differences may have to be ironed out in the full cabinet.[8] By contrast, the president may decide to ignore the secretaries of state and defense and be his own foreign policy maker, aided only by personal advisers. On balance, however, the chief executives in both countries customarily have a greater degree of independent authority in the foreign policy area than they have in domestic affairs.

CABINET GOVERNMENT

It is increasingly suggested that British government ought to be called "cabinet government" instead of "parliamentary government," the former term more accurately indicating the actual location of political decision-making power in Britain today. When one speaks of the government in Britain, one often means the cabinet, including the prime minister as its leader. The cabinet is the directing force within the governmental machinery; as such, the cabinet makes the most important policy decisions, supervises the policy execution, and coordinates the work of the whole executive machinery.[32]

Although the cabinet is important in the United States government, it is clearly subordinate to the president. In contrast to the British collective executive, the American executive is a single one. With this difference in mind, we can now analyze and compare the roles of the cabinets in the two political systems.

ROLE OF THE CABINETS

The increase in political strength of the British cabinet parallels and is in part the consequence of the development of the two-party system and the tradition of strong party discipline and legislative cohesion. The cabinet is the source of all major policy, the overseer and coordinator of administration, and essentially an executive committee of the House of Commons; it organizes the work of the House, shepherds bills through it, and explains and defends its policies and programs in that arena. Of the essence of cabinet government is the fact that the executive is chosen by the legislature, remains in it, and governs so long as it retains the confidence of the legislature. As has been seen, in contrast to the separation between legislative and executive powers which characterizes the American government, the British cabinet is the one body in which these two powers are joined. The juncture is achieved because the members of the cabinet who exercise the executive powers also, in actuality, control most of the legislative power. While cabinets come and go, the cabinet continues. Whereas any one cabinet can be deprived of its power, that does not result in legislative recapture of power; the same authority is simply given to a new set of individuals who compose a new cabinet.[33]

Cabinet members in Britain combine two other roles besides the legislative-executive combination. Most head particular ministries, while at the same time serving as part of the chief executive and, as such, standing above the ministries. This combination is essential to a plural executive. The centrifugal tendencies of the departmental interests may tempt ministers to lose sight of government-wide responsibilities. It is sometimes complained that at cabinet meetings, whatever is being discussed, some members are ill-informed because they are mainly occupied with their own departments and with the problems of coordination with other departments whose affairs impinge directly upon their own. This also presents a problem for coordination among the United States cabinet members, especially because, unlike the British case, there is no collective cabinet to deal with substantive decision making as a body. In Britain, however, there is a better chance that the pluralism inherent in the cabinet may be overcome on occasion and that ministers can fully realize both responsibilities. When this is achieved, a high degree of coordination in administration and coherence in policy can be attained.[34] By their common membership in the cabinet, ministers are aided and obliged to make the actions of their various departments both compatible and mutually supportive. Thanks to their party majority within the legislature, they are freed from the inconsistencies that the more casual majorities of a leaderless legislature, such as the American, will impose on public policy.[35]

The entire relationship between the American president and his cabinet is markedly different, and the term "cabinet government" in no way applies. The heads of the United States cabinet departments are clearly subordinate to the president, both formally and substantively, and the president and his cabinet do not together constitute a plural executive. The cabinet heads are certainly part of a whole administration, but their only real policy focus is toward their separate departments. Advice to the president usually comes separately from each department, and he must make the final decisions himself, resolving problems of conflict and duplication between departments. Departmental ties that develop with clientele interest groups and with groups inside Congress work to limit the degree of the president's overall control over policy, but he is free of any collective links with his cabinet and can accept or ignore cabinet members' advice as he sees fit.

CABINET SELECTION AND COMPOSITION

The British prime minister in theory has a free hand in selecting his cabinet members. In fact, the power to appoint to cabinet posts is one of his key party leadership resources. However, in practice, there are strong party constraints which limit his freedom of choice. Inevitably, there are leading members of Parliament in his party who must be included. Some of these may lead wings or factions of the party and have considerable support of their own. While the prime minister is literally forced to work with some associates, the American president is not. For example, President Kennedy selected a cabinet which did not include one major legislative figure of his party, and President Nixon's original cabinet contained only one of these legislative party leaders. Although customary limitations have evolved, to which the president must pay attention in forming his cabinet, these are general and do not infringe on his freedom of choice. On the other hand, those constraints on the prime minister's cabinet selections are definite and particular; the leader of each important party faction must be included in order that allegiance from the factions be maintained.[36]

Some of the chief factional leaders that must be included in the British cabinet may be the main rivals of the prime minister for his position. It would be politically impossible to hold the parliamentary party together without including these rivals, and, in addition, it may in fact benefit the prime minister to have them there. If the key political rivals within his party are in the cabinet with him, they are blanketed under cabinet collective responsibility, rather than left out, free to raise storms of criticism on the back benches and within the country. Some measure of harmony in the cabinet itself has to be sacrificed for the sake of a greater measure of unity within the parliamentary party as a whole. Thus, the policy-making autonomy of the prime minister is significantly curtailed because of the composition of the cabinet.

The British leader of the opposition, heading the political party which does not hold a majority of legislative seats, operates under the same basic constraints and freedoms in selecting the shadow cabinet. Yet, the actual formation of the government and assumption of the post of prime minister tends to confer on the chief executive a greater degree of freedom of choice in staffing cabinet posts, in moving individuals from post to post, and even in dismissing ministers than he had as leader of the opposition. The added status of the top executive office carries with it an edge of resources beyond that of simply party leader.

The prime minister is theoretically free to shift ministers from post to post, or to dismiss them altogether. Again, however, political reality constrains his freedom to do so. He cannot risk frequent changes, dismissals or resignations, or even incurring weakened support for his policies from his cabinet members, lest he undermine either the solidarity of his parliamentary party support on which he and the rest of the government depend, or the solidarity of party support in the country on which his party's legislative majority in the next election depends. It is often suggested, for example, that after Prime Minister MacMillan dismissed one-third of his cabinet members, although his right to do so was unquestioned, his position as party leader was badly undermined. On balance, the leader's power of appointment and dismissal give him an edge over other party members; because cabinet posts are so clearly steps to the top of the political ladder, he can exert a strong impact on their future careers. However, he is limited in his freedom to do so by important party constraints.

In the United States, a cabinet post is not an essential step toward the presidency; in fact, no cabinet member has been nominated for the presidency from that post since the first third of this century. Cabinet members are appointed to their positions by the president with Senate approval. Many come from the private sector, with no previous political experience, and move back into it when their cabinet term ends. In making his cabinet selections, the president is less constrained by his party than is the case in Britain. He may choose his cabinet in part to try to gain party unity with support from factional wings, in part to enlist support on a regional or ethnic basis, in part to repay old political debts, or in part to gain expertise or administrative ability. Whatever the reason, the choice is basically his own to make. Unlike the prime minister, he need not confine his selections to members of the legislature, and, in fact, if an American cabinet member holds a legislative seat prior to his cabinet appointment, he must resign his position in one branch to join another. The president often turns to state-level offices, and to industry, labor, or academia for cabinet appointees. He may even select members of the opposition political party, something a prime minister never does unless a coalition cabinet has to be formed.

Overall, the British cabinet ministers are generally more experienced in political life than are the American cabinet chiefs. Ordinarily they have served an apprentice period in the legislature and in subcabinet level executive posts. While American cabinet secretaries may have had little or no executive or legislative experience, they are more likely to have special training and expertise in the subject area over which their department has jurisdiction. In addition, they often have strong ties with their departments' constituent groups from which they frequently come. Since the British cabinet ministers are likely to be moved from post to post and to come from the national political leadership ranks, they are unlikely to have either the specialized expertise and technical knowledge or, in most cases, the longterm close links with groups in the private sector whose affairs are vitally affected by ministry and cabinet decisions.

When a president selects his cabinet heads, he is choosing leaders to manage departments for him. The prime minister is not doing *only* this; his first consideration is to select a parliamentary team to occupy the front benches in the House of Commons. The main concern of this team is to continue to carry the support of its own backbenchers.[37]

CABINET COLLECTIVE RESPONSIBILITY

The most important of the customs governing the work of the British cabinet is that of cabinet collective responsibility, for which there is no American counterpart. It derives from the fact that the government in Britain is a creature of Parliament and is responsible to it. Since the government survives only so long as it has the support of a majority in the House of Commons, it must present a united front to that body. Thus, all cabinet ministers must at all times support the cabinet decisions, collectively shouldering the responsibility for its policies and actions. During discussions in cabinet, a minister may vigorously oppose a decision, but once the decision has been made, he may not evidence any disagreement with it. Even if a minister has taken no active part in the preliminary discussions of issues on which he disagrees with the final position, he must support it wholeheartedly in public. If he cannot do this, and is unable to refrain from public criticism of a cabinet decision, he must resign his cabinet post.

Cabinet responsibility allows for a united front to be presented not only to Parliament—thus helping maintain party discipline and answer opposition criticism—but also to the party outside Parliament and to the electorate at large.[38] Voters are thus able to assign responsibility for policies and programs to the party instead of to individual ministers of departments and to vote accordingly.

Although it by no means involves agreement by all ministers with all cabinet policies, collective responsibility works to curb sharp and excessive disagreement among them.[39] It also promotes a degree of compromise among factions within the party in order to obtain the necessary uniform stand. This in turn works to stimulate a more unified and focused opposition than could otherwise be achieved. By contrast, in the United States, one of the major reasons why there is no organized, cohesive opposition is that there is no collective government position to oppose.

Although some American cabinet heads may develop the feeling that they are indeed a team supporting the president in his administration, this is often not the case. At no time does the whole cabinet answer together to the legislature. The president himself is not a cabinet member, and the cabinet meets as a full body only at the president's will and initiative. The heads of the departments have not ordinarily worked together over a long period of time, while British ministers usually have; before their appointment many do not know one another, and they sometimes do not even know the president. No one, neither the legislature, the party, nor the public, expects the cabinet to present a common position on all major issues, and neither the president nor the cabinet members expect his party members in the legislature to vote in support of all measures he recommends.

RELATIONS BETWEEN CHIEF EXECUTIVES AND THEIR CABINETS

With no specific ministry of his own, the prime minister is free to serve as coordinator-in-chief for the cabinet, chairing its meetings, aided by the secretariat. Since he combines this role with that of a party and parliamentary leader, his authority within the cabinet is great. The coordinating role has increased as other ministers have become more and more absorbed in their complex and time-consuming departmental business, giving the prime minister a greater personal role in the overall planning and coordinating of government policy.

While the American cabinet meets only at the behest of the president, the prime minister cannot fail to have the cabinet meet regularly as a full body to discuss and debate policy issues. The extent of mastery that he can exercise over the rest of the cabinet depends largely on his own personality and leadership position in the party, as well as on his own view of his role. However, he is ultimately limited by the basic collective nature of the body, the positions and support of the other ministers for his leadership, and his need for their continued backing. The possibility that their support may be withdrawn is an important constraint upon his actions. When a prime minister is confronted with a substantial amount of discontent in the cabinet or in the party generally, he can be driven from office.

Thus, the relationship between the prime minister and key cabinet ministers is a mutually supporting and restraining one. To some extent, the tenure in office of the ministers themselves and their continued support from the parliamentary party depends upon the prime minister. Reciprocally, their attacks, threats of resignation, or actual resignation from the cabinet may imperil the leadership position of the prime minister. In addition, while the prime minister shapes the cabinet agenda and hence may be able to delay discussion of controversial measures within the cabinet, he cannot postpone indefinitely full cabinet discussion of such issues.[40]

With the great increase in the scope of governmental activity, the full cabinet has become less concerned with details and more with making and approving top-level broad policy decisions. The cabinet secretariat prepares and circulates materials for the cabinet meetings in advance, so that they can be studied prior to discussion. In addition, much of the more detailed and technical work has been increasingly delegated to cabinet committees and to individual ministers. A trend toward "superministries" has evolved, with several ministries combined and headed by one minister aided by several others.[41] Samuel Beer has suggested that this works to strengthen the coordination among groups of departments, but at the same time has had a tendency to fragment cabinet authority because the centers of power thus created are harder to control than were their constituent parts when they were dispersed. For a department to commit the whole cabinet to a policy is a more serious matter when it is one of these superministries that operates out of a complex of power.[42]

When the American cabinet meets as a full body, it is more often than not on a formal rather than on a substantive basis. Normally, the president deals with department heads individually. The large personal staffs which presidents appoint have tended to lessen somewhat the importance of the cabinet. Depending upon the inclinations of a particular president, the key policy advisers may not be in the cabinet at all, but in his circle of personal advisers and executive staff agency officials. Since the cabinet members often have no political base of their own and have no direct power over the president's tenure in office, he may meet with them or not, and heed their advice or not, at his own discretion. The president alone is responsible for major policy decisions; hence, he alone must finally make and stand behind them.

In any cabinet, the British as well as the American, some departments' business is felt to be more vital to the policy-making process than is that of others. This depends in part on the problems which seem paramount in a country at a particular time and in part on the priorities which a particular administration sets. In the United States, the term "inner cabinet" has been coined to cover the heads of the state, defense, justice, and treasury departments, those with whom the president spends much time and on whom he relies for policy advice. By contrast, the outer cabinet consists of those chiefs whom he generally consults with less regularity and frequency; those under this rubric include the departments of the interior; housing and urban development; health and human services; and transportation. Sometimes those heading outer cabinet departments complain of the lack of contact with the president for long periods of time.[43]

Individual cabinet members may have considerable independence from the president in their actions because of the ties which they develop with congressional committees and their clientele groups. For example, the agriculture secretary may have closer contacts with the Senate and House of Representatives agriculture subcommittees and with farm interest groups than with the rest of the administration or the president. In any department or ministry, there are centrifugal forces pulling the individual in charge away from the cabinet or administration as a whole and toward the more particular concerns of the specific department. In the United States, counterforces overcoming this tendency are relatively weak when compared to the counteracting effects of cabinet collective responsibility and party government in Great Britain.

BRITISH GOVERNMENT: A PRIME MINISTERIAL GOVERNMENT?

If one intends by the use of a title for a form of government to convey the location of final decision-making power, it is probably true that it is no longer accurate to label British government as a "parliamentary government." The political system is still parliamentary in the sense that legal supremacy continues to rest in Parliament and that the cabinet is part of the legislature and continues in office only as long as it has the support of the legislature. But, with the development of centralized party organizations and party cohesion in the legislature, the cabinet is assured of remaining in office and having its policies and programs enacted so long as its members fill a majority of the seats in the House of Commons. Hence, the system can be described with greater accuracy in pinpointing political decision-making power as a cabinet government. Parliament plays a supervising, criticizing role, rather than a basic policy-making role.

It has recently been suggested that prime ministerial government might be a more accurate description than is cabinet government. Among others, R. H. S. Crossman and J. P. Mackintosh have maintained that either the prime minister or the departmental ministers, backed by strong civil servants in top positions, make the policy decisions. The cabinet has shrunk in importance to the extent that it is now only form, lacking substance, according to this argument. At the same time, it is alleged that the prime minister can and does act in a high-handed manner, on his own initiative or together with a small group of ministers.[44] This is not to say that prime ministerial government implies "presidential government." On the contrary, Crossman points out that the prime minister's encounters with the leader of the opposition differ from presidential press conferences most importantly in that the former take place in the parliamentary ambience. It is this regular conflict between the two leaders in the parliamentary setting which most clearly marks off the parliamentary system from the presidential. The prime minister must be present in Commons, fighting his contender, and thus is constantly tested in a process covered by the press.[45]

It is true that the prime minister's prominence—as government leader, party leader, and in the public view generally, as he receives greater coverage by the mass media—has markedly increased. More and more it appears that the elections, formally held to fill the 635 seats in the House of Commons, have come to be personal contests between the two major party leaders, one of whom will become prime minister. The May 1979 general election followed a campaign in which the Labor party highlighted its leader, James Callaghan, whereas the Conservative party conducted a much more typical campaign which focused principally upon party and gave less attention to Margaret Thatcher. Although both party leaders campaigned widely throughout the country, the difference in their emphasis on leader or party points up the extent to which elections in Britain are still fought between parties rather than between two potential prime ministers.

It is also accurate to list, as Crossman does, a number of powers which the prime minister has at his disposal. He is the principal successor to the powers that formerly accrued to the monarch. With the chancellor of the exchequer, he prepares the budget outside the cabinet, and, by means of his authority over the treasury, he has control over finances and civil service personnel. He has relative freedom in dismissing cabinet members. In addition, the prime minister has the final word on cabinet agenda and on the organization of cabinet committees. He also has a monopoly on patronage and a high degree of control over government publicity.[46]

Others reach different conclusions from the same facts, interpreted differently. Finer concludes that while the prime minister is clearly the single most important individual within the cabinet, by far overshadowing his colleagues there, the final decision-making power continues to rest in the cabinet, because it is that body which must keep the confidence of Parliament.[47]

Stacey believes that Crossman's arguments confuse the cabinet meetings with the cabinet itself as an institution. Indeed, Stacey states, the cabinet, including the committees responsible to it, has not lost substantial power to the prime minister. That body does not have to agree with the recommendations of the committees or with the leader. On the several occasions when the prime minister has acted on his own initiative or in concert with a small group of ministers and when these actions were not approved of by the cabinet, countervailing forces were produced. For example, Stacey cites the major role played by Anthony Eden in formulating a Suez policy unpopular with his cabinet. Until a late stage in the policy development, he kept his cabinet colleagues in the dark. The countervailing forces subsequently forced him from office. Granted, he was ill when he resigned, but similar illness has not resulted in the resignation of other prime ministers not in such disfavor with their cabinets.[48] Thus, even though the prime ministerial office has risen in status and the holder of the office has authority different in kind from that of his colleagues, he is not independent of that body. It is his sole source of political authority. Although occasionally a major policy matter may be dealt with by a partial cabinet, the regular procedure is for the cabinet to discuss and decide all major issues and emergencies. The prime minister's position will carry great weight with the other cabinet members, but, unlike the president, the prime minister can be, and on occasion is, overruled by his cabinet. In fact, the prime minister can exercise his greatly increased powers only by carrying his cabinet with him.[49]

Stacey concludes that the so-called emergence of "government by prime minister" is probably a myth because the tradition of collective responsibility of the cabinet to Parliament still obtains and the complexity of modern government makes prime ministerial government unlikely. The sheer burden of the office prevents a prime minister from intervening at all closely, except in the most urgent matters.[50] G. W. Jones confirms this, pointing out that the prime minister lacks the administrative resources and knowledge that would be needed to make a large impact on a wide range of governmental responsibilities.[51] Although the personal staff available to him has increased in size in recent years, it does not begin to approach the staff at the disposal of an American president.

Samuel Beer has probably best cut through to the heart of the matter, pointing out that what is lacking from the descriptions of prime ministerial government can be summed up in the word politics. For example, the prime minister knows that if the cabinet, or those members in it who are most prominent politically, should resign, his own leadership position would be gravely discredited. Furthermore, this does not actually have to occur to make its possibility a continuing influence on cabinet interaction. There are, in addition, other dangers constraining the prime minister within the cabinet. Dissension within the cabinet is likely to spread to the parliamentary backbenchers of the party, making Parliament more difficult to handle. It can even spread to the civil service, creating problems of administrative control.[52]

Part of the essence of the British cabinet government lies in the fact that many of the cabinet members will be men with their own strong party bases in Parliament, in the party, and in the country, unlike American cabinet secretaries. The prime minister is constrained by his cabinet in a way that the American president is not. All of the energizing, directing, and coordinating which the prime minister, like the president, can provide for the government does not change the essentially collegial nature of the cabinet system.

AMERICAN GOVERNMENT:
AN INSTITUTIONALIZED PRESIDENCY?

When evaluating the modern presidency, some authors note a twentieth-century change in the dimensions of that office which has been labeled the "institutionalization of the presidency."[53] This refers to the growth of a large presidential bureaucracy, an ongoing institution composed of the White House office and the executive office of the president. Although individual presidents come and go, the institutionalized presidency persists and functions with a great deal of power and no political accountability. It is suggested that while this presidential bureaucracy was developed and expanded by presidents to gain greater control over the sprawling executive branch and over policy making, it has taken on a life of its own. Thus, the argument runs, the institutionalization poses a danger of actually reducing a president's influence on policy.

Thomas Cronin has observed that, ironically, the addition of numbers of administrators and functions to the presidential establishment has resulted in a presidency afflicted with the very ills of those traditional departments that the expansions were designed to remedy. Since the presidency has itself become a large, complex bureaucracy, it is rapidly acquiring many of the problems characteristic of all large bureaucracies—layering, overspecialization, communication gaps, inadequate coordination, and the impulse to become consumed with short-term concerns of operation at the expense of systematic thinking about the long-run consequences of policies and priorities. Dealing with this monster takes so much of the president's time that he has little left to consult with cabinet officials, for example.[54]

A markedly different interpretation of the modern presidency stresses its personalized rather than its institutionalized nature.[55] The closest advisers are personally selected by the president, and each president shapes the office he holds in a highly individual way. Style and personality are viewed as key factors in molding the presidency, particularly in light of the media focus on candidate image in the course of presidential campaigns and on the personality of the incumbent president. The most often cited drawback to this personalization of the office is the corollary tendency toward enlarged presidential powers, especially in relation to those of Congress which cannot be similarly personalized, and the charismatic nature of the popular attachment to personalized authority. Both of these developments are felt to thwart the democratic values of limited authority and executive accountability.

By implication, these perceived problems inherent in the nature of the modern presidency might appear to pose similar dangers in the future for the prime minister's office in Britain. Currently, since the attention paid to the personality of the prime minister does not approach that directed toward the president, and since the bureaucratic institutions surrounding that office have not grown to the scale of the American presidential bureaucracy, the magnitude of the problems facing the British executive position appear slight by comparison. However, if current trends persist, they may develop to equal proportions.

It is accurate to conclude that personalities give much shape to the office of the presidency. Koenig observes that far more than most offices, the presidency is plastic and responsive to the variations in the political personalities of its different incumbents. Although lesser offices can be regulated, institutionalized, and bureaucratized, the presidency has eluded rigidity.[56] However, because the presidency is an institution with constitutional restraints that are designed to curb excesses of power, there are outer limits to the degree that any incumbent can expand the office. Beyond the institutional checks on executive power that were built into the governmental framework at its origin, political realities also work to inhibit presidential abuse of power. For example, Congress has demonstrated its ability to collect and exercise its potential checking power with surprising speed and strength, once sufficiently aroused. Public opinion, on which the personalized power of the president depends, can reverse its direction, abandoning support of a president deemed guilty of power abuse. Perhaps most important in the long run is a basic tendency exhibited in the American political culture toward suspicion of political authority; the American people are less inclined to stand in awe of top officials than to topple them from any pedestals they might attempt to ascend.

It is perhaps in this ability to make large, personal impact on the office that presidents can best hope to overcome the potential immobilizing effects of institutionalization of their office. Similar to all institutions that increase in size and scope of activity and function over time, the presidential bureaucracy has developed a degree of autonomy. On a smaller scale, the office of the prime minister has also expanded and developed some autonomy with the creation and growth of the cabinet secretariat and other advisers to aid the prime minister in guiding and coordinating the increasingly complex cabinet business. It is probably inevitable that present-day chief executives be aided by such expanded staffs and that coordinating and controlling them will call for much effort and creativity. As Koenig observes, the institutionalized presidency may provide the best guarantee that the multiple specialists a major problem requires will be addressed to it, which is especially important in light of the enormity of the President's problems and the potential dangers of the times.[57] What may enable future presidents to remain in control of the presidential bureaucracy is the ability they have to give personal direction to the institutions surrounding their office.

CHAPTER SEVEN

LEGAL SYSTEMS

Legalism runs throughout modern liberal government. It takes many forms: constitutional prescriptions and prohibitions; statutory authorizations and restraints; writs and processes; procedural and substantive standards; and a host of others. The fabric of legal relationships, institutions, values, and expectations gives meaning and force to the idea of a rule of law. The very idea of authority, as opposed to mere power or force, implies legitimacy, and legitimacy in the liberal tradition means at least that the competence of governors to collect taxes, make policy decisions, administer laws, and do a myriad of other things is conferred and controlled by law. But, political liberalism also means that the governed must have opportunity to challenge what the governors do and how they set about doing it.

Political accountability enforced by means of political processes is an essential part of the grand design, but redress of individual injuries inflicted by abuse of authority requires more specific and direct remedies. Provision of those remedies is a major function of legal systems in the Anglo-American tradition of constitutional government. In both societies, the legal culture embodies, informs, and vitalizes the rule of law. In both, legalism penetrates most important phases of political and social life. To ignore its prominence would do violence to the reality of contemporary constitutionalism in Britain and the United States. Also, in both the norms of the political culture condition the content and function of law; the legal systems embrace the values, beliefs, styles, expectations, and attitudes of the respective societies but also act upon those societies.

Although the American system owes much to its British antecedents, the origins of British and American legal systems lie largely in different milieus. Different pressures and different times shaped the emergent systems. By the middle of the eighteenth century, British domination of America south of Canada ensured permanent establishment of the already advanced system of common law jurisprudence. American colonials were mostly of English origin; those who were not lived in British North America subject to the authority of British colonial governments which reflected the traditions and institutions of the British cultural heritage. The common law was chief among them. The substance of that law and the basic structure of the English judicial system were brought to America by colonial governments, by English-trained lawyers and judges, and by the fervent reception given to Blackstone's *Commentaries on the Laws of England* during the second half of the eighteenth century.

In the pre-Revolutionary era, America was an essentially frontier society given to a developing tradition of local self-government. It was separated from the mother country by long, slow communication routes across three thousand miles of water. Americans therefore began almost immediately to adapt the substance of the common law to the needs and conditions of the new society, and, in a modified form, the inherited common law in America survived the 1776 Revolution. Although it continued after 1776, the American common law system took on a greater flexibility and adaptability than had been possible before that year, for slow growth by evolution had long been the formative process of the parent English legal system. The American legal system fell almost immediately under heavy legislative control. By 1820, statutory law had become its principal method of development, but, from 1820 to 1875, statutory expansion of the legal system gradually lost prominence, until by 1875 the judiciary had regained that primary control over its own branch of government that it exercises today.[1] In sum, Americans inherited the substance and structure of a developed legal system. Independence from the mother country did not end the common law in America and mark the start of a new and unique indigenous legal system, but, it did facilitate the growth of a native version, built by trial and error on a foundation of English law. The present American legal system is the product of experimental growth and development at state and national levels.

The range of judge-made law varies between the British[2] and American legal systems. In both jurisdictions, statutory law in modern times has tended to curb the range of common law, but most modification along that line in America has taken place in the states where the range of common law has been mainly limited to torts, contracts, and real property.[3] In general, there is no national common law, especially not in the criminal law arena, for no common law crimes are recognized, and none is enforced by national courts. Approximately half of the states do recognize and enforce common law crimes, however.

Another point of difference between British and American legal systems involves variant degrees of judicial regard for the force of precedent. *Stare decisis,* or the rule of precedent, is the formative rule of judge-made common law. British judges hold previously decided cases in much higher esteem than American judges do, perhaps because American judges are not involved with the Britisher's respect for gradualism, heritage, and stability. American judges and law are more pragmatic, more aware that law must adapt quickly to changing needs of society if it is to be an effective instrument of social control. Judges of both systems recognize that internal consistency, predictability, certainty, and stability are desirable attributes of a legal order. But, American judges are more willing than British to abandon, distinguish, ignore, or repudiate prior decisions; whereas British judges adhere with much fidelity to the rule of precedent, those of American national tribunals do not so conscientiously feel themselves bound by past decisions.

The welfare state has affected the development of the British and American legal systems. An increased output of statutory law in Britain and the United States has inevitably followed rapid societal change and the tremendous expansion of governmental functions that has occurred since the industrial revolution. In both countries, the welfare/service state has dominated the older norms of political laissez faire, with the result that increased demands on government have been translated into statutory law. In both places the volume of administrative rules and regulations that have the force of law has surpassed that of judge-made and enacted law. The statutes of both governments have increasingly come to deal with general principles, delegating authority to administrative departments and other units to supplement general enactments by detailed rules and regulations. Neither Congress nor Parliament has the ability or knowledge necessary to legislate rapidly and with specific content. Because British and American societies have undergone the vast changes that accompany burgeoning technology and industry, both have tended to see statute law and administrative rules grow to overshadow but not displace judge-made law. Nevertheless, both systems have remained common law systems in which many legal rules are made and enforced by judges, although the days are gone when more leisurely government permitted judges alone to play a major role in keeping the law attuned to societal needs, expectations, and conditions.[4] In spite of these shared characteristics, American courts play a major role in keeping administrative procedures and rules within the boundaries of delegated authority and due process of law. British judges, in contrast, exercise only minimum control over administrative action, but they can decide actions interpreting grants of authority by Parliament to administration and thereby add interpretative gloss to Britain's unwritten constitution. British judges traditionally preside over fact-finding parliamentary Tribunals of Inquiry created to look into allegations of corruption or other improprieties in administration. That is a nonjudicial role, of course, and is undertaken in the face of a strong tradition of judicial independence from political functions of government. But, these developments notwithstanding, English and American legal systems have adhered to the principle that all persons shall be subject to ordinary law administered by regular courts, and both have refused to create separate systems of tribunals to try charges of alleged wrongdoing brought against government administrators.

JUDICIAL ORGANIZATIONS

It will be impossible here to do more than notice some major differences in the judicial organizations of England and the United

States, for the subject is broad and both are the products of their respective political and legal heritages and cultures. Adaptation of the American judicial system to the principles and structure of government under the national Constitution has produced features and processes that depart from its English progenitors in many ways.

THE AMERICAN JUDICIAL SYSTEM

It is next to impossible to compare in detail the judicial system of England and Wales with that of the United States and especially with the national court system. The unitary government of the former permits a single integrated structure of courts embracing what in the United States would be local, state, and national tribunals. American federalism mandates that instead of one system, the states united under the Constitution shall operate fifty separate systems and the national government yet another. American state and local courts embrace justices of the peace, magistrates, domestic relations, juvenile, traffic, probate, small claims, landlord-tenant, and other specialized courts of a local nature; state, country or circuit courts of general jurisdiction, and intermediate and high appellate courts complete the patterns.

But, those courts are mentioned here only to fill in the picture. The American courts relevant to this examination make up a specialized judiciary of limited jurisdiction but nationwide scope. Congress created them by virtue of authority conferred on it to establish courts inferior to the Supreme Court to exercise the judicial power of the United States. They consist today of district courts, courts of appeals, and the Supreme Court. They hear and decide civil and criminal cases arising under the Constitution, laws, and treaties of the United States or that originate in a local or state court but raise a federal question. Jurisdiction over other sources of litigation belongs in general to the state court systems. It is only slightly inaccurate, but it is deceptively simplified to assert that national courts enforce national laws, and state courts enforce state laws.

These national constitutional tribunals are geographically decentralized, so that at least one district court operates in each state of the union.[5] Trial juries operate only in these courts, and the rights of criminal defendants are most meaningful and most often invoked during proceedings before them. Trial is normally by a single judge, with or without a jury, and any case tried by a district court can be appealed to a court of appeals. States are grouped into circuits of varying size, with each circuit containing one court of appeals. It supervises the district courts of its circuit and receives cases on appeal from them. Each court of appeals has at least three judges assigned to it and must take jurisdiction over any case brought up to it. When more than three judges make a bench, they sit in panels of three except in rare instances when decisions are rendered by a full court. Above the courts of appeals is the Supreme Court at the top of this nominal hierarchy of constitutional tribunals. The highest court consists of a chief justice and eight associate justices who always sit as a unit, exercise almost complete discretion over the cases they review, and supervise the inferior courts in the interests of systemic uniformity and harmonious operation.

The American constitutional courts, along with those of the states, make up a complex mechanism for administering justice to the people, but one consistent with federalism. It is a system of multiple tribunals having confusing and overlapping jurisdictions. It embraces fifty-one systems of civil and criminal law, procedures, and rules. To it all, the nationalizing decisions of the Supreme Court have imparted only a modicum of uniformity and simplification.

THE ENGLISH JUDICIAL SYSTEM

The integrated judicial system of England and Wales is less complicated from that of the United States because of the unitary nature of its constitutional setting. One structure of centrally administered and staffed courts incorporates justices of the peace and stipendiary magistrates at the bottom, trial and appellate courts in midstructure, and the House of Lords at the top. Instead of multiple systems of rules, procedures, laws, and everything else that make up a judicial system, as found in the American situation, the English judiciary utilizes only one nationwide pattern applied with a high degree of uniformity. Hence, it comprises a relatively more symmetrical, simple, tidy, and integrated arrangement of relationships and jurisdictions than does the American.

Another notable structural difference between the English and American arrangements lies in the fact that the English system maintains one pattern of courts to handle criminal matters and a separate one for civil. They come together under the same judicial roof only on those rare occasions when the appellate jurisdiction of the House of Lords is invoked. In American judicial structures, there is no comparable division; regardless of court, the same judges alternately hear civil and criminal cases as they become ready for trial.

Although limitations of space require an abbreviated description of the English judicial structure, the treatment will be more extended than that devoted to American constitutional courts on the assumption that most American students are less familiar with it than with their own judicial system.[6] As a concession to brevity, and because civil litigation involves only private rights and private law, no attention will be paid to the civil side of the structure.

LOCAL COURTS

Approximately nine hundred rural justice of the peace courts and fifty urban magistrates courts make up the local base of the British criminal court structure. The justices are part-time, unpaid laymen, but the magistrates are full-time, paid lawyers. Together they try ninety-eight percent of all British defendants and dispose annually of an estimated 1.7 million cases involving minor offenses carrying penalties of not over £150 in fines or six months in jail or both. Proceedings are formal and handled with dispatch but with great care for the defendant's rights, despite the fact that juries are not used; defendants are not usually represented by counsel, and a senior police officer normally prosecutes. Although these courts are at the bottom of the structure, they are highly respected and dispense justice in an atmosphere of decorum.

The office of the English justice of the peace (JP) is a very different position from that found in many American states, where JPs have done much to disgrace local justice. The ancient English office predates the reign of Elizabeth I and is the forerunner of the hapless American JP. But, whereas the American office of JP is under heavy attack by proponents of judicial reform, its continued importance in England is based on solid acceptance and on the tradition that it provides citizens opportunity to render valuable public service.[7] No counterpart of the English lay judge serves on American national constitutional courts, all judges of which are full-time and professionally trained.

CROWN COURTS

After having a preliminary hearing before a justice of the peace or a magistrate, and following indictment of the accused, more serious criminal cases are sent up to a crown court for trial. The crown courts have original jurisdiction over more serious offenses and, on appeal, review decisions of magistrate's courts. When a defendant charged with a major felony such as rape, murder, robbery, or larceny is before a crown court, he must be tried by jury unless he pleads guilty. Justices from the high court preside over those trials, and Morrison points out that this service on crown courts brings professional justices who normally sit on the collegial high court in London into contact with the more localized judges. In that way, the senior justices of the system keep in touch with their junior colleagues throughout the country who are engaged in local administration of civil and criminal justice. Therefore, the crown courts bridge the gap between the central courts of London and the decentralized administration of justice by localized tribunals closer to the people.[8]

When a crown court hears an appeal from a local court's decision, a panel of magistrates from other jurisdictions sits with a professional judge from the crown court. That arrangement brings the lay justices into contact with a professional judge at the only point in the judicial system where it occurs, for the justices are otherwise a self-regulating group whose administration of justice is largely self-contained and carried on apart from contact with professional judges.[9]

CRIMINAL DIVISION, COURT OF APPEAL

The criminal division of the court of appeal stands above the crown courts. It is composed of fourteen lords justices and the master of the rolls, and it is the intermediate appellate court of the British judicial system. The criminal division usually hears appeals in panels of three judges who embody a mixture of appellate and trial experience. The criminal division, like the American Supreme Court, can control most of the cases it takes on review, and it typically takes about only 10 percent of those brought to it.[10] Most appeals are taken against convictions on the ground that the evidence leading to conviction was faulty or failed to support the verdict reached. Appeals against sentences are less frequent and can be taken only with the prior consent of the appeal court. But, unlike American national appellate courts, the British tribunal does not often order new trials, an option normally taken only when it finds that a mistrial has occurred. It otherwise limits its action to revising the conviction if it finds an insufficiency of legitimate evidence, or revising the sentence if it finds an excessive penalty has been imposed.[11] Relatively few appeals against either sentence or verdict are attempted in the British criminal justice system, and even fewer raise questions of law that are the normal requirement for appeal in the United States. Solicitors and barristers discourage baseless appeals, and appellate judges frown upon them. The opportunity for appeals is also limited by the fact that with only fourteen justices, the high court cannot hear a large volume of them.

British appellate procedure differs appreciably from that used in American courts. American appeals are predominantly taken on points of law, whereas British appeals are on issues of fact; American procedure draws heavily on the written record and on briefs, supplemented by only limited oral presentation; English proceedings are mainly oral. American judges study records and briefs before oral presentations are made, but many English judges will not do so for fear of becoming biased by them; American oral pleadings stress the law of the case, that of English counsel stress the facts; American appellate decisions are usually reached only after a conference of judges has evaluated the records, briefs, and arguments, but English decisions are often immediately announced from the bench following a hasty whispered consultation among the judges; written appellate opinions are commonly prepared by American judges but are infrequently used by English judges to explain the reasoning behind their decisions; the strong tradition of dissent that operates among American appellate judges is not part of English usage; and whereas American judges spend relatively little time in court, English judges spend proportionally more.[12]

THE HOUSE OF LORDS

Above the criminal division, court of appeal, stands the House of Lords, when it acts as Britain's highest court. The incompatibility inherent in using a legislative body colored by partisan outlooks as a court of law is neutralized by a usage of the constitution. Except for the fact that the lord chancellor functions as both senior judge of the realm, vocal spokesman for the government and presiding officer of the chamber, the political and judicial roles of the Lords are fully separated. When the Lords sit as a court, custom decrees that only the lord chancellor, the law lords, and a few judges who are also peers may participate in the adjudicatory function of the House of Lords. Each case is decided by a panel of five appointed by the lord chancellor to hear it. The House of Lords does not serve as an active court, because only a few cases come to it from the judicial systems of Scotland and Northern Ireland and from the court of appeal. Like the American Supreme Court, it hears second appeals, for the most part, and it also is insulated from litigation both by the lower courts and by its own ability to choose the cases it will review. The court of appeal protects the Lords from being swamped by appeals, just as the American court of appeals and its own control of its docket protects the United States Supreme Court from the same fate. Both the Supreme Court and the House of Lords accept only important issues, but the Supreme Court is a public law court only incidentally concerned with justice for individual litigants, whereas the law lords fulfill a general appellate role in the English judicial system without special attention to public as opposed to private legal questions. Unlike the Supreme Court, however, the law lords are never required to impose binding rules of national law on hostile state judges, for they are at the top of a unified hierarchy of courts, all parts of which apply controlling national law to the adjudication of conflicts.[13]

THE LEGAL PROFESSIONS

The personnel as well as the machinery of judicial administration are crucial to the quality of legal justice dispensed and to public confidence in and acceptance of a judicial system and its product. If the courts are accessible, if the judges are trained and professionally competent, and if the rules are impartially, speedily and properly applied, the stability of the judiciary in its constitutional setting will be greatly enhanced. It is the judges who operate the judicial machine, and they make, interpret, apply, modernize, and enforce the legal rules. Hence, we look next at the selection of British and American judges and at their professional backgrounds. A cursory glance shows that American constitutional court judges do not comprise a closely knit collegial group. Most of them are separated by space, status, and assignment from one another, especially those of inferior courts distant from justices of the Supreme Court. They share the bond of being judges over the affairs and persons of their fellow citizens that is known as the cult of the robe, but they do not share the bond of common class origin, education, professional practice, and associations that unite all barristers in Britain and identify the senior members of the British judicial system.

The quality of justice administered by a judicial system is extensively conditioned by the calibre of its judges. They, in turn, reflect their professional training, personal backgrounds, and experiences at law prior to becoming judges. Because British and American judges are selected from the ranks of practitioners and are appointed to the bench, a brief examination of the British and American bars is necessary before examining selection procedures.

It is from the ranks of the legal professions of the United States and Britain that judges are chosen by executive appointment. Much of their professional socialization and many of the internalized values they hold about the legal system and its purposes, institutions, and functionaries have been derived from their training and experiences before becoming judges. Hence, we believe this brief examination will contribute a significant dimension to an understanding of the subject.

The legal professions of the United States and Britain are carried on for private economic benefit; they exist primarily in the private sector and are internally organized and largely self-governing. Contacts between them and government in the United States most commonly arise out of public examination and licensing of attorneys and from the role of public authority in expelling a member from the profession by disbarment. The profession actively lobbies government, and its individual members hold many public offices. In Britain, government plays almost no part in controlling the profession, and its members are less active in government than is the case in America.

The British and American professions are diversely organized. In America the profession is undifferentiated. American law students do not prepare for only one phase of practice by taking a program of instruction that commits them to a lifetime of specialized activity; British students do. An American law student is not tested for eligibility to become either an office attorney serving the general legal needs of the public or a trial attorney. Instead, legal education in the United States is intended to enable students to pass state bar examinations and be licensed to practice law. Once admitted to the bar, an attorney may enter any phase of professional work he desires and may move freely from one phase to another, usually without further training or testing. American law schools turn out generalists who may later move into a subject or functional speciality.

The legal profession of Britain is not only differently structured but also makes specialized demands upon those who seek admission to its ranks.[14] It is divided into two mutually exclusive categories of practitioners. Approximately twenty thousand office lawyers known as solicitors advise clients on all legal matters, prepare legal documents and instruments, negotiate transactions, and prepare cases for presentation in court. They deal with the general public, handle the lion's share of legal work, and have barristers and lay members of the public for clients.

About three thousand barristers make up an elite group of attorneys, most of whom practice in London where the major British courts sit and where the four historic Inns of Court are located. Every barrister must be a member of one of the Inns, which control the professional education, examinations, admissions, discipline, and professional standards of their members by means of joint councils. They are free of governmental control.[15] Most barristers are "juniors," but approximately two hundred have been designated "Queen's Counsel" (QC), in recognition of their outstanding professional achievements. Most nominees for judgeships in Britain are selected from the QCs by the lord chancellor, who recommends their appointment to the monarch. For that reason the British bar (all barristers) will occupy our attention to the exclusion of the solicitors.

Several unique features of a barrister's activity are relevant to the professional conditioning that he will take to the bench should he become a judge. His primary responsibility in advocacy is to serve the interests of justice. This almost trite statement is supposedly also true in the American context. But, although American attorneys are officers of the courts, the principal duty of a defense attorney is widely accepted as being to represent the interests of his defendant client, to defend him at trial, and to get him acquitted if possible. Whereas service to abstract justice is a major internalized value of the British bar, it is a vague idea in American practice that is easily dominated by the client-attorney relationship and the exigencies of a successful defense. It leaves an American defense lawyer free to do virtually anything that his professional conscience and the canons of ethics will tolerate.

Yet another divergent dimension emerges from British practice. In the United States, all criminal prosecutions are conducted by a public officer. Defense attorneys are either privately retained or are supplied by court appointment, legal aid, or other arrangement. In Britain, prosecution and defense of criminal charges are normally in the hands of barristers retained for the purpose on a case-by-case basis. Thus, a barrister may appear in one case for the prosecution and in another on the opposite side. As a result of this alternation of professional role, members of the British bar tend to develop attitudes of mutual respect and tolerance for and cooperation with their colleague on the other side of a case. In an American criminal trial, virtually nothing can bridge the gap separating the interests of the prosecutor and defense counsel. The barrister learns from experience to see cases from both sides; he gains experience on both sides, and the common element in both perspectives is not conviction or acquittal of the defendant as primary outcome, but a fair result achieved by fair procedures.

The barrister's objectivity and commitment are aided because his profession shields him, as an American attorney's does not, from becoming closely identified with a particular client or category of clients. There is no distinct criminal law bar in Britain, and the norms, organization, and culture of his profession protect a barrister from the realities and practices that have so badly tarnished the image of the American criminal bar. The British bar enjoys a uniformly high reputation and public standing, especially when contrasted to the low estate to which some segments of the American legal profession have fallen; members of the British bar are well-trained, honest, disciplined, and free from compromising influences.

Morrison points out still other consequences that flow from the separation of solicitors from barristers. First, that division is the principal basis for assigning civil and criminal cases to different courts in the British judicial system.[16] Second, allocation of privileges and responsibilities within the legal profession causes both groups to resist all but minor reforms of the status quo, of the court system, and of its operation that would enable one to make incursions into the protected territory of the other or blur the distinct identity of either. Third, a most telling result is a strong desire by the barristers to remain the sole source of nominations to higher judgeships. Fourth, the segregation of the barristers into the four guild-like Inns of Court has aided in making them into a small group of closely knit professionals, highly socialized and politically strong.[17] Fifth, barristers, by virtue of the narrow focus of their professional activity, tend to regard only those issues on which solicitors prepare them for court as appropriate for adjudication. They do not, conversely, identify problems that solicitors deal with as presenting truly justiciable questions, with the result that only matters important to the trial work of barristers acquire prominence in their professional outlooks. Sixth, when a barrister assumes a judgeship, he therefore takes that same professional outlook with him to his new position, where it doubtless colors his perception of his judicial role and its proper performance.[18]

It is from the professional ranks of legal practioners that British and American national judges are chosen. We now turn attention to how those selections are made.

SELECTION AND TENURE OF JUDGES

Of the various methods by which judges can be selected, that of executive appointment is employed by the American and British judicial systems, but the similarity of process ends at that point. Executive appointment of judges is often alleged to politicize the judiciary and to give the executive too much power over it, thereby threatening its independence. But, comparison of the American and British selection procedures indicates that the legal and political cultures that control their operation, not the processes themselves, determine their outcomes.

AMERICAN JUDICIAL QUALIFICATIONS AND SELECTION PROCEDURES

For an American to be appointed to a national judgeship, the only necessary qualifications are to be an attorney twenty-one years of age or older and to possess the right political credentials.[19] The method by which we choose judges for the national bench is a thoroughly politicized one in which political factors play a central and perhaps the controlling role.[20] Judgeships on national courts are sometimes used to pay off political debts and to reward partisan aid. Personal friendships may be a determinant, and close attention is paid to party affiliations of nominees. Availability normally requires strong backing from local and state party and other interests. Names of aspirants are advanced for presidential consideration by state and local business people, the legal profession, partisan politicians, labor leaders and other sources, and by the U.S. senators and representatives of the state in which a judgeship is located. Hopefuls bring with them aggregations of backers, including as much partisan political leverage as can be derived from contacts and allegiances grown out of past public service and party activity. Senatorial courtesy bears fully upon the selection of U.S. district court judges but less upon the selection of appeals court judges. Tenure for "good behavior" puts a heavy premium upon the selection of nominees whose social, economic, and political outlook is right as viewed through the eyes of [the] appointing president. Although judges become fully independen[t] once on the bench, most presidents have made more than 90 p[er] cent of their judicial appointments from the ranks of their resp[ec]tive political parties.

Some formalized screening procedures are utilized. Scrutiny [of] professional standing and reputation by the American Bar Ass[o]ciation's Committee on the Federal Judiciary is supposed to pr[o]vide assurance that a prospective nominee possesses a respectab[le] professional record and standing in the eyes of his colleagues. T[he] Federal Bureau of Investigation conducts a full inquiry into ea[ch] prospect's background to ascertain that it is free from blemish[es] that would be embarrassing if they should come to public atte[n]tion. After the president submits a nomination to the Senate f[or] its confirmation, the Senate Judiciary Committee may conduct [a] hearing on it; but only nominees to the Supreme Court are no[r]mally subjected to close examination. In sum, if a prospect has [a] law degree, a reasonable record of professional achievement, [a] personal history devoid of descrediting blemishes, and the rig[ht] combination of political backing, his chances of being nominat[ed] and appointed by the president to a federal judgeship are excelle[nt.]

Qualifications for national judicial positions are almost whol[ly] undefined. A prospective district court judge does not need [to] know anything about federal rules of civil or criminal procedu[re;] about bankruptcy rules or the statutes he will be called upon [to] adjudicate; about rules of evidence; or about how to empanel a[nd] charge a jury, impose sentence, maintain order and decorum, [or] ensure a fair trial. The absence of prescribed qualifications f[or] district court judgeships in the American judicial selection proce[ss] goes far to assure that a new judge must learn how to be a jud[ge] after he ascends the bench. Judgeships on U.S. courts of appea[l] are often filled by nominees from the ranks of district judges, b[ut] no minimum period of experience as a trial judge has been fixe[d] to qualify one for elevation to the higher court. No promotion[al] ladder exists within the national judicial hierarchy, so presiden[ts] can go outside the judiciary to select nominees from state judici[al] systems, the houses of Congress, law school faculties, the Depar[t]ment of Justice political overhead, and the ranks of U.S. attorney[s.]

The foregoing also applies to selection of justices of the Supreme Court. That tribunal is unique and occupies such a central position in our constitutional system that it is a thing almost apart from the district and appellate courts below it. The lower courts are primarily concerned with applying national law to the solution of litigant-centered cases; the Supreme Court is a public law court that exists to interpret the Constitution and laws of the United States, promote nationwide uniformity and symmetry in national law, supervise the lower courts, lead and educate public opinion, police American federalism, and maintain the constitutional separation of powers. Yet, no agreement has ever been reached about what qualifications are requisite to perform these special functions, with the result that appointees have brought to the bench a wide variety of experiences, ideologies, temperaments, and personalities. The criteria and processes of their selection have been as open-handed and politicized as those that influence the selection of lower court judges.

BRITISH JUDICIAL QUALIFICATIONS AND SELECTION PROCEDURES

The British judicial selection process differs strikingly from the American and operates as follows: The lord chancellor is the central figure.[21] He is a member of the cabinet, is appointed and removed by the prime minister, and presides over the House of Lords. At the same time, he is the highest ranking legal officer of the government but sits as Britain's highest judge when the House of Lords acts as the system's supreme court. In spite of his anomalous position, however, he selects nominees for British judgeships, usually alone, though for the highest judicial positions he sometimes consults with the prime minister. Almost all nominations are drawn from the ranks of senior barristers for appointment by the monarch, who acts only on the advice of the lord chancellor, the responsible minister in the matter.

In contrast to the politicized American selection process, British legal culture forbids outside sources to submit the names of qualified persons to the lord chancellor and forbids a barrister to nominate himself. It gives the bar as an organized group no voice in the selection procedure and excludes the political leanings of eligible barristers from consideration. The lord chancellor draws freely from the ranks of the senior barristers without regard to party affiliation or history of partisan activity. For more than twenty-five years, politics have been wholly absent from all judicial selections, and, for longer than that, there has been no discernible correlation between judicial decisions and the political backgrounds of British judges. No executive clearance or legislative or other confirmation precedes submission of the lord chancellor's recommendations to the monarch. The lord chancellor is often familiar with the professional standing of the senior barristers, who number only two to three hundred. He usually has first-hand knowledge of the principal candidates for higher judicial posts, but it is not uncommon for him to seek the advice of senior judges and barristers.

British judicial selection practice has also evolved more of a career ladder within the judiciary than American practice has. A number of part-time positions at trial court level are used by the lord chancellor to test the qualifications of prospective appointees for full-time judgeships. Hence, many British judges have been moved in the judicial phase of their legal careers first from part-time to full-time status; thereafter, by succeeding appointments, from trial to appellate courts; and finally, for a chosen few, to the House of Lords. Rarely is a senior judgeship filled by an appointee who has had no prior experience on the bench.

Morrison suggests that several consequences flow from the British selection process. The small population of barristers from among whom British judges are drawn has resulted in the judiciary having a highly uniform upper-class identity. Its homogeneity is alleged by many to be a source of strength, but the judges have been strongly criticized as unrepresentative of the people and their interests. Although British judges when appointed are probably better qualified than are American judges, they embody a much narrower range of origins, orientations, experiences, and perceptions than are found among the latter.[22] The structure of their profession and of the British judiciary largely isolate them from political experience and from the social, economic, and other conflicts of life that leaven and season judicial outlooks from American national court benches.[23] Nevertheless, British selection procedures normally assure that trial court judges will have had years of trial experience before going onto the trial bench and that appellate judges will have sat on trial courts before being elevated to the appellate level. That relationship of experience to selection smooths the transition from lawyer to judge and imparts unity to the judges' legal careers. By way of contrast, in the United States the practice of law is one career; serving as judge is another professional activity, often looked at as a second career unrelated to the first. Ascending the British bench is more the second phase of a unified career at law than it is the start of a new one.

New British judges are less likely to take their places encumbered by irrelevant baggage than are American judges. They do not bring with them to the bench the nonprofessional experiences, contacts, and commitments accumulated during antecedent careers. In America, judges' antecedent careers commonly have included partisan activity, party service, elective or appointive office, business ventures, and other similar doings, much of it restricted to a limited geographic area. The British barrister is forbidden to engage in other professions while practicing law.[24] He cannot work in a law firm where his participation shifts from case to case, and he seldom has opportunity to form continuing relationships with clients the way that many American attorneys do. He rarely is identified with partisan politics, for although barristers may sit in the House of Commons, almost none stand for election; between the scope of competitive civil service coverage and the demands of their practice, they have no real ability to serve in appointive positions either.[25] Once they become judges, their isolation from the events and pressures of ordinary daily life reinforces the formality and symbolism of British courts and enhances the reputation of their judges for professionalism, impartiality, and legitimacy.[26]

The foregoing should be sufficient to indicate that the guidelines and procedures for selecting British judges bear little resemblance to those of the United States. Both recruit by executive appointment from the ranks of the legal profession and forego subjecting new judges to preadjudicative training. But, whereas the American selection process is thoroughly politicized, that of Britain is virtually untouched by political considerations in its present form and operation. Although politically accountable members of the executive choose British judges, the legal culture has developed to neutralize the appointment process. Even appointment of lay justices of the peace has been depoliticized. The local advisory committees in the counties and boroughs help the lord chancellor to identify persons qualified to hold the office and make nominations regardless of party preference.

Nominees are drawn for the respective benches from strikingly different sources by the British and American selection procedures. American judges come from the entire spectrum of socio-economic and educational backgrounds, in keeping with American egalitarianism. Judges of the British superior courts and many of the lower ones as well are recruited from a narrow band of upper-class and upper middle-class society. The British bench is characterized by Morrison as a surviving haven preserved for the elite classes by the educational system and by the organization and practices of the British bar.[27] Its members also differ from American judges in being generally older, a characteristic attributable to the years of service at the bar needed to prove their qualifications for judgeships. Their professional standing and reputation among their fellow barristers, rather than the senatorial endorsements, public service, party support, and localized influence that gain nominations for American aspirants, are the principal qualifications for British judgeships.

REMOVAL OF JUDGES

Self-removal of judges can be accomplished in both systems by resignation, medical retirement, or retirement for length of service. Appointment of judges to serve during good behavior does not imply indentured servitude. Both the United States and England utilize retirement with pensions to induce elderly judges to leave the bench and to make it easier for them to do so voluntarily. American national judges who enter "senior" (retired) status may sit on call by the chief justice of the United States.

Involuntary removal of judges is necessary but ought not be by procedures easily invoked for political reasons. Impeachment is the sole means of removing American constitutional judges. It has been invoked twelve times against various of them in the United

ates, and politics has entered into both the actual and threatened
e of the process. Most British judges are virtually beyond re-
oval. The lord chancellor may remove justices of the peace at his
easure and judges of the county courts for misbehavior and in-
ility to perform their duties, but removal of all other judges is
ntrolled by the Judicature Act of 1925. That statute provides for
eir removal by the Queen upon address to her by the houses of
rliament; but only one judge has been removed since 1701, and
was ousted in 1830. This British statutory arrangement, how-
er, does not afford the same degree of security the American
nstitutional procedure of impeachment does, inasmuch as a
rliament disposed to do so may alter it at any time by new
gislation.

REGARD FOR PRECEDENT

Among the judges of American national courts, regard for the
nding force of precedent has never been as strong as it is among
e lawyers and judges of England. American judges have never
en reluctant to differentiate or even to ignore the principle by
nich an earlier case was decided. They have generally been all
o willing to create law to suit the case at bar. Beginning in the
lonial era, judges adapted the common law to conditions on this
de of the ocean. After independence was gained, the new federally
uctured legal system, embracing those of the separate states and
at of the new national government, tended to produce even
eater deviation. Rapid change and sectional economic, religious,
cial, geographic, and other diversity fostered an attitude recep-
e to judicial experimentation and adaptation of law to shifting
cietal expectations and demands. So did judicial application,
pecially by national courts, of a written national constitution that
und all judges and required adaptation as well as implementa-
on by judicial interpretation and decision making. American con-
tutional precedents are both by nature and by necessity transi-
ry to a degree that the English rule of precedent rejects.[28] The
merican practice of judicial review, not known in Britain,
ightened awareness that the practical test of a legal system is its
ility to respond to social need and that law embraces political,
onomic, sociological, and psychological elements.[29] Judicial re-

view thrust American national judges into the making of importan
public policy which in England is left to the politically representa
tive and accountable parts of the government. The predominantl
political method used to select judges of American national tribu
nals reinforces the other influences operating to give American law
a sociological dimension unknown to that of England. On th
whole, the socio-legal climate of the United States has not been a
favorable to the rule of precedent as has that of its historic home.

CERTAINTY IN THE LAW

The high regard of English judges for the rule of precedent i
doubtless attributable also to their love for certainty in the law
Although comparisons are always chancy, it is probably safe to sa
that English judges place greater stress on certainty in the law tha
do American judges. American judges emphasize that certainty i
but one value to be served in a legal system—that flexibility an
adaptability of legal rules to changed social conditions are of equa
if not superior importance for an efficacious rule of law. Man
American national judges believe that they should effectively an
actively join in the process of societal modernization. Many o
them therefore regard the principle of *stare decisis* as a policy t
be generally observed, but depart from it when, in their estima
tions, circumstances justify it.

The idea that the law is a consistent, coherent whole seems t
have a looser grip on the minds of American judges than it doe
on those of English jurists. American judges seem more willing t
decide cases with an eye to present and future consequences o
their decisions than to be controlled by the backward-looking focu
of prior decisions. Geldart has written that the force of preceden
so controls English judges that they cannot adequately correct it
deficiencies by the force of later decisions. In consequence, majo
portions of judge-made English common law are periodicall
negated and displaced by statutory rules.[30] High courts o
England are reluctant to overrule long-standing decisions of lowe
tribunals, even ones thought to have been wrongly decided, whe
the decisions have been acted on in good faith by persons who re
garded them as making good law; English judges often feel tha
certainty in the law is more important than efforts to attain perfec

ion by endless adjustments of its rules.[31] The first duty of the English judge is not to act as a social engineer but to decide legal issues dividing parties to legal conflicts.[32]

JUDICIAL POLICYMAKING AND ACTIVISM

Although English judges regard precedents as more rigidly binding than do American judges, they nevertheless have played something of an active role by creating law embodying new policy purposefully made from the bench to reflect urgent societal pressures of the day. In this context, policy decisions can be thought of as ones that prescribe new patterns of administrative goals or that alter the substance of existing policies. Policy decisions result from the application of judicial power to those problems of society that generate justiciable controversies. They are the products of judicial discretion which judges always possess in some degree but may or may not feel justified to exercise. In American national courts, policy decisions are products of very broad judicial discretion to interpret the provisions of statutes, executive orders, administrative rules and regulations, and the Constitution of the United States.

Whether they be American or English, however, judges indisputably incorporate their preferences regarding what government ought to do into their decisions; English law no less than American must be adapted to the changing needs of men if it is to remain vital and claim their allegiance. English jurists are far more respectful of the primacy of Parliament in the lawmaking field than American national court judges are of American statutory and constitution-making processes. Nevertheless, the growth of the common law has been a vehicle for juristic innovation, and not all British judges have agreed with Lord Patrick Devlin that a precedent, once established, "becomes as rigid as the branch of a tree."[33] The sovereignty of Parliament stands available like a loaded shotgun behind the door to undo any development of British judge-made law, whether constitutional, statutory, or common, that might upset the legislature, just as the "necessary and proper" clause gives Congress ample authority to react to nonconstitutional rulings of American national court judges. Compared to the ebullience with which American national judges enter the policymaking arena, British judges are shy and reticent and very willing to leave constitution and statute making to Parliament and the voters. Far more than their American counterparts, they accept the idea that they interpret and apply law, not make it.

Certainty and stability nevertheless remain the dominant characteristics of British law; adaptability and challenge are those of the American. Yet, there is no reason to think that English judges more than American can throw off the influence of their times and sterilize their decision making so that it reflects only purely legal principles. They influence the development of English law, but more subtly and with lower profiles than typify the American national judiciary, and more in concert with Parliament than as a complement to it. English judges have high regard for their role as purveyors of dispassionate justice and are concerned that the British people would lose faith in the impartiality of British courts if their judges decided cases according to public policy interests rather than by a narrow focus of law. Overt lawmaking such as the U.S. Supreme Court continually practices is beyond the pale of judicial propriety to most British judges. But, in Britain as in the United States, the judges have historically made new law, with or without a statute to interpret, when great societal need was met only by legislative inactivity. Still, despite their judges' preference for syllogistic reasoning, the modernization of British law is largely due to judicial innovation instead of parliamentary enactments. Britain no doubt has a smaller, more uniform, and more conservative society than does the United States, but, like the American Congress, its unaided Parliament is incapable of meeting the need of a modern society for modern legal rules that only courts can prescribe. Yet, British judges generally do not use powers of statutory construction to legislate within the interstices of the acts at bar nor to interpret statutory language according to their felt perceptions of contemporary policy needs. Literal statutory language, not considerations of abstract justice or legislative intent, tends to control them. Innovative, creative judges do sit on British courts, but, in the main, English legal tradition is marked by a strong respect for certainty and stability in the law maintained by the controlling force of precedent and by judicial self-restraint.

The attitudes and practices of American national judges stand

n sharp contrast—most British judges conscientiously endeavor
o avoid making policy from the bench, but American national
udges assume an almost unlimited activism over policies, programs, and expenditures of national (and state) administrative
agencies. The bounds of their contemporary assertiveness seem-
ngly know no limits. In the execution of their own judicial
powers, judges of American national courts since the days of John
Marshall have interpreted the Constitution and statutes in determining matters of national policy that in Britain, according to
democratic theory and practice, should be reserved for the legisla-
ive and executive branches. Making policy by public administra-
ion is an inherently political function. In recognition of that fact,
British judges do but American judges do not endeavor to refrain
from engaging in it. Although the U.S. Supreme Court is the most
visible and active judicial agent that makes policy decisions, any
national judge may participate in the exercise.

Congress and the executive branch aid and abet the practice.
Groups representing commerce, manufacturing, finance, agriculture, labor, human rights, religion, education, patriotism, and almost every other interest have used the courts to attain policy
objectives they could not realize by using the ballot or pressuring
egislators or administrators. Class action suits brought by public
nterest groups—the Sierra Club, Natural Resources Defense Council, Environmental Defense Fund, Center for Law and Social Policy,
Wilderness Society, or Izaak Walton League—may end in a court-
supervised consent decree committing a governmental agency to a
court-approved program lasting several years and requiring expenditure of many millions of dollars, all in the absence of legislative
discussion and approval. American national courts have even
ordered administrators to undertake broad long-range programs
that legislators have refused to enact.

Congress enhances the role of national courts in the policymaking arena. In the Water Pollution and Control Act and in the
Clean Air Act,[34] Congress extended a clear invitation to citizens
and organizations to bring private suits to compel administrative
compliance with statutory duties, even providing for payment of
the attorney's fees of successful plaintiffs. Such reliance on the
courts to compel administrators to execute statutory mandates

places the American national judiciary in the position of acting a
a legislative enforcement arm protecting against bureaucratic reca
citrance. The expectation is that American judges will assum
leadership in social engineering by judicial decision making. Th
result of this expectation is that numerous American nation;
judges are exercising judicial power in areas heretofore considere
appropriate only for legislative or executive attention. They hav
for example, recently mandated: that pregnant women have
limited constitutional right to abortions; how police must inte
rogate suspects; that imprisonment can be a cruel and unusu;
punishment; that states must provide treatment for persons invo.
untarily confined in mental institutions; and how state welfar
agencies must run their programs. They have operated a sta
mental health system, a prison system, and a major urban publi
school system. In earlier times they have integrated public school;
restructured legislative representation, defined public morality, an
tried to prescribe a "fair" margin of profit. In contrast, the Britis
legal culture does not tolerate as much judicial activism as th
American does, and most British judges are not as activist as mo;
American judges are inclined to be. Different cultural tradition
have shaped their crafts of judging and determined the manner i
which they carry it out from the bench. British judges have en
deavored since the middle of the nineteenth century to leave polic
decisions to the government and legislature of the day. They tr
for the most part, to decide only the cases before them, answerin
only specific legal questions of individual right and obligatio
They endeavor to adhere to the judges' role as neutral third-part
arbiters in the adjudication of disputes. They also try to avoid pre
scribing broad policies for future application by legislative o
executive personnel.

Ehrmann characterizes the British judiciary as a small group c
remarkably homogeneous judges, proud of their reputation fc
consistency and predictability,[35] who have traditionally regarde
the creation of social policy by the bench as subversive of consis
tency and an invitation to arbitrariness. Their propensity has lon
been to adhere rigidly to precedents, even when doing so carrie
standards adapted to a bygone era over into contemporary day;
They look at statutes with an eye to the literal meaning of th

stated language, disregarding legislative history and intent, although doing so might defeat the clearly understood purpose of a statute.

More recently, however, a few British judges have begun to exhibit attitudes and practices toward policy making from the bench more in line with that of their American counterparts. They have avoided inconvenient precedents by distinguishing them or by limiting their application to original cases. British judges can also use their discretion to preserve an appearance of loyalty to *stare decisis* while adapting law to contemporary needs. But the British judge more than the American is hemmed in by numerous traditions and taboos, many of them centuries old, and he carries with him a heavy burden of internalized as well as of externally imposed constraints.[36] Ehrmann concludes that in spite of their common law heritage, British judges have begun to read their principled views into the meaning of statutes, a practice particularly indulged by judges of the highest courts. Like that of American judges, their practice is subject to the scrutiny of public opinion and peer judgment and to the possibility that it may provoke retaliatory corrective legislation.[37] To that degree, American and British judges operate subject to like constraints, and it is likely that the courts of both systems tend to avoid antagonizing the legislature. Certainly, American judges resort to interpretation of statutes far more often than they invoke their power to declare a statute unconstitutional. While the American national judiciary has provoked congressional ire numerous times, British judges have only rarely been drawn into overt controversy with Parliament over differences of policy or other issues. They have largely escaped retaliatory legislative acts.

JUDICIAL REVIEW

Congressional retaliation has most often been directed at the Supreme Court of the United States in reaction to specific exercises of its power to declare acts of Congress unconstitutional. In England, the sovereignty of Parliament is a fundamental principle of the English constitution, just as judicial review is recognized as a fundamental principle of the American. It is Parliament alone that determines the bounds of judicial power as well as of its own competence. British judges, therefore, cannot instruct Parliament what statutes it can enact, how it can use its investigative authority, how its chambers shall be composed, whether it has used proper procedures, or what means it can select to attain a desired social objective. They can and do use their power to read meaning into statutory language. But if Parliament disagrees with the judges' construction and expresses its disagreement in amendatory legislation, there is no way the judicial power can withstand the corrective mandate from the legislature. Consequently, British judges do not become locked in constitutional struggles with the partisan parts of the governmental system, as when our Supreme Court's invalidation of major economic measures of the New Deal in America led to presidential proposal of a court packing plan in 1937. Neither has the Parliament acted against British courts as Congress has against American national courts to alter their jurisdiction, to change the number of their judges, or to shift their jurisdictional boundaries for partisan political reasons.

The job of British judges is made simpler by the fact that they do not concern themselves with questions of constitutional validity. They are not encumbered during trials with broad questions of social policy brought before them in the form of often thinly disguised questions of law. They are not forced to consider the variety of evidentiary materials considered by American national judges who are concerned with issues of legislative intent,[38] and they do not need rules governing constitutional construction. The application of a precedent or the interpretation of meaning in a statutory phrase are more precise legal questions than is the power of Congress to compel an employer to accommodate the religious preferences of an employee whose theology forbids him to work at a time when the business normally operates.

The absence of judicial review in England rests on several bases. The evolved nonassembled constitution operating in a unitary governmental system may preclude the need for a final arbiter. The same evolutionary process also produced a sovereign Parliament whose legal supremacy is inconsistent with the existence of a controlling judicial power competent to direct it. However, Fred H. Morrison takes the position that the most significant explanation is found in the role assigned to English judges by the legal heritage of the system. The generally held perception of their function in the system denies them power to judge the validity of statutes of the national legislature, and judges, Parliament, lawyers, the public, and all other participants in the system accept that perception. Any attempt by the judiciary to enlarge their authority by assuming a power of judicial review would meet with aroused opposition from every quarter. Such a change could come about only if numerous judges of the Court of Appeal concurrently sustained the reform; if the bar were willing to present allegations of unconstitutionality to the judges for decision; and if judges could overcome the contrary socializing forces of their earlier legal training, bar practice, and judicial experience, all of which strongly militate against the transformation coming to pass.[39]

PUBLIC ATTITUDE TOWARD THE JUDICIAL SYSTEM

The attitudes of British and American citizens toward their respective judicial systems contrast sharply. In England, the general public both in and out of court holds the judicial system in high regard. Throughout the polity, a general confidence prevails that the system operates to produce impartial justice administered by eminently qualified judges employing the fairest procedures human wit and experience can devise. The British people, like many Americans, do complain that their criminal justice system is weighted in favor of defendants, is excessively rule-bound, and is unjustifiably cumbersome.[40] The record of British judges for probity and professionalism is perhaps the best among all legal systems of the world, however, and the quality of British judges is widely regarded as the greatest strength of their legal system. It is safe to say that no such laudatory conclusions prevail among Americans about the quality of the American judges, judicial system, or justice. Respect for British law and for the personnel and agencies of judicial administration contrast sharply to the widespread criticism of, hostility toward, and loss of confidence in the American judicial processes of the last decade. The British citizenry predominantly leans toward support for and cooperation with the personnel and institutions of the legal order. American rebelliousness toward authority, particularly that associated with law and order, is lacking in the typical Englishman. The British take a more complacent, acquiescent attitude toward legal controls and are more respectful and calm, reflecting a much more deeply internalized tradition of support for law and order. None of these characteristics is a marked feature of the American legal culture.

Yet, British justice has not retained popular respect and support by being lenient or by rendering popular verdicts. Its sentencing standards are at least as rigorous and fair as those of American judges. The difference in attitude toward the courts and judges stems partly from the fact that the British are more stoic than Americans and more disposed than Americans to accept the outcome of judicially imposed adversity without displays of intemperate emotion and ill-considered actions. The roots of respect for the law penetrate much more deeply into the British character than into that of most Americans. Americans seemingly believe that every law is made to be broken under appropriate circumstances and for legitimate purposes, that laws are made to be observed by the other fellow, and that the spirit of revolution must be fertilized, to paraphrase Thomas Jefferson, by individual decisions about the obligation to obey the mandates of particular laws. The influence of British deference can perhaps be seen once again in the absence of spirited rebelliousness from the British character.[41]

But, like American judges, those in English courts are human, and British judges sometimes exhibit personality traits and biases that affect their attitudes toward crimes and sentences.[42] Given sufficient provocation, they may lose their composure and even act prejudicially to the administration of even-handed justice, but that conduct is almost certain to precipitate appeal and reversal of the defendant's conviction. It is an uncommon occurrence for spectators, defendants, or attorneys to disrupt the decorum of a British courtroom by the sort of unseemly conduct or intemperate remarks that often occur in American courts. Occasional disorders outside as well as inside British courtrooms do occur and are just as apt to trigger judicial intemperance as they would in this country. Such instances are very much the exception to decorum and good order in British judicial experience, however.

INDEPENDENCE OF THE JUDICIARY

The independence of the judiciary from partisan influences is widely regarded in the Anglo-American legal tradition as the indispensible prerequisite of justice. It is the keystone of impartiality in the administration of legal justice by courts of law. British and American jurisprudence attach equal significance to the principle, but the British have probably attained a higher degree of its realization in practice than Americans have, thereby contributing to recognition of the British judiciary as probably the most respected in the world.

Judicial independence has several aspects. It embraces freedom of the judge from partisan political bias and influence. Thus, although a peer judge may assume his seat in the House of Lords, he must assiduously refrain from identifying with any political party upon pain of irrevocably compromising his judicial neutrality. It is not statutory or other formal restraints that have produced public confidence in the judicial independence. Some English judges have revealed personal opinions and values that have sometimes colored their interpretations of statutes, but, on the whole and in contrast to the performance of American national judges, those of the mother country have attained and maintained a very high level of impartiality. No political scandal has touched the English judiciary for over a century.

Formalized protections of judicial independence exist in both systems of courts. Because the level of professionalism is probably not as high in the American national judiciary as it is among the judges of English superior and appellate tribunals, formal guarantees substitute for internalized values to a greater extent among American than among English judges. The independence of American national court judges is protected by constitutional guarantees. They are given tenure during good behavior. To protect them from coercion, they are guaranteed salaries that cannot be reduced by Congress, and they are protected from removal by any process but conviction on impeachment. But, despite constitutional protection, partisan political motives have guided Congress' use of the impeachment process, its structuring of the national judiciary, its denial of salary increases, and its control of substantive jurisdiction over cases and controversies. Partisan politics permeates the selection of all national judges, and the judiciary's own policy-making activities have reached proportions that threaten the good name of the judiciary. Such considerations undermine public confidence in its competence and impartiality.

The stated constitutional protections may be distorted in other ways. Tenure during good behavior and removal by impeachment can even be regarded as paradoxically placing national judges in jeopardy, for no one knows what impeachable offenses are subsumed by the ambiguous words "treason, bribery and other high crimes and misdemeanors." The impeachment process is an essentially political mechanism. In our constitutional history, it has acquired a record of use against the judiciary for political reasons. It has not been an effective safeguard for the independence of national court judges; it has been used or its use threatened more than once as a political lever to move the ideological position of judges, especially of those of the Supreme Court.

The tenure of British judges is guaranteed by the Act of Settlement of 1701. That document requires both houses of Parliament to petition the crown for removal of a judge.[43] The Parliament acts of 1911 and 1949 left that process undisturbed, so that the House of Commons cannot bypass the House of Lords and remove one or more British judges. Participation by the House of Lords in matters affecting the legal system also assures that the opinions of the law lords will be heard and given great, probably determinative, weight by that house.[44] The security of British judges is imperfectly guaranteed, for the existing arrangement may of course be upended by act of Parliament withdrawing the exempted status.

The British also recognize that the pocketbook is one of man's most vulnerable points and have moved to protect their judges from financial coercion by authorities who for political reasons would influence judicial decisions or force a judge out of office by reducing or terminating his salary. To attain that end, the British have removed judicial salaries from the politically controlled annual appropriations process wherein they would be subject to executive control. Judges' salaries have been made a permanent charge on the consolidated fund and need not be voted annually by Parliament, which is controlled by the partisan executive. That arrangement is a statutory one authorized by Parliament and, given a favorable political environment, may be altered by the legislature acting in its sovereign capacity. But, it would be answerable at the polls and would doubtless pay a heavy price for any blatant transgression against the principle of judicial independence.

In the United States, estimates of expenditures for support of the national judicial branch are prepared as a basis for the annual Congressional appropriation process. However, the judicial estimates are compiled in the judicial branch and are merely transmitted to the executive for inclusion in the budget document. They must be submitted to Congress just as they are received from the judiciary, for if a president could revise the judicial estimates, he could exercise a degree of control over the judiciary that would violate the doctrine of separated powers. The national judiciary attains only a degree of financial independence by the arrangement. It is not as great as that enjoyed by the British judicial system, for Congress enjoys the power that goes with control of the purse whereas Parliament does not. Congress has many times tried to guide the judiciary by tightening or loosening the pursestrings, a recent instance occurring in 1975 when it denied a salary increase to justices of the Supreme Court because it disliked some of their recent decisions.

TRIAL CHARACTERISTICS

British and American trial judges preside over their courts as neutral third parties, maintain order and decorum, rule on point of law, and apply rules of procedure and evidence; but, British judges more than American are the centers of attention. The centrality of their position is emphasized by the effects of socialization upon the public, bar, and bench; by courtroom decorum, judicial wigs, and robes; and by the formal nature of British advocacy, the elevated bench, and counsel's inability to move about during proceedings. British judges enter into courtroom proceedings in an active way, but American district judges infrequently do so. British judges commonly interrogate witnesses of both sides, but the American version of the adversary process makes the prosecutor and defense attorney the main actors in the courtroom drama. Their roles, freedom of movement, latitude of expression, and behavior before the courts overshadow the role of the judge, who is hemmed in by rules of procedure and evidence. Upon completion of the trial, British judges sum up the case for the jurors. They state the law of the case for them, as American district judges do; they may also comment to them about the weight of the evidence and testimony of witnesses, unlike American judges. British sentences can be imposed by judges other than those who presided at trial, whereas it is the task of American national trial judges to fix and impose sentence. Despite their central role during trials, the British judges' exercise of their wide discretion rarely provides a basis for appeal on a procedural issue. A presumption of finality and legitimacy attaches to their rulings and judgments that is unknown to American legal culture. In American practice, almost any challenged procedural step or bench ruling may provide a foundation for appeal. Although both systems assume that a convicted defendant is entitled to one post-conviction appeal, finality in the American tradition seemingly comes only when an appellate court has passed on the conviction's validity. The rate of appeal from national district courts to courts of appeals in the United States is high, and it almost seems as though the finality and fairness of an American trial are not conclusively established unless and until an appellate court has validated them for the defendant, his counsel, and the public.

Other differences distinguish British criminal trials from those of American national courts. British pretrial proceedings are characterized by a definite propensity of judges and counsel to bring defendants speedily to trial, forgoing the delaying tactics typical of pretrial strategies by American attorneys trying to gain an advantage. British judges are intolerant of dilatory tactics. When trial is held by jury, little time is lost in British courts; they do not follow the often time-consuming procedures of interrogation and challenge found in the American jury-selection process. British trials are also expedited because defense counsel goes to trial knowing the prosecution's full case. Because it is assumed that any barrister can present a case on short notice from a solicitor's brief, British judges do not willingly tolerate or accommodate requests for delays and continuances. Lawyers, defendants, police, judges, and public understand that offenders shall be proceeded against; unlike the situation in too many American criminal trials, counsel, police, and parties appear at the designated times ready for trial. A lapse of two months between arrest and start of trial is considered unduly long. Minor offenses are quickly, fairly, and smoothly disposed of before magistrates and crown courts; before higher courts, trials move expeditiously to conclusion and are only rarely interrupted for any reason other than daily adjournment.[45] Karlen reports that speedy completion of British trials is aided by the fact that defense counsel only infrequently register objections to the prosecutor's introduction of evidence.[46] That is due to the fact that the defense knows the prosecution's evidence before trial starts and is unlikely to be caught off guard in court during trial. In American criminal trials, on the other hand, much time is typically consumed by defense counsel's seemingly endless motions and objections. Many reasons for those tactics exist, but Karlen suggests that the chief motive of American defense lawyers is to get every possible objection into the record of trial proceedings so that they can be used later as grounds for a postconviction appeal. An American lawyer's failure to object may leave him vulnerable to allegations of professional incompetence. Further, American defense lawyers in criminal trials do not know the prosecution's case in advance, as do British defense counsel. Their frequent and seemingly automatic objections may therefore be a knee-jerk defense against being caught off guard. Finally, American prosecutors and defense attorneys who go to trial normally operate in an atmosphere of intense rivalry, with the result that they take more and deeper differences with them into the courtroom to be settled by the adversary process. It will be recalled that British barristers go to trial more concerned with obtaining a just outcome than as armed adversaries.[47]

British and American legal cultures also offer different traditions about the prosecution of criminal cases. The prosecution of crimes in American national courts is always conducted by a public officer, never by a private party or counsel. As early as 1704, the private prosecution of crimes began to disappear from criminal procedure on this side of the Atlantic,[48] and in 1789 Congress created the position of United States district attorney to prosecute alleged violations of national criminal laws. Consequently, private prosecution of national crimes before national courts has never existed under the Constitution. Violations of national criminal laws have always been regarded as breaches of the public peace to be prosecuted by a public officer in the name of the people. Today, a United States attorney is assigned to every district court and often has a staff of assistants and investigators under his direction. He prosecutes national crimes before his court; investigates and prepares cases for prosecution; and decides such matters as what cases to prosecute, what charges to bring, when to go to the grand jury and to trial, whether to plea bargain, and how the prosecution's case shall be presented. In other words, he exercises great discretionary control over the enforcement of national criminal laws. In Britain, however, no public official performs the functions or exercises the authority of a U.S. attorney. He has no counterpart there. Contemporary practice in Britain combines two partly incompatible principles. First is the ancient idea that criminal acts are personal injuries that the injured party must redress against the perpetrator by private action. Hence, prosecution continues to be thought of as a private matter for the victim, his family, relatives, and friends. The second principle reflects the idea that the peace of the realm is part of the monarch's right and must be preserved by actions of the monarch's officers. Debate over the second idea continued from at least the time of Henry VIII until the position of director of public prosecutions was established in 1879.[49]

The director continues today as a full-time officer of the Crown concerned only with public business. His office advises the police and government agencies on prosecution, but it has no investigative responsibilities or capacity such as U.S. attorneys have. He must prosecute all cases begun by government agencies; all formerly capital offenses; those of particular importance or complexity, such as those coming under the Official Secrets Act; and those he is ordered to prosecute by his superior, the home secretary. He can personally take over and prosecute any case in those categories that is sufficiently complex and important to justify that unusual step. But, the director of public prosecutions notwithstanding, private parties in Britain have the right to bring criminal charges and to prosecute them. The British system of criminal justice continues to be essentially one of private prosecution. To prevent abusive or irresponsible accusations being brought against persons by their personal enemies or for other baseless reasons, a defendant may sue a wrongful accuser. Much initiative in the matter has passed in Britain to the police, who normally begin criminal actions by filing sworn allegations of criminal conduct with a court against accused individuals. In the lower criminal courts, a senior police officer usually prosecutes cases against defendants; in the higher courts, a police solicitor ordinarily retains a barrister in private practice to present the case in the name of the Crown. The barrister holds no public office, argues only the case he was retained to present, and plays no role in police or investigative activities similar to that of a U.S. attorney.[50] The relationship of the barrister to the police solicitor on those occasions is the same as that of any barrister to a solicitor who retains and briefs him.

LEGAL AID

The problem of providing legal aid for indigent defendants who cannot afford to hire their own attorneys is a major one for the American and British criminal justice systems. The legal professions in both countries regularly provide some charitable assistance for indigent accuseds, and judges in both have for many years provided court-appointed attorneys. In the United States, of course, most legal aid is supplied in state courts by state judges who act under a wide variety of plans. In national courts, judges may also appoint attorneys and provide other assistance for indigent defendants. Congress has authorized each district judge, with the consent of the judicial council of his circuit, to provide those charged with more than petty offenses with legal aid. It may include not only assistance of a lawyer but also "investigative, expert, and other services necessary to an adequate defence." The judicial councils may also make appellate counsel available to defendants unable to afford it. And if a defendant at any stage of a trial or appellate proceeding can no longer afford to pay a private attorney retained by him, a court-appointed counsel may be substituted in the interest of justice.[51]

Provision of counsel in British courts differs from the American arrangement in two notable respects. Counsel is provided on a nationally uniform basis under both statutory and common law procedures. But, the major difference lies in the fact that the availability of counsel in Britain is not an essential constitutional right of the defendant as it is in the United States.[52] It may be judicially authorized on request of an indigent defendant whenever a judge believes that free legal aid is necessary to a just trial. British defendants are permitted to choose lawyers from approved lists of available professionals. But court clerks designate solicitors when their services are authorized, and solicitors retain the services of barristers. In that way, the burden of legal aid work is distributed equitably within the profession. Competent attorneys paid by the public at the prevailing rate for professional services afford indigent defendants adequate representation of their interests before the courts, but British legal aid does not provide as wide a variety of defense services as Congress has made available in American national courts. British judges are generous, however, in providing available aid, with the result that a high proportion of British defendants benefit from it.

PLEA BARGAINING

Plea bargaining is a method of inducing accused persons to plead guilty in return for a prosecutor's recommendation that charges be reduced or that lighter sentences be imposed. United States attorneys extensively employ it in national district courts and defend its use as an expeditious way to dispose of cases without going to trial. It is indispensable, its supporters insist, to the system's ability to keep up with case loads. But plea bargaining has a seamier side; its use means that prosecutors can build impressive conviction records without having to develop cases that prove the guilt of defendants beyond a reasonable doubt; it deprives defendants of their constitutionally guaranteed trial protections; it gives prosecutors great leverage over defendants and may subject them to irresistable pressures to yield up their right to trial; it truncates the adversary process by keeping the cases out of court; it makes the status of courts' dockets depend in part on the bargaining record of prosecutors; and, in many other ways, it short-circuits the due process ideal that determinations of guilt shall rest on trial verdicts supported by convincing evidence. Plea bargaining dominates the processing of criminal defendants by district courts. It depends on the discretion of U.S. attorneys and on the cooperation of national judges who know what goes on and must from considerations of practical need accept the bargains on which the system is built. It is subject to an almost infinite variety of abuses and involves the judiciary in a hypocritical charade. It is nevertheless the mainstay of the American national criminal justice process.

Bargained pleas are not unknown in Britain, where they are called "negotiated pleas." Their use is common, but they by no means play the central part that they do in American practice. Barristers who prosecute and defend have no independent authority to make bargains, as American prosecutors and private defense counsel can do. Charges cannot be reduced except by permission of the courts. British judges do authorize reductions in order to induce guilty pleas by defendants, but British judges do not encourage or readily tolerate deals, and British practice takes particular care to shield the system, and especially its judges, from its perverting influences.

OTHER COMPARISONS AND CONTRASTS

In addition to the similarities and contrasts identified above, there are other lesser points that deserve to be noted. British and American national courts are geographically dispersed, bring administration of justice conveniently near to the people, and are hierarchically structured. Both distribute jurisdiction to courts according to whether proceedings are civil or criminal, original or appellate. The tribunals of both systems perform allocative as well as adjudicative functions and are parts of their national political processes. All judges must wait for litigation to be brought before their courts; none can initiate trials of cases, and all preside to umpire proceedings in a basically passive way. The level of judicial competence of British judges is probably superior to that of American national judges. British jurists play a more central and active role in court proceedings than do American judges, who tend to take a back seat to the role of attorneys. British judges are more involved in developing all the evidence of a trial and in excluding irrelevancies from the proceedings. They function under simpler, less technical procedures and rules which enhance their role in the courtroom over that of their American counterparts. Judges of British and American national courts cannot give advisory opinions, and American judges can only decide cases that present a genuine adversary relationship between contending parties. Neither may decide hypothetical questions, but both will decide any real litigation, whether in the nature of a friendly suit or not. Judges of both systems are absolutely immune from criminal suits brought against them by persons who have suffered harm or injury as a result of judges' action or utterance from the bench. Both systems disqualify judges from trying cases in which they have a personal interest or possible bias.

British and American tribunals employ the accusatorial trial process; both have a high regard for the right of defendants to a fair trial; both administer costly justice that burdens poor litigants; and both experience difficulty in keeping abreast of their case loads so that justice is not unjustifiably delayed.

In both systems, the use of juries endures, but juries—both grand and trial—are now more deeply rooted in the American judicial culture than in the British, where both originated. Use of the grand jury is still widely employed in American national courts for indictments and investigations, but it has been abandoned in Britain. Trial by jury is used by courts of general trial jurisdiction in both systems, but, in Britain, it is not extensively employed except when its use is mandatory for the trial of serious felonies. In American national courts, use of trial and grand juries is limited to district courts. Their survival and enduring strength in American practice and legal culture is due in part to their being rooted in the national Constitution. Their use is further reinforced by a widely held belief among Americans that participation of citizens on juries injects a popular leavening influence of common sense, practical experience, and pragmatic justice into a criminal justice process that might otherwise become too dehumanized, rule bound and professional. Doubtless, some of the respect popularly felt for the Constitution rubs off on the institutions it fosters. In both systems, trials—whether by bench or jury—are open to the public and press and are subject to the measure of confidentiality necessary to protect personal reputations or national interests.[53]

SUMMARY

Despite their many differences of structure and procedures, the judicial systems of the United States and Britain are grounded on the rule of law and operate to make it real. Neither fully attains the ideal in practice, but the role they fill is central to the operation of both. Neither courts, law, nor the rule of law exists as an end in itself. Each separately and all together enhance the possibility of freedom for individuals living subject to the coercive powers of government. Courts, statutes, and lawyers in Britain do not constitute a main line for the defense of individual freedom as they are regarded as doing in the United States, but the British legal system nevertheless plays a part in constraining unwarranted power and improper procedures. The British judiciary is more conservative than the American and is not expected, nor does it expect, to play the activist part in social control and modernization that the American legal culture assigns to its judiciary. Thus, the British judiciary is not prominently featured in the public mind as a policy maker and agent of societal reform. But it is no less a valuable part of the democratic mechanism for all of that.

Our purpose in this examination has been to acquire comparative perspectives on the two judicial and supporting systems. It has not been to lay a foundation for concluding that one is better than the other. The adequacy of a judicial system as an agency of social control is measured by the sense of confidence that people feel in it. Although neither system approaches perfection, and both exhibit their human and conventional origins, they are well-adapted to their respective social orders. Differences between them fall more on the level of detail than on that of fundamental principles. The place of each in its society is consonant with expectations and demands, and each is conditioned by its political and legal culture. Each remains an essential proponent of private rights and interests against abusive public power. Both traditions adhere firmly to the proposition that a single body of law should control private citizen and public officials alike.

Because British judges only touch the periphery of policy making from the bench, they do not raise the troubling questions about democracy that American judicial review and activism generate. To the extent that British judges may step over the line between statutory enforcement, interpretation, and adjudicative policy making, they may immediately encounter the harsh realities of parliamentary repercussions. Control of policy in Britain remains firmly in the hands of politically accountable portions of the government. But, Americans must ask themselves whether, when their judges and justices declare an act of Congress unconstitutional, they are undemocratically substituting their conception of desirable policy for that of the elected representatives of the people. Are judicial review and judicial activism consistent with the principles of liberal democratic government? Most questions of constitutional construction are political issues more appropriate for the application of legislative than judicial power, and that fact is more clearly recognized and respected by the British judges and legislators than by American. The American tradition of judicial activism seems stronger today than ever before and ignores the fact that judges and justices are not bound by the letter of constitutional and statutory language, by precedents, or by the intent of legislating bodies unless they desire to be. They make law; they do not merely find it in preexisting form. To a far greater degree than British judges, American judges play an allocative as well as a mediating role in society. The processes of which they are a part are inherently political and produce results far beyond those of direct concern to the litigants.

On the other hand, American judges play a far greater part in refining, applying, communicating, and protecting the values of political liberalism and the rights of the citizenry than British judges do, and American judges are sometimes more responsive to political and social changes in society than the other branches are. In sum, their overall task is more difficult than that of their British counterparts; in addition to injecting a dynamic element into American law, they must also superintend federalism, police the separation of powers, and educate the citizenry about the principles, values, and operations of their constitutional system.

CHAPTER EIGHT

CONSTITUTIONALISM AND RESPONSIBLE GOVERNMENT

The major functions of constitutional government are to provide systems of effective restraints on the exercise of governmental power, to render the government responsible, and to set forth means for calling leaders to account.[1]

Both the British and the American governments can be accurately characterized as responsible governments. Basically, responsible government is government constitutionally limited by values which imply responsibility on the part of the decision makers for their decisions and by institutions which provide legitimate means for holding decision makers accountable for their actions. Placing high value on both liberty and authority leads to empowering the governmental systems to act authoritatively while at the same time placing limitations on their exercise of power in order to protect individual liberty. Popular control over decision makers is maintained by requiring that officials answer to the people for their actions.

The presence of a constitution and of constitutionalism promotes responsible government. Constitutional government is almost synonymous with responsible, limited government. Most basic to constitutional government is constitutionalism, the belief in and reverence for the constitutional traditions, limited government, and protection for the individual against the abuse of power. Without the presence of constitutionalism, paper documents count for little; their guarantees remain empty phrases.

Robert Fluno suggests that constitutionalism contributes several important elements to limited government. Constitutionalism:

1. supports the constitution, uniting and legitimizing power and authority;
2. ensures that the formal scheme of government is normally followed, contributing to the orderliness of constitutional regimes and making it simpler to locate responsibility;
3. provides efficiency, making elements of a political system relatively stable and knowable;
4. helps to encourage innovation by rendering the processes of government clearer;
5. helps to inhibit tyranny by indoctrinating those who govern against acting arbitrarily.[2]

With the strong constitutional traditions present in both Great Britain and the United States, the actual documents and formal rules simply make explicit the fundamental underlying beliefs and values within each country. As constitutional governments, they differ one from the other in that the British government evolved from the ancient past, with its constitutional beginning impossible to date, whereas the American Constitution can be dated precisely. In addition, the United States has one assembled, written constitutional document, but Britain's unassembled constitution derives from several sources. However, the governments of both countries qualify as constitutional governments and both political cultures are deeply pervaded by constitutionalism.

Political responsibility and accountability are linked to political responsiveness, but are distinguishable from it. Whereas responsibility and accountability involve accepting praise or blame and answering for decisions made or not made, after the fact, responsiveness refers to the degree to which the governmental office-holders take action, or not, in response to perceived demands and supports of the various individuals and interests within the population. The link between responsibility and accountability, on the one hand, and responsiveness, on the other, derives from the officials' awareness that since they are subject to be held responsible for their decisions and to be called to account for them, they must attempt to determine citizen needs and expectations, to anticipate reactions to their decisions, and to satisfy enough of the demands so that they will continue to receive adequate support from those whom they govern. Otherwise, the legitimacy of the officeholders and of the institutions themselves will eventually be called into question. Responsiveness as a guiding political value involves incentives or spurs to positive action as well as negative blocks or hindrances to prevent action.

DEMOCRATIC PROCESSES

Responsibility in governmental systems is inextricably related to democracy regarded as a process. Because the keystone of democratic government is the ultimate responsibility of the governors to the governed, certain minimal institutions and practices must exist and operate to bring that relationship about. An electorate as broadly based as possible must have regular, periodic opportunities at the polls to make real choices between competing alternatives. Access to positions of public power and responsibility must be open to all segments of the people with no arbitrary and the fewest possible substantive exclusions. Alternatives must be made available to the electorate by organized political parties in order that voters can make an effective choice at the polls and that opposition to and criticism of the government can be expressed clearly. In systems in which one or two parties are dominant, their representative capabilities must be supplemented by minor parties and interest groups able to enjoy some measure of access to, influence over, and participation in identifying issues and formulating policies to deal with them. Parties must present to the voters sufficiently distinct options to offer them meaningful alternatives.

The preceding comparative analyses of the political cultures, the constitutions, and the political processes and governmental institutions in Britain and the United States clearly indicate that responsibility in government obtains in both political systems. In part, responsible government in both the British and the American systems derives from the fact that both rest title to exercise authority upon the shifting foundation of voter support. Each electorate contains a significant segment of voters who must be cultivated to be kept loyal and who will be lost in the course of time if the government's strategies are planned or its actions taken without consideration of probable popular reaction. No government in either system can take for granted that it will indefinitely receive popular acceptance. The possibility of losing the next election thus operates as a definite limitation on what a government can do, and the sharper the party differences are that constitute alternatives presented to the voters, the less precise the government's right to authority will be as long as the choices offered are compatible with the system's political culture and underlying consensus of values.

However, there are important differences in the ways in which responsible government is achieved within each of the two countries. In Great Britain, responsible government results from the long evolution of traditions and values which place fundamental importance on limiting power and from the development of institutions which concentrate governmental power and authority in the cabinet, the elected leaders of the majority party within Parliament.

In contrast to the governmental system of the United States, that of Britain has shown over the centuries a remarkably high degree of stable processes and institutional continuity. These characteristics seem to go hand in hand with the pronounced conserving tendency of the British political culture and its disposition toward a retrospective traditional gradualism that passes to each successive generation the values of moderate civil conduct and institutional conservation.[3]

Responsibility in the British political and governmental system is more highly perfected than it is in the American. Behaviorally, perceptually, institutionally, and procedurally, British party government embodies the principles of constitutionalism and of legal accountability of decision makers to persons over whom they exercise their authority, the governed. British deference to superior merit and a willingness to let the bureaucracy operate free from close attention by press and public opinion do not combine to produce abject civic submissiveness in the British people. Belief that government will act responsibly and acceptance of responsible leadership are ingrained parts of the British political character; submission to irresponsible power is not. But although the British civic culture tolerates a higher degree of political, legal, and administrative centralization and a wider range of bureaucratic discretion operating in a closed hierarchical environment than does the American, the British are less tolerant of authority gone wrong.

But while the British system is tuned to democratic responsibility, it is not as committed to the democratic ideals of responsiveness, representation, consent, and popular sovereignty. The American political culture teaches and American attitudes anticipate that the political parts of the government must and will be responsive to the perceived needs and wants of the electorate. The American system more nearly than the British realizes that goal in practice, for the British political heritage and the Conservative party ideology stress the right of the party when elected to office to rule as its leadership believes to be in the best interest of the body politic. So construed, the function of the electorate is to choose the governors and periodically to hold them accountable at the polls, but not to determine what they should do while in power. Only the Labor and the weakened Liberal parties subscribe to the views that powers of government originate with the people and that decision makers have an obligation to be responsibly representative of electoral opinions on public matters. On the whole, therefore, the British system operates more on the basis of party-formulated programs to which voters react than it does on ones constructed by parties out of electoral inputs. The idea that those political leaders who control the Commons hold all power essential to govern is deeply imbedded in British political heritage and consciousness;[4] the diffusion of power among Parliament, cabinet, prime minister, civil service, administration, and political parties operates as a practical limitation upon its exercise, whatever legal theory may teach to the contrary.

Both political systems possess a developed capacity to respond to expressed mass demands, but the American, perhaps reflecting its fractionated party organization, its heightened sense of social egalitarianism, and its allocation of powers among a large number of semi-independent centers, is expected to do so whereas the British is not. The parts of the American system are less articulated, less interdependent, and less subordinated to the whole than are those of the British, with the result that, whether by design or consequence, within it the principal guarantors of responsibility are competition and rivalry between multiple centers. The reality of separated powers extends far beyond the constitutional embodiment in the system's basic tripartite division. Despite the fact that the British system also contains multiple points at which decision makers and key influentials can be persuaded, bargained with, and otherwise influenced, in the British political machinery not all interests are thought to be equally entitled to access. The government as inheritor of Crown power selects those interests it desires to bring into the decisional framework. Not all are regarded as having an equal right of access to centers of formal power. The doctrine of popular sovereignty that is so central to American pluralism has no place in the British system. Neither is the responsiveness of government to the governed given a similar central position in British political values.

Within the context of these differences between the two systems, elections hold the key to both responsibility and responsiveness, to the extent that it is present, in the United States and in Britain. However, the fusion of legislative and executive power and thus of policy-making authority in Parliament concentrates political responsibility within that body. By contrast, governmental power and authority in the United States is constitutionally separated among the formally coequal legislative, executive, and judicial branches of government, and between the state and national governments. There are numerous American elections, taking place at different times, which disperse the focus of political party activity. Therefore, the lines of accountability are less clearcut and less well developed within the American system than they are in the British.

A British government has several advantages that an American administration lacks in its struggle to win continuing support from the voters:

1. The prime minister can determine the time for an election that is usually advantageous to his party;
2. The government can count on party loyalty firm and extensive enough to prefer its leaders rather than to abandon them and risk an opposition party victory;
3. The government knows that a significant portion of the elec-

torate is deferential to authority holders who have responsibility for deciding and acting on common problems;

4. It can count on a political culture that views government as essentially good, an agent for collective action to be taken on policies arrived at in an absence of deep seated hostilities, suspicions, and rivalries between contending power centers in society and government.

If appropriately used, these considerations may enhance maximum responsibility of the government to the electorate, but they have been criticized as lending themselves to possible manipulation by the incumbent party, derogating from responsible government.

In Great Britain, the political party is clearly the principal agent of accountability. British government is essentially party government because the general election provides for the voters a choice between two highly cohesive and disciplined political parties with relatively clearcut and distinguishable programs. The election returns give the answer to the question, Which party shall govern? Once that is determined, governing involves an ongoing dialogue between the party in power and the monarch's loyal opposition.[5] Political parties also structure the electoral choice in the United States, but the dispersal of both governmental authority and power diffuses political responsibility. American parties are less cohesive, less disciplined, and less programmatic than are the British parties. Whereas the lines of accountability in Britain run clearly and directly from the electorate to the decision makers through the political parties, accountability by means of American parties is somewhat impeded by their decentralized organization. This does not mean that responsible government does not obtain in the United States or that political parties are unimportant there, but rather that other, more diverse means of calling decision makers to account must be relied upon more extensively. Interest group activity, elections at state and local levels, litigation, and public opinion impact on specific issues contribute to achieving responsible government in America.

The differences between British and American political parties highlight the differences between the overall patterns of responsible, accountable government in the two countries. Operating in a unitary, parliamentary system in which the people remain relatively deferential to political authority, the British parties concentrate power and provide the electorate with relatively clearcut alternatives. The 1979 general election campaign presented sharp differences in proposed programs, policies, and philosophies of governing between the Conservative party, led by Margaret Thatcher, and the Labor party, led by James Callaghan.

At the end of a five year period, but in practice usually more frequently, the government party stands before the voters, awaiting their evaluation. The opposition party presents itself as an alternative government, running on both its electoral program and its record of questioning and of criticizing the government in the parliamentary setting. Whichever party is chosen is expected to govern and is deferred to in this function by the voters. The party's perceived success or failure in governing the country is the principal judgment rendered in the next election. Thus two key elements for responsible and accountable government can be seen clearly: the British electorate holds the governing party responsible for what it does and fails to do, and the cohesive, disciplined opposition party calls the government to account daily within Parliament.

Unlike the formal concentration and centralization of decision making power and authority which characterizes the British system, greater diffusion of authority and dispersal of decision-making points are present in the American system. The pluralism in American society, different from the more organic pluralism found in Britain, shapes the political and governmental institutions. This opens more access points for citizens and groups to attempt to influence officials, but it impedes pinpointing responsibility. The number of American issue-oriented groups appears to be increasing steadily, encouraged in part by the potential that is present in the United States for stimulating responsiveness at multiple decision-making points. The localism that pervades the American political culture, in contrast to the more national orientation in Britain, contributes to the system's responsiveness. In addition, there are strong political incentives for American officials to respond directly to demands of local groups to which their future election chances are tied. Similar incentives do not exist in Britain;

instead, the future of the elected representatives rests almost entirely with the national party organization and the party in Parliament.

LEGISLATIVE-EXECUTIVE RELATIONS

Significant differences exist between the two political systems in the relationship of legislative power to responsible government. Legislative-executive relations in the two systems stand in sharp contrast. Executive control of the House of Commons is so complete that the British legislature no longer has an autonomous capacity to resist the executive, to formulate and enact policy independent of the government leadership within the chamber, or effectively to control public finance. In such matters, the ability of Commons to disregard the government leaders has become a systemic aberration to be undertaken only at the risk of endangering its right to rule. In modern-day Britain, the principal function of the House of Commons is to support the government. The opposition, although formally recognized, is limited to criticism that is muted by its recognition that a difference exists between opposition and obstruction and by its acknowledgment of the proposition that the proper function of the government in power is to govern. In Commons, both government and opposition state their positions on policy matters, not with the objective of convincing the other side to shift its ground, but to educate the electorate to its viewpoint, thereby strengthening its political position by weakening that of its opponent.

The fusion of legislative and executive powers in the British system of government has all but totally subordinated the Commons to the government of the day. To make this statement is not to assert that the functions and procedures of the Commons in no way contribute to curbing the executive power. The changes which have come about in legislative-executive relations are fully compatible with the logic of responsible party government, but they have gone far to strip the House of Commons of its character as an independent law-making body. The British legislature seems now to have yielded much of its hard-won former independence to the executive.

On the American side of this comparison, Congress is found in a much stronger position than is the House of Commons. Under the American separation of powers, Congress has yielded little or nothing to the executive in these major policy areas. In foreign affairs and defense policy, the president probably holds an irresistible position in his relations with Congress. In most arenas of domestic policy and sometimes in foreign affairs and defense policy as well, the president has a decidedly rougher path to the attainment of his policy objectives than does a prime minister. Congress retains and does not hesitate to use its power to initiate authorizations and to increase and to reduce executive revenue and expenditure proposals. The executive originates general proposals for legislation also, but Congress disposes of executive suggestions and is in no manner or degree subservient to the president's leadership.

A number of features within the American system contribute to make the president's success in policy making uncertain:

1. weak party organization, loyalty, and control, and a near absence of party unity and discipline;
2. Congress' extensive constitutional authority to control the exercise of presidential powers and its control of the purse and of administrative organization, personnel, and authority;
3. the existence of a large, decentralized, and geographically dispersed bureaucracy that is difficult to control;
4. a constitutional assumption that legislative-executive conflict will be generated by the separated powers.

These combine to virtually preordain that American government will be conducted by presidential influence, bargaining, and persuasion, mixed with large increments of frustration, of obstruction, and, often, of defeat.

The success a president experiences in getting his legislation through Congress is dependent upon a host of political variables, of course, but even those who have the clout of a John Kennedy or the legislative savvy and contacts of a Lyndon Johnson must often fight for their policies on Capitol Hill. Party misalignment may count strongly against a president, but party alignment is no guarantee of enactment. Neither organized opposition nor party government exists in American legislative-executive relations, but despite the bumps and potholes in the road of its dealings with the American executive, the Congress probably better fulfills the traditional functions of representing, legislating, managing public finance, and controlling executive power than does the Commons today. Popular sovereignty and the representative principle continue strong in the American political tradition and impart vitality to the centrality of Congress' constitutional position. Yet, the president's highly visible roles as head of party, constitutional chief executive, and representative of all the people cause the American electorate to hold him responsible for the record of his administration in spite of his limited authority and imperfect political power in relation to policy development, enactment, and implementation. Dispersed responsibility is the American model.

The two situations are simply different. Whether one believes the American Congress or the British Commons to be more consonant with the assumptions and procedures of responsible democratic government is a judgment that must be formed within the context of each system. Both legislative bodies have lost credibility in the eyes of their beholders; both continue to be the objects of proposed reform, but loss of institutional integrity to the executive appears to be the major worry of British parliamentary reformers. Most corrective measures there could only be taken to enhance parliamentary autonomy at the expense of responsible party government. The fact that those measures for that purpose have not been initiated by any government backed by a working majority in the House of Commons suggests that public opinion and party and government leaders remain unconvinced that changes are necessary. The enforcement of executive responsibility by means of party government remains the primary value. Reinforcing responsibility for concentrated decision making by a few national leaders in a highly visible center is the pattern preferred by the British.

It almost goes without saying that the democratic processes essential for responsible government do function in both the British and American political systems in ways that approximate the ideals. However, many unresolved problems for which no certain cures are known endure in both. For example, although its present composition and means of identification satisfies most Britishers, British leadership is not democratically recruited from all elements of their society. Thus, it must be assumed that elements and interests of British society not directly represented by persons identified with them will be given adequate regard by those who have successfully entered their decision-making elite. However, if they are not taken into account by policy makers, effective responsibility within the system will be impaired to the extent that the neglected interest is unable to command support. And on its side, American leadership, despite recent modest gains, still fails to incorporate minority representation in its top decision-making elite. But whatever may be its other shortcomings, neither system recognizes that a preemptive right to leadership positions belongs to any segment of society.

LEGAL CULTURES AND THE JUDICIARIES

Responsible government is not dependent in either the British or the American system upon the protection of political processes alone. The two legal cultures in the examination before us have produced different values, institutions, and practices to protect personal freedoms from irresponsible government, but in both the rule of law and the principle of limited government operate. In the American legal culture, responsible government is that which is constitutionally and statutorily limited, administratively controlled, closely scrutinized by a nervous, cynical, and suspicious public opinion, and legally answerable to courts of law for the substance of its authority and the manner of its exercise. This is the American framework for the rule of law.

The British, no less than the Americans, insist on controlled, answerable, limited, and responsible government, but they are far less prone to depend upon formal legal sanctions for protection against infringement of their rights than Americans are. Increased recognition of personal rights by American courts has greatly stimulated litigation in an already litigious people, with the result that the American principle of judicial supremacy has moved the judiciary farther into the realm of substantive policy than had been customary in our tolerant legal culture.

It is impossible for the decisions of British courts to be devoid of policy implications and consequences, particularly when the meaning of a parliamentary enactment is at issue, but the involvement of British judges in active policy making would offend not only the principles of parliamentary sovereignty and political neutrality of the judiciary but also that of accountable party government. The principle that politics shall not be permitted to intrude upon judicial objectivity conversely imposes a systemic requirement that judicial policy making in the American manner shall not compromise the right of the government to make policies beyond the inescapable minimum and its obligation to answer for them at periodic intervals. For the most part, the British remain comfortable in their freedom, secure in the knowledge that common law remedies and acts of Parliament are sources of ample protection. Perhaps more than Americans, they understand that the security of the individual against arbitrary power depends more on a public opinion and an active parliamentary insistence that demand respect for it than it does upon a documentary enumeration of particular guarantees. But the American Bill of Rights and judicial power notwithstanding, the most elemental and ultimately effective guarantor of responsible government in both systems is an insistently supportive public opinion.

In spite of the differences between the institutions and processes in the two countries, both political cultures retain a fundamental belief in the value of limited, constitutional government. It is primarily because of this belief that responsible government exists in the two countries.

NOTES

CHAPTER 1

1. Richard Rose, *Politics in England* (Boston: Little, Brown, 1964), p. 37.
2. Karl W. Deutsch, *Politics and Government* (Boston: Houghton Mifflin, 1970), p. 207.
3. R. A. Williams, Jr., *American Society*, 3d ed. (New York: Alfred A. Knopf, 1960), chap. 11 presents an extended analysis.
4. David M. Potter, *People of Plenty* (Chicago: University of Chicago Press, 1954), pp. 112–16 develop this idea at greater length.
5. Walter A. Rosenbaum, *Political Culture* (New York: Praeger, 1975), p. 79.
6. Ibid., p. 86.
7. Ibid., p. 82.
8. Richard H. Tawney, *Religion and the Rise of Capitalism* (Gloucester, Mass.: Peter Smith, 1962), p. 23.
9. See especially Richard Hofstadter, *Social Darwinism in American Thought* (Boston: Beacon Press, 1955).
10. Rosenbaum, *Political Culture*, p. 52.
11. Ibid., pp. 52–55.
12. Ibid., p. 66.
13. Rose, *Politics in England*, p. 79. A thoroughly revised analysis in the second edition also supports the author's original conclusion. See *Politics in England*, 2d ed., chap. 5, especially pp. 176–81.
14. Ibid., p. 38.
15. Ibid., p. 39.

16. Ibid., p. 40.
17. Ibid., p. 48.
18. Lawrence C. Mayer and John H. Burnett, *Politics in Industrial Societies: A Comparative Perspective* (New York: John Wiley and Sons, 1977), p. 88.
19. Gwendolyn M. Carter, *The Government of the United Kingdom* 3d ed. (New York: Harcourt, Brace, Jovanovich, 1972), pp. 10–11.
20. Douglas V. Verney, *British Government and Politics: Life Without a Declaration of Independence*, 3d ed. (New York: Harper and Row, 1976), p. 22. See also Samuel H. Beer, *British Politics in the Collectivist Age* (New York: Alfred A. Knopf, 1965).
21. Rose, *Politics in England*, 2d ed., pp. 153–58.
22. Mayer and Burnett, *Politics in Industrial Societies*, p. 71.
23. Carter, *Government of the United Kingdom*, 3d ed., p. 12.
24. R. M. Punnett, *British Government and Politics*, 2d ed. (New York: W. W. Norton and Co., 1971), pp. 16–17.
25. Mayer and Burnett, *Politics in Industrial Societies*, p. 72.
26. Ibid., p. 74.

CHAPTER 2

1. J. A. Corry and Henry J. Abraham, *Elements of Democratic Government* (New York: Oxford University Press, 1964), p. 40.
2. Robert Y. Fluno, *The Democratic Community* (New York: Dodd Mead, 1971), p. 182.
3. Gwendolyn M. Carter, *The Government of the United Kingdom* 3d ed. (New York: Harcourt, Brace, Jovanovich, 1972), pp. 40–41.
4. S. E. Finer, *Comparative Government* (Baltimore, Md.: Penguin Books, 1970), p. 147.
5. Frank Stacey, *The Government of Modern Britain* (Oxford: Clarendon Press, 1969), p. 238.
6. Carter, *Government of the United Kingdom*, 3d ed., p. 39.
7. Ibid., p. 38.
8. William H. Young, *Ogg and Ray's Introduction to American National Government* (New York: Appleton-Century-Crofts, 1970), p. 45.
9. Samuel H. Beer, *The British Political System* (New York: Random House, 1974), pp. 24–25.
10. Corry and Abraham, *Elements of Democratic Government*, p. 112.
11. Carl J. Friedrich, *Constitutional Government and Democracy* (Boston: Ginn and Company, 1950), pp. 137–38.
12. Ibid., p. 139.
13. David F. Roth and Frank L. Wilson, *The Comparative Study of Politics* (Boston: Houghton Mifflin, 1976), p. 110.

14. Sydney K. Bailey, *British Parliamentary Democracy* (Boston: Houghton Mifflin, 1971), p. 5.
15. Roth and Wilson, *Comparative Study*, p. 112.
16. Ibid., p. 120.
17. R. M. Punnett, *British Government and Politics*, 2d ed. (London: Heinemann, 1971), pp. 162–63.
18. This section draws heavily on Samuel Huntington, *Political Order in Changing Societies* (New Haven: Yale University Press, 1968), chap. 2.
19. Carter, *Government of the United Kingdom*, 3d ed., p. 42.
20. A. F. Pollard, *Factors in American History* (New York: Macmillan, 1925), pp. 32–35.
21. Richard Rose, *Politics in England Today* (London: Faber and Faber, 1976), p. 110.
22. Stacey, *Government of Modern Britain*, p. 55.
23. Finer, *Comparative Government*, pp. 149–50.
24. Rose, *Politics in England Today*, p. 111.
25. Friedrich, *Constitutional Government*, p. 369.
26. Bailey, *British Parliamentary Democracy*, p. 6.
27. Carter, *Government of the United Kingdom*, 3d ed., pp. 41–42.
28. Harry Street, *Freedom, the Individual, and the Law* (Baltimore, Md.: Penguin Books, 1967), pp. 10–11.
29. See Anthony Lester and Geoffrey Bindman, *Race and the Law in Great Britain* (Cambridge: Harvard University Press, 1972) for treatment of equality of rights in the British context.

CHAPTER 3

1. Jean Blondel, *Voters, Parties and Leaders: The Social Fabric of British Politics* (Harmondsworth, Middlesex: Penguin Books, 1974), pp. 55–57.
2. Ibid., p. 55.
3. E. E. Schattschneider, *Party Government* (New York: Rinehart and Company, 1942), p. 129.
4. Peter Merkl, *Modern Comparative Politics*, 2d ed. (New York: Holt, Rinehart and Winston, 1977), p. 93.
5. The involvement of rank-and-file members of British parties in party organization is discussed by Blondel, *Voters, Parties and Leaders*, pp. 89–102.
6. Richard Rose, *Politics in England* (Boston: Little, Brown, 1964), p. 157.
7. Ibid., pp. 156–57.
8. David B. Truman, *The Congressional Party* (New York: John Wiley and Sons, 1959), pp. 280–89.
9. Judson L. James, *American Political Parties* (Indianapolis, Ind.: Pegasus Press, 1969), p. 129.

10. C. P. Cotter and B. C. Hennessey, *Politics Without Power: The National Committee* (New York: Atherton Press, 1964), pp. 230–31.
11. James P. Anderson, *Public Policy-Making,* 2d ed. (New York: Holt, Rinehart and Winston, 1978), p. 73. Anderson draws on D. W. Brady, "Congressional Leadership and Party Voting in the McKinley Era: A Comparison to the Modern House," *Midwest Journal of Political Science,* 16 (August 1972), and James Turner, *Party and Constituency: Pressures on Congress* (Baltimore, Md.: Johns Hopkins University Press, 1970), p. 17.
12. Lawrence C. Mayer and John H. Burnett, *Politics in Industrial Societies: A Comparative Perspective* (New York: John Wiley and Sons, 1977), pp. 318–19.
13. Merkl, *Modern Comparative Politics,* 2d ed., p. 120.
14. Ibid.
15. Rose, *Politics in England,* p. 128.
16. Peter Bromhead, *Britain's Developing Constitution* (London: George Allen and Unwin, 1974), p. 176.
17. Rose, *Politics in England,* p. 126.
18. Ibid., p. 124.
19. Ibid.
20. Gwendolyn M. Carter, *The Government of the United Kingdom,* 3d ed. (New York: Harcourt, Brace, Jovanovich, 1972), p. 144.
21. Samuel H. Beer, "Pressure Groups and Parties in Britain," *American Political Science Review,* 50 (March 1956), pp. 1–23.
22. Samuel H. Beer, *The British Political System* (New York: Random House, 1974), p. 150. See also chap. 10.
23. Ibid. p. 178.
24. Ibid.
25. A discussion of American reaction to the impact of the new politics can be found in Joe McGinniss, *The Selling of the President,* 1968 (New York: Trident Press, 1969).
26. See, for example, Judson L. James, *American Political Parties in Transition* (New York: Harper and Row, 1974); James L. Sundquist, *Dynamics of the Party System* (Washington, D.C.: The Brookings Institution, 1973); and C. B. MacPherson, *The Life and Times of Liberal Democracy* (London: Oxford University Press, 1977).

CHAPTER 4

1. M. Pinto-Duschinsky, "The Conservative Campaign: New Techniques Versus Old," in Howard Penniman, ed., *Britain at the Polls: The Parliamentary Elections of 1974* (Washington, D.C.: American Enterprise Institute for Public Policy Research, 1975), p. 90.
2. Ibid., p. 89.

3. Frank Stacey, *The Government of Modern Britain* (Oxford: Clarendon Press, 1968), p. 20.
4. See *Smith* v. *Allright,* 321 U.S. 649 (1944), overruling *Grovey* v. *Townsend,* 295 U.S. 45 (1935), which had held that a party primary for the nomination of candidates for public office was a function of a private political organization and therefore could not violate the Fourteenth Amendment to the U.S. Constitution.
5. R. M. Punnett, *British Government and Politics,* 2d ed. (New York: W. W. Norton and Co., 1971), pp. 50–56.
6. Punnett reports that Wilson's use of national electronic media was so successful in projecting his own vote-getting appeal into Labor constituencies and so dominated their local campaigns that constituency associations were left with little to do but build up their candidates' identities with the voters. Punnett, *British Government,* 2d ed., p. 55.
7. Anthony King, "The Election that Someone Won—More or Less," in Penniman, ed., *Britain at the Polls,* p. 210. See also D. Leonard, "The Labor Campaign," in Penniman, ed., *Britain at the Polls,* pp. 61–83.
8. The negative influence on his party's electoral fortunes while he was prime minister and Conservative party leader is recounted by Anthony King. See note 7 above.
9. Philip Purser, "Box Pop and the Poll," *Sunday Telegraph,* May 6, 1979, p. 16.
10. Comment, "The New Era," *Evening Standard,* May 4, 1979, p. 19.
11. Pinto-Duschinsky, "The Conservative Campaign," in Penniman, ed., *Britain at the Polls,* p. 88.
12. J. G. Blumler, "Mass Media and Reactions in the February Election," in Penniman, ed., *Britain at the Polls,* p. 133.
13. Richard Rose, *Politics in England Today* (London: Faber and Faber, 1974), p. 274.
14. Pinto-Duschinsky, "The Conservative Campaign," in Penniman, ed., *Britain at the Polls,* pp. 100–101.
15. Jean Blondel, *Voters, Parties and Leaders: The Social Fabric of British Politics* (Harmondsworth, Middlesex: Penguin Books, 1974), p. 96.
16. Ibid., pp. 95–96.
17. Gwendolyn M. Carter, *The Government of the United Kingdom,* 3d ed. (New York: Harcourt, Brace, Jovanovich, 1972), p. 78.
18. Austin Ranney, "Selecting the Candidates," in Penniman, ed., *Britain at the Polls,* pp. 34–36. More extended analyses of British procedures for selecting candidates can be found in Austin Ranney, *Pathways to Parliament* (Madison: University of Wisconsin Press, 1965); M. Rush, *The Selection of Parliamentary Candidates* (London: Thomas Nelson and Sons, 1969); and P. Paterson, *The Selectorate* (London: MacGibbon and Kee, 1967).

19. Ranney, "Selecting the Candidates," in Penniman, ed., *Britain at the Polls,* p. 37.
20. Ibid., p. 38.
21. Ibid., pp. 38–39.
22. Ibid., p. 42.
23. Ibid., pp. 36–37.
24. Ibid., p. 43.
25. The 1979 general election in Britain reduced the number of women MPs from the 27 returned by the October 1974 vote to approximately 20 in the house of 635 members. The American Senate includes but one woman and the House of Representatives only a handful.
26. Malcolm E. Jewell and C. S. Patterson, *The Legislative Process in the United States,* 3d ed. (New York: Random House, 1977), p. 91.
27. Public Law 93-443. This act is summarized in *Congressional Quarterly Weekly Report,* October 12, 1974, pp. 2866, 2868.
28. Punnett, *British Government,* 2d ed., p. 55.
29. For example, in the 1974 February election, the Conservatives spent the equivalent of about $2,160,000 for 635 constituency campaigns (an average of $3,300 each). An additional sum of approximately $1,000,000 was spent on its national campaign in spite of the fact that much more could legally have been expended because no limitations apply at that level of activity. Pinto-Duschinsky, "The Conservative Campaign," in Penniman, ed., *Britain at the Polls,* p. 104.
30. Ibid., pp. 106–7.
31. Carter, *Government of the United Kingdom,* 3d ed., p. 77. For an account of the use of polls in the first 1974 campaign see Richard Rose, "The Polls and Election Forecasting in February 1974," in Penniman, ed., *Britain at the Polls,* pp. 109–13.
32. Rose, "The Polls and Election Forecasting," in Penniman, ed., *Britain at Polls,* p. 110.
33. Rose, *Politics in England,* p. 175.
34. Ibid., p. 176.
35. Stacey, *Government of Modern Britain,* p. 310.
36. T. Brennan, *Politics and Government in Britain* (Cambridge: At the University Press, 1972), pp. 107–9.
37. An extended analysis of the political roles of the British media of mass communications can be found in Blumler, "Mass Media Roles and Reactions," in Penniman, ed., *Britain at the Polls,* pp. 131–62.
38. Punnett, *British Government,* 2d ed., p. 11.
39. Blumler, "Mass Media Roles and Reactions," in Penniman, ed., *Britain at the Polls,* p. 134.

40. Ibid., p. 135.
41. Federal Elections Campaign Act of 1971, Public Law 92-225.
42. Federal Elections Campaign Act of 1974, Public Law 93-443. See n. 27.
43. Gerald M. Pomper, "The Presidential Election," in M. M. Pomper, ed., *The Election of 1976* (New York: David McKay, 1977), p. 74.
44. Samuel H. Beer, *The British Political System* (New York: Random House, 1974), p. 208.
45. Ibid., pp. 201–14.
46. Brennan, *Politics and Government*, p. 91.
47. David Butler and D. Stokes, *Political Change in Britain* (New York: St. Martin's Press, 1971), p. 106.
48. J. H. Goldthorpe, "Social Inequality and Social Integration," in Richard Rose, ed., *Studies in British Politics*, 3d ed. (London: Macmillan, 1976), p. 90.
49. Brennan, *Politics and Government*, p. 102.
50. Ibid.
51. Butler and Stokes, *Political Change*, p. 14.
52. Brennan, *Politics and Government*, p. 101.
53. Butler and Stokes, *Political Change*, pp. 15–17.
54. Ibid., p. 27.
55. Blondel, *Voters, Parties and Leaders*, p. 78.
56. Derived from Beer, *British Political System*, Appendix, p. 228.
57. Blondel, *Voters, Parties and Leaders*, p. 68.
58. Beer, *British Political System*, p. 140.
59. Butler and Stokes, *Political Change*, pp. 256–57.
60. Blondel, *Voters, Parties and Leaders*, p. 58.
61. Gallup Poll, "Voting Behavior in Britain, 1945–1974," in Rose, ed., *Studies in British Politics*, 3d ed., p. 214.
62. Ibid., p. 210.
63. Ibid., pp. 210–11.
64. Lester W. Milbrath and M. L. Goel, *Political Participation*, 2d ed. (Chicago: Rand, McNally, 1977), pp. 39, 48.
65. The vagaries associated with the concept of social class and application of the concept to political behavior analysis are explored at length by Butler and Stokes, *Political Change*, pp. 47–70, and by Brennan, *Politics and Government*, pp. 68–72.
66. Brennan, *Politics and Government*, p. 93; Butler and Stokes, *Political Change*, p. 47; P. G. J. Pulzer, *Political Representation and Elections* (London: George Allen and Unwin, 1968), p. 98.
67. Brennan, *Politics and Government*, p. 94, citing J. R. Alford, *Party and Society* (London: Murray, 1964), in which correlations between class and voting behavior in Britain, Canada, Australia, and the United States were studied.

68. Gallup Poll, "Voting Behavior in Britain," in Rose, ed., *Studies in British Politics,* 3d ed., pp. 204–15.
69. Rose, *Politics in England,* 2d ed., p. 266.
70. Butler and Stokes, *Political Change,* p. 256.
71. Rose, *Politics in England,* 2d ed., pp. 169–71.
72. D. Kavanagh, "The Deferential English: A Comparative Critique," in Rose, ed., *Studies in British Politics,* pp. 74, 78.
73. Rose, "Social Structure and Party Differences," in Rose, ed., *Studies in British Politics,* 3d ed., p. 236.
74 . G. Pomper, "The Presidential Election," in M. Pomper, ed., *Election of 1976,* pp. 74–75.
75. Blondel, *Voters, Parties and Leaders,* p. 59.
76. Ibid., p. 101.
77. G. Pomper, "The Presidential Election," in M. Pomper, ed., *Election of 1976,* p. 62.
78. D. Studlar, "Political Culture and Racial Policy in Britain," in Rose, ed., *Studies in British Politics,* 3d ed., p. 107. See also Rose, *Politics in England,* 2d ed., pp. 26–31.
79. Ibid., p. 106.

CHAPTER 5

1. Harold Wilson, *The Governance of Britain* (New York: Harper and Row, 1976), p. 171.
2. Frank Stacey, *The Government of Modern Britain* (Oxford: Clarendon Press, 1969), p. 71.
3. Kenneth Bradshaw and David Pring, *Parliament and Congress* (London: Quartet Books, 1972), pp. 289–90.
4. Richard Rose, *Politics in England Today* (London: Faber and Faber, 1974), pp. 88–89.
5. Wilson, *Governance of Britain,* pp. 186–87.
6. Bradshaw and Pring, *Parliament and Congress,* pp. 292–93, 297.
7. Ibid., p. 325.
8. Gwendolyn M. Carter, *The Government of the United Kingdom* 3d ed. (New York: Harcourt, Brace, Jovanovich, 1972), p. 111.
9. Wilson, *Governance of Britain,* p. 169.
10. Stacey, *Government of Modern Britain,* pp. 110–15.
11. Bradshaw and Pring, *Parliament and Congress,* p. 355.
12. Samuel Huntington, *Political Order in Changing Societies* (New Haven: Yale University Press, 1968), pp. 106–7.
13. Ibid., p. 108.
14. Kenneth Prewitt and Sidney Verba, *Principles of American Government* (New York: Harper and Row, 1977), pp. 260–61.
15. Arnold J. Heidenheimer, Hugh Heclo, and Carolyn Teich Adams, *Comparative Public Policy* (New York: St. Martin's Press, 1975), p. 164.

16. Carter, *Government of the United Kingdom*, 3d ed., p. 90.
17. David F. Roth and Frank L. Wilson, *The Comparative Study of Politics* (Boston: Houghton Mifflin, 1976), p. 278.
18. R. M. Punnett, *British Government and Politics* 2d ed. (London: Heinemann, 1971), p. 91.
19. Roth and Wilson, *Comparative Study*, p. 278.
20. Jean Blondel, *Comparative Legislatures* (Englewood Cliffs, N.J.: Prentice-Hall, 1973), pp. 145–47.
21. Peter Bromhead, *Britain's Developing Constitution* (London: George Allen and Unwin, 1974), pp. 112–13.
22. Stacey, *Government of Modern Britain*, p. 63.
23. Richard H. Watson, *The Promise and Premise of American Democracy* (New York: John Wiley and Sons, 1975), p. 332.
24. Samuel H. Beer, *The British Political System* (New York: Random House, 1974), pp. 93–94.
25. Punnett, *British Government*, 2d ed., p. 91.
26. Watson, *Promise and Premise*, pp. 330–31.
27. Beer, *British Political System*, pp. 127–30.
28. Ghita Ionescu and Isabel de Madariaga, *Opposition* (Baltimore, Md.: Penguin Books, 1972), p. 9.
29. Ibid., p. 60.
30. Beer, *British Political System*, pp. 120–22.
31. Theodore J. Lowi and Randall B. Ripley, *Legislative Politics U.S.A.* (Boston: Little, Brown, 1973), chap. 9.
32 . Lawrence C. Mayer and John H. Burnett, *Politics in Industrial Societies: A Comparative Perspective* (New York: John Wiley and Sons, 1977), pp. 182–83.
33. Blondel, *Comparative Legislatures*, pp. 134–35.
34. Ibid., pp. 134–36.

CHAPTER 6

1. For further information on political socialization in the early years and the attitudes of children toward chief executives, see Fred I. Greenstein, *Children and Politics* (New Haven: Yale University Press, 1965); David Easton and Jack Dennis, *Children in the Political System* (New York: McGraw-Hill, 1969); and Robert D. Hess and Judith V. Torney, *The Development of Political Attitudes in Children* (Chicago: Aldine, 1967).
2. R. M. Punnett, *British Government and Politics*, 2d ed., (London: Heineman, 1971), p. 257.
3. Clinton Rossiter, *The American Presidency* (New York: Mentor Books, 1960), p. 16.
4. Frank Stacey, *The Government of Modern Britain* (Oxford: Clarendon Press, 1969), p. 249.
5. Ibid., p. 253.

6. Ibid., p. 241.
7. Graeme C. Moodie, *The Government of Great Britain* (New York: Thomas Y. Crowell, 1971), pp. 95–96.
8. Austin Ranney, *The Governing of Men* (Hinsdale, Ill.: Dryden Press, 1975), p. 387.
9. Peter Bromhead, *Britain's Developing Constitution* (London: George Allen and Unwin, 1974), p. 25.
10. Ibid., p. 46.
11. Marian Irish and Elke Frank, *Introduction to Comparative Politics* (Englewood Cliffs, N.J.: Prentice-Hall, 1978), p. 299.
12. Punnett, *British Government,* 2d ed., p. 201.
13. Stephen V. Monsma, *American Politics: A Systems Approach,* 3d ed. (Hinsdale, Ill.: Dryden Press, 1976), pp. 187, 194.
14. Samuel H. Beer, *The British Political System* (New York: Random House, 1974), p. 45.
15. Richard Rose, *Politics in England Today* (London: Faber and Faber, 1974), pp. 278–79.
16. Stacey, *Government of Modern Britain,* p. 182.
17. Beer, *British Political System,* p. 131.
18. Derived from David Butler and Jennie Freeman, *British Political Facts* (New York: St. Martin's Press, 1976) and J. N. Kane, ed., *Facts About the Presidents* (New York: H. W. Wilson Co., 1968).
19. Peter H. Merkl, *Modern Comparative Politics,* 2d ed. (New York: Holt, Rinehart and Winston, 1977), p. 145.
20. Ruth Silva and others, *American Government: Democracy and Liberty in the Balance* (New York: Alfred A. Knopf, 1976), pp. 350–62.
21. See James David Barber, *The Presidential Character* (Englewood Cliffs, N.J.: Prentice-Hall, 1972).
22. Rose, *Politics in England Today,* pp. 75–76.
23. P. J. Madgwick, *Introduction to British Politics* (London: Hutchinson Publishers, 1970), p. 89.
24. See Punnett, *British Government,* 2d ed., chap. 10.
25. Beer, *British Political System,* p. 81.
26. R. H. S. Crossman, *The Diaries of a Cabinet Minister,* vol. 1 (Cambridge: Harvard University Press, 1976), p. 511.
27. Silva and others, *American Government,* p. 335.
28. See Punnett, *British Government,* 2d ed., chap. 10.
29. Gwendolyn M. Carter, *The Government of the United Kingdom,* 3d ed. (New York: Harcourt, Brace, Jovanovich, 1972), p. 111.
30. Punnett, *British Government,* 2d ed., p. 203.
31. Rose, *Politics in England Today,* pp. 307–27.
32. Punnett, *British Government,* 2d ed., p. 191.
33. Beer, *British Political System,* p. 27.
34. Ibid., p. 35.

35. Ibid., p. 27.
36. Louis W. Koenig, *The Chief Executive* (New York: Harcourt, Brace, Jovanovich, 1975), p. 397.
37. R. H. S. Crossman, *The Myths of Cabinet Government* (Cambridge: Harvard University Press, 1972), p. 31.
38. Punnett, *British Government*, 2d ed., p. 180.
39. Ibid., p. 182.
40. Alexander J. Groth, "Britain and America: Some Requisites of Executive Leadership Compared," *Political Science Quarterly* 85 (April, 1970), p. 227.
41. Punnett, *British Government*, 2d ed., p. 214.
42. Beer, *British Political System*, p. 41.
43. Thomas E. Cronin, *The State of the Presidency* (Boston: Little, Brown, 1975), pp. 191–92.
44. Stacey, *Government of Modern Britain*, pp. 277–78.
45. Crossman, *Myths of Cabinet Government*, pp. 12–16.
46. Ibid., pp. 51–52.
47. S. E. Finer, *Comparative Government* (Baltimore, Md.: Penguin Books, 1970), p. 147.
48. Stacey, *Government of Modern Britain*, pp. 277–79.
49. Patrick Gordon Walker, *The Cabinet* (London: Cape, 1970), pp. 95–96.
50. Stacey, *Government of Modern Britain*, p. 279.
51. G. W. Jones, "Development of the Cabinet," in *The Modernization of British Government*, ed. William Thornhill (Totowa, N.J.: Rowman and Littlefield, 1975), p. 57.
52. Beer, *British Political System*, pp. 45–47.
53. See Koenig, *Chief Executive*, chap. 8, and Richard E. Neustadt, *Presidential Power* (New York: Thomas Y. Crowell, 1971), for development of the concept of the institutionalized presidency.
54. Cronin, *State of the Presidency*, p. 120.
55. See Koenig, *Chief Executive*, chap 8; Neustadt, *Presidential Power*, passim.; Cronin, *State of the Presidency*, chap. 2; and Barber, *Presidential Character*, passim., for analyses of the impact of personality on the presidential office.
56. Koenig, *Chief Executive*, p. 326.
57. Ibid., p. 210.

CHAPTER 7

1. J. W. Hurst, *The Growth of American Law* (Boston: Little, Brown, 1950), p. 85.
2. On the British side of this chapter, the treatment is applicable only to England and Wales, for the legal systems of Scotland and Northern Ireland are different and separate.

3. Jay A. Sigler, *An Introduction to the Legal System* (Homewood, Ill.: Dorsey Press, 1968), p. 13.

4. W. S. Carpenter, *Foundations of Modern Jurisprudence* (New York: Appleton-Century-Crofts, 1958), p. 198 ff. examines the impact of statutory upon common law.

5. This brief description can be amplified by reading Henry J. Abraham, *The Judicial Process,* 3d ed., (New York: Oxford University Press, 1975), chaps. 4 and 5; H. R. Glick and K. N. Vines, *State Court Systems* (Englewood Cliffs, N.J.: Prentice-Hall, 1973); F. J. Klein, *Federal and State Court Systems—A Guide* (Cambridge: Ballinger, 1977); and Herbert Jacob, *Urban Justice* (Englewood Cliffs, N.J.: Prentice-Hall, 1973).

6. Serious students who wish to go beyond this treatment may do so by reading R. M. Jackson, *The Machinery of Justice in England,* 6th ed. (Cambridge: At the University Press, 1972); F. L. Morrison, *Courts and the Political Process in England* (London: Oxford University Press, 1973); and Abraham, *Judicial Process,* 3d ed. in appropriate parts.

7. Delmar Karlen, *Anglo-American Criminal Justice* (New York: Oxford University Press, 1967), p. 61.

8. Morrison, *Courts and the Political Process,* pp. 52–54.

9. Ibid., p. 57.

10. Ibid., p. 42.

11. Abraham, *Judicial Process,* 3d ed., pp. 246–47.

12. Morrison, *Courts and the Political Process,* p. 44.

13. Ibid., pp. 37–40.

14. More extended treatments of this subject may be found in R. M. Jackson, *The English Courts of Law,* 6th ed., (Cambridge: At the University Press, 1972); H. G. Hanbury, *English Courts of Law,* 4th ed., prepared by D. C. M. Yardley (London: Oxford University Press, 1967); and Abraham, *Judicial Process,* 3d ed. Legal education in England is described in Jackson, *The English Courts of Law,* 6th ed.

15. Hanbury, *English Courts of Law,* 4th ed., p. 141.

16. Morrison, *Courts and the Political Process,* p. 58.

17. Ibid., pp. 62–63.

18. Ibid., p. 64.

19. Extended examinations of American judicial selection procedures can be found in numerous readily available studies of the constitutional courts, such as Abraham, *Judicial Process,* 3d ed.; J. R. Schmidhauser, *Constitutional Law in the Political Process* (Chicago: Rand McNally, 1962); James Eisenstein, *Politics and the Legal Process* (New York: Harper and Row, 1973).

20. In an effort to improve the quality of judges and to reduce the impact of nonprofessional considerations upon the American national judicial selection process, President Carter has called for

reforms in the procedures used by Senators to identify prospective district and appellate judges for presidential nomination. However, results produced by efforts to fill the 152 new judgeships created by Congress in 1979, the survival of politics in the new mechanisms, and the bickering and infighting their creation and use has generated do not hold out much promise that political partisanship and maneuvering will be diminished or that the quality of nominees will be appreciably enhanced.

21. The lord chancellor consults with the prime minister when selecting persons to be lord chief justice and master of the rolls, but the prime minister, who often is not a barrister and is encumbered by other duties, plays only a minor role in the judicial selection process.

22. Morrison, *Courts and the Political Process*, pp. 78, 81.

23. Henry W. Ehrmann, *Comparative Legal Cultures* (Englewood Cliffs, N.J.: Prentice-Hall, 1976), pp. 71–73.

24. Morrison, *Courts and the Political Process*, p. 81.

25. Ibid., pp. 86–87.

26. Ibid., p. 82.

27. Ibid., p. 83.

28. An interesting analysis of this distinctly American phenomenon can be found in Edward H. Levi, *An Introduction to Legal Reasoning* (Chicago: University of Chicago Press, 1962), pp. 1–8, 57–104.

29. Ehrmann, *Comparative Legal Cultures*, p. 115.

30. W. Geldart, *Elements of English Law*, 7th ed., by D. C. M. Yardley (London: Oxford University Press, 1966), p. 3.

31. Ibid., p. 7.

32. Ibid., p. 8.

33. Quoted in L. L. Jaffe, *English and American Judges as Lawmakers* (London: Oxford University Press, 1969), p. 1.

34. 77 *Statutes at Large* 392 and 86 *Statutes at Large* 816, respectively.

35. Ehrmann, *Comparative Legal Cultures*, p. 113.

36. W. Friedman, *Legal Theory*, 5th ed. (New York: Columbia University Press, 1967), p. 464.

37. Ehrmann, *Comparative Legal Cultures*, p. 140.

38. Harrold Stannard, *The Two Constitutions* (Toronto: VanNostrand, 1949), pp. 162–63.

39. Morrison, *Courts and the Political Process*, pp. 100–101.

40. Jackson, *The English Courts of Law*, 6th ed., p. 169.

41. See F. Kessler, "Order in the Courts," *Wall Street Journal*, Vol. 79, No. 63 (March 30, 1972), pp. 1, 17.

42. Jackson, *The English Courts of Law*, 6th ed., p. 170.

43. Except for those of county courts and justices of the peace who are removable by the lord chancellor of England.

44. Hanbury, *English Courts of Law*, 4th ed., pp. 124–30 examines the theory of judicial independence at greater length.
45. Jackson, *The English Courts of Law*, 6th ed., p. 169.
46. Karlen, *Anglo-American Criminal Justice*, p. 186.
47. Ibid., pp. 186–87.
48. B. A. Grossman, *The Prosecutor* (Toronto: The University of Toronto Press, 1967), p. 13.
49. Ibid., pp. 11–12.
50. Ibid., p. 12.
51. 78 *Statutes at Large* 552. This provision may also be found as Title 18, section 3006A of the United States Code.
52. *Argersinger* v. *Hamlin*, 407 U.S. 25 (1972). In *Argersinger*, the United States Supreme Court held that ". . . no person may be imprisoned for any offense, whether classified as petty, misdemeanor, or felony, unless he was represented by counsel at his trial" or before trial had knowingly and intelligently waived his right to assistance of counsel at trial. 407 U.S. 25, 37.
53. Hanbury, *English Courts of Law*, 4th ed., pp. 129–30.

CHAPTER 8

1. Carl J. Friedrich, *Limited Government* (Englewood Cliffs, N.J.: Prentice-Hall, 1974), pp. 13–14.
2. Robert Y. Fluno, *The Democratic Community* (New York: Dodd, Mead and Company, 1971), pp. 185–88.
3. Walter A. Rosenbaum, *Political Culture* (New York: Praeger, 1975), p. 15.
4. J. P. Mackintosh, *The Government and Politics of Britain*, 3d ed. (London: Hutchinson Publishers, 1975), p. 116.
5. Graeme C. Moodie, *The Government of Great Britain* (New York: Thomas Y. Crowell, 1971), p. 220.

BIBLIOGRAPHY

Abraham, Henry J. *The Judicial Process*. 3d ed. New York: Oxford University Press, 1975.

Alford, J. R. *Party and Society*. London: Murray, 1964.

Anderson, James P. *Public Policy-Making*. 3d ed. New York: Holt, Rinehart and Winston, 1978.

Bailey, Sydney K. *British Parliamentary Democracy*. Boston: Houghton Mifflin, 1971.

Barber, James David. *The Presidential Character*. Englewood Cliffs, N.J.: Prentice-Hall, 1972.

Beer, Samuel H. *British Politics in the Collectivist Age*. New York: Alfred A. Knopf, 1965.

_____. "Pressure Groups and Parties in Britain." *American Political Science Review* (March, 1956) 50:1-23.

_____. *The British Political System*. New York: Random House, 1974.

Blondel, Jean. *Comparative Legislatures*. Englewood Cliffs, N.J.: Prentice-Hall, 1973.

_____. *Voters, Parties and Leaders: The Social Fabric of British Politics*. Harmondsworth, Middlesex: Penguin Books, 1974.

Bradshaw, Kenneth and David Pring. *Parliament and Congress*. London: Quartet Books, 1972.

Brennan, T. *Politics and Government in Britain*. Cambridge: At the University Press, 1972.

Bromhead, Peter. *Britain's Developing Constitution*. London: George Allen and Unwin, 1974.

Butler, David and Jennie Freeman. *British Political Facts*. New York: St. Martin's Press, 1976.

Butler, David and Donald Stokes. *Political Change in Britain.* New York: St. Martin's Press, 1971.

Carpenter, W. S. *Foundations of Modern Jurisprudence.* New York: Appleton-Century-Crofts, 1958.

Carter, Gwendolyn M. *The Government of the United Kingdom.* 3d ed. New York: Harcourt, Brace, Jovanovich, 1972.

Corry, J. A. and Henry J. Abraham. *Elements of Democratic Government.* New York: Oxford University Press, 1964.

Cotter, C. P. and B. C. Hennessey. *Politics Without Power: The National Committee.* New York: Atherton Press, 1964.

Cronin, Thomas E. *The State of the Presidency.* Boston: Little, Brown, 1975.

Crossman, R. H. S. *The Diaries of a Cabinet Minister,* Vol. I. Cambridge: Harvard University Press, 1976.

————. *The Myths of Cabinet Government.* Cambridge: Harvard University Press, 1972.

Deutsch, Karl W. *Politics and Government.* Boston: Houghton Mifflin, 1970.

Easton, David and Jack Dennis. *Children in the Political System.* New York: McGraw-Hill, 1969.

Ehrmann, Henry W. *Comparative Legal Cultures.* Englewood Cliffs, N.J.: Prentice-Hall, 1976.

Eisenstein, James. *Politics and the Legal Process.* New York: Harper and Row, 1973.

Finer, S. E. *Comparative Government.* Baltimore, Md.: Penguin Books, 1970.

Fluno, Robert Y. *The Democratic Community.* New York: Dodd, Mead and Company, 1971.

Friedman, W. *Legal Theory.* 5th ed. New York: Columbia University Press, 1967.

Friedrich, Carl J. *Constitutional Government and Democracy.* Boston: Ginn and Company, 1950.

————. *Limited Government.* Englewood Cliffs, N.J.: Prentice-Hall, 1974.

Geldart, W. *Elements of English Law,* ed. D. C. M. Yardley. 7th ed. London: Oxford University Press, 1966.

Glick, H. R. and K. N. Vines. *State Court Systems.* Englewood Cliffs, N.J.: Prentice-Hall, 1973.

Greenstein, Fred I. *Children and Politics.* New Haven: Yale University Press, 1965.

Grossman, B. A. *The Prosecutor.* Toronto: The University of Toronto Press, 1967.

Groth, Alexander J. "Britain and America: Some Requisites of Executive Leadership Compared." *Political Science Quarterly* (April, 1970) 85:217–39.

Hanbury, H. G. *English Courts of Law,* ed. D. C. M. Yardley. 4th ed. London: Oxford University Press, 1967.

Heidenheimer, Arnold J., Hugn Heclo, and Carolyn Teich Adams. *Comparative Public Policy.* New York: St. Martin's Press, 1975.

Hess, Robert D. and Judith V. Torney. *The Development of Political Attitudes in Children.* Chicago: Aldine, 1967.

Hofstadter, Richard. *Social Darwinism in American Thought.* Boston: Beacon Press, 1955.

Huntington, Samuel. *Political Order in Changing Societies.* New Haven: Yale University Press, 1968.

Hurst, J. W. *The Growth of American Law.* Boston: Little, Brown, 1950.

Ionescu, Ghita and Isabel de Madariaga. *Opposition.* Baltimore, Md.: Penguin Books, 1972.

Irish, Marian and Elke Frank. *Introduction to Comparative Politics.* Englewood Cliffs, N.J.: Prentice-Hall, 1978.

Jackson, R. M. *The English Courts of Law.* 6th ed. Cambridge: At the University Press, 1972.

_____. *The Machinery of Justice in England.* Cambridge: At the University Press, 1972.

Jacob, Herbert. *Urban Justice.* Englewood Cliffs, N.J.: Prentice-Hall, 1973.

Jaffe, L. L. *English and American Judges as Lawmakers.* London: Oxford University Press, 1969.

James, Judson L. *American Political Parties.* Indianapolis, Ind.: Pegasus Press, 1969.

_____. *American Political Parties in Transition.* New York: Harper and Row, 1974.

Jewell, Malcolm E. and C. S. Patterson. *The Legislative Process in the United States.* 3d ed. New York: Random House, 1977.

Kane, J. N., ed. *Facts About the President.* New York: H. W. Wilson, 1968.

Karlen, Delmar. *Anglo-American Criminal Justice.* New York: Oxford University Press, 1967.

Klein, F. J. *Federal and State Court Systems—A Guide.* Cambridge: Ballinger Publishing Co., 1977.

Koenig, Louis W. *The Chief Executive.* New York: Harcourt, Brace, Jovanovich, 1975.

Lester, Anthony and Geoffrey Bindman. *Race and the Law in Great Britain.* Cambridge: Harvard University Press, 1972.

Levi, Edward H. *An Introduction to Legal Reasoning.* Chicago: University of Chicago Press, 1962.

Lowi, Theodore J. and Randall F. Ripley. *Legislative Politics U.S.A.* Boston: Little, Brown, 1973.

Mackintosh, J. P. *The Government and Politics of Britain.* 3d ed. London: Hutchinson Publishers, 1975.

MacPherson, C. B. *The Life and Times of Liberal Democracy*. London: Oxford University Press, 1977.

Madgwick, P. J. *Introduction to British Politics*. London: Hutchinson Publishers, 1970.

Mayer, Lawrence C. and John H. Burnett. *Politics in Industrial Societies: A Comparative Perspective*. New York: John Wiley and Sons, 1977.

McGinniss, Joe. *The Selling of the President, 1968*. New York: Trident Press, 1969.

Merkl, Peter. *Modern Comparative Politics*. 2d ed. New York: Holt, Rinehart and Winston, 1977.

Milbrath, Lester W. and M. L. Goel. *Political Participation*. 2d ed. Chicago: Rand McNally, 1977.

Monsma, Stephen V. *American Politics: A Systems Approach*. 3d ed. Hinsdale, Ill.: Dryden Press, 1976.

Moodie, Graeme C. *The Government of Great Britain*. New York: Thomas Y. Crowell, 1971.

Morrison, F. L. *Courts and the Political Process in England*. London: Oxford University Press, 1973.

Neustadt, Richard E. *Presidential Power*. New York: Thomas Y. Crowell, 1971.

Paterson, P. *The Selectorate*. London: MacGibbon and Kee, 1967.

Penniman, Howard, ed. *Britain at the Polls: The Parliamentary Elections of 1974*. Washington, D.C.: American Enterprise Institute for Public Policy Research, 1975.

Pollard, A. F. *Factors in American History*. New York: Macmillan, 1925.

Pomper, M. M., ed. *The Election of 1976*. New York: David McKay, 1977.

Potter, David M. *People of Plenty*. Chicago: University of Chicago Press, 1954.

Prewitt, Kenneth and Sidney Verba. *Principles of American Government*. New York: Harper and Row, 1977.

Pulzer, P. G. J. *Political Representation and Elections*. London: George Allen and Unwin, 1968.

Punnett, R. M. *British Government and Politics*. 2d ed. New York: W. W. Norton, 1971; 2d ed. London: Heinemann, 1971.

Ranney, Austin. *Pathways to Parliament*. Madison: University of Wisconsin Press, 1965.

————. *The Governing of Men*. Hinsdale, Ill.: Dryden Press, 1975.

Rose, Richard. *Politics in England*. Boston: Little, Brown, 1964; 2d ed. Boston: Little, Brown, 1974.

————. *Politics in England Today*. London: Faber and Faber, 1976.

————, ed. *Studies in British Politics*. 3d ed. London: Macmillan, 1976.

Rosenbaum, Walter A. *Political Culture*. New York: Praeger Publishers, 1975.

Rossiter, Clinton. *The American Presidency*. New York: Mentor Books, 1960.

Roth, David F. and Frank L. Wilson. *The Comparative Study of Politics*. Boston: Houghton Mifflin, 1976.

Rush, Michael. *The Selection of Parliamentary Candidates*. London: Thomas Nelson and Sons, 1969.

Schattschneider, E. E. *Party Government*. New York: Rinehart and Company, 1942.

Schmidhauser, J. R. *Constitutional Law in the Political Process*. Chicago: Rand McNally, 1962.

Sigler, Jay A. *An Introduction to the Legal System*. Homewood, Ill.: Dorsey Press, 1968.

Silva, Ruth, and others. *American Government: Democracy and Liberty in the Balance*. New York: Alfred A. Knopf, 1976.

Stacey, Frank. *The Government of Modern Britain*. Oxford: Clarendon Press, 1969.

Stannard, Harrold. *The Two Constitutions*. Toronto: VanNostrand, 1942.

Street, Harry. *Freedom, the Individual, and the Law*. Baltimore, Md.: Penguin Books, 1967.

Sundquist, James L. *Dynamics of the Party System*. Washington, D.C.: The Brookings Institution, 1973.

Tawney, Richard H. *Religion and the Rise of Capitalism*. Gloucester, Mass.: Peter Smith, 1962.

Thornhill, William, ed. *Modernization of British Government*. Totowa, N.J.: Rowman and Littlefield, 1975.

Truman, David B. *The Congressional Party*. New York: John Wiley and Sons, 1959.

Verney, Douglas V. *British Government and Politics: Life Without a Declaration of Independence*. 3d ed. New York: Harper and Row, 1976.

Walker, Patrick Gordon. *The Cabinet*. London: Cape, 1970.

Watson, Richard H. *The Promise and Premise of American Democracy*. New York: John Wiley and Sons, 1975.

Williams, R. A., Jr. *American Society*. 3d ed. New York: Alfred A. Knopf, 1960.

Wilson, Harold. *The Governance of Britain*. New York: Harper and Row, 1976.

Young, William H. *Ogg and Ray's Introduction to American National Government*. New York: Appleton-Century-Crofts, 1970.

INDEX